We Must March My Darlings

Also by Diana Trilling

Diana Trilling

We Must March My Darlings

A CRITICAL DECADE

New York and London
HARCOURT BRACE JOVANOVICH

"Lawrence and the Movements of Modern Culture" copyright © 1973 by George Weidenfeld and Nicolson Limited. Reprinted courtesy of Harper & Row, Publishers.

"Celebrating with Dr. Leary" © 1967 by Encounter Ltd. Used by permission.

Portions of this book originally appeared in *Commentary, Partisan Review, Redbook, Harper's Magazine, Atlantic Monthly,* and *Saturday Review,* to whose editors the author expresses her gratitude.

Library of Congress Cataloging in Publication Data

Trilling, Diana.
We must march my darlings.

1. United States—Social conditions—1960–
2. Radicalism—United States. 3. United States—
Intellectual life. I. Title.
HN65.T74   309.1'73'092   76-54566
ISBN 0-15-195599-9

First edition
BCDE

To my son Jim

Contents

Introduction

IN publishing a collection of essays, it has been the custom for their author to supply an introduction in which a theme or "position" is identified which unites the volume, and gives reason for the essays to be read in conjunction with one another. This was not always so: as literary criticism was traditionally practiced, the fact that a single voice, that of the writer, made itself heard in a group of essays, and that a single mind and sensibility had been directed to the works that were being discussed, was all that was demanded in justification of their being brought together in a book. This situation has been altered by the commanding presence on the literary scene of writers whom we speak of as "literary intellectuals," who venture into many more areas of their culture than were once thought to fall within the literary domain. With this broadening of the critic's range, it is now virtually a requirement of publication that in any collection of essays a unifying principle be located or contrived for it. The introduction to a volume of essays is no longer merely iconographic of its author's intention of seriousness; it has the practical purpose of indicating what is presumably the chief path that the reader should keep in view as he moves through the scattered territory that lies before him.

The foreword to my own previous volume, *Claremont Essays,* which was indeed a collection of disparate pieces, called attention to an opinion which, so it seemed to me, ruled my writing, whatever its subject: my belief that even in an unsatisfactory society the individual is best defined by his social geography. That I still maintain this belief will be apparent to any reader of the present volume. In the present collection, however, its re-assertion is, I think, less crucial. As I have gone through my writing since *Claremont Essays* appeared in 1964, what has most forcefully impressed itself upon me is the nature of its historicity—historical time, as we took it for granted even so few years ago, would now seem to have vanished. In the essays of the last decade—from, roughly, 1965–75—we observe a procession of events each of which had its full dramatic or even melodramatic moment, only to be virtually wiped from memory by a next event, a next dramatic moment. As something to be relied upon for evidence of cultural continuity, history—one might put it—has become non-history.

Painters once used to speak of something they called "negative space," by which they meant that between such objects as were represented in a picture, enough distance had to be suggested to permit the introduction into the painting, if the artist desired it, of any other objects which in reality might occupy the space. Metaphorically speaking, there is no negative space in this new volume such as there was in *Claremont Essays*. Space and time are in important ways inseparable, and space has disappeared in an acceleration of time so sharp as almost to constitute a mechanism for obliteration. I am not implying that the lethal assault upon history which we have experienced in this last decade was not foreshadowed in a volume which, as in the case of my earlier collection, could concern itself with, say, the moral radicalism of Norman Mailer or the meaning of the meaninglessness of Albee's *Who's Afraid of Virginia Woolf?* But around these prognosticative phenomena of an earlier period there was still space in which the life of culture had its relatively orderly growth; social and moral possibility, including good possibility, could still have been introduced into the canvas without violating its circumstantial accuracy. Now this useable if unused space has been blotted out. "Protean man," as Robert Lifton called him in proposing that the character of modern life had produced a man unprecedentedly attuned to cultural influence and almost infinitely susceptible of change, is replaced by man in solution; indeed, by man dissolved—so the New New Criticism, that most self-imposing critical system of recent years, would have it—into mere constructs of language.

I offer the present volume with its reports on Dr. Leary and on the drug culture of the sixties, on the early passions of women's liberation, on the emotions and deportment of the university disruptions and of the protests of the Vietnam War, on the student attitudes of the early seventies, all of them cultural manifestations which a few years ago were so tall on the horizon and so fraught with portent, in documentation of this self-destruct history which is now the time-measure by which we undertake to assess our cultural and social progress or lack of it. To cite what is perhaps the most urgent instance to which we can make reference: like the word Watergate, like the name Nixon, the Vietnam War still of course has its emblematic uses; but even in the memories of those who were of draft age while the War went on, its protest has become weightless. The steps of the Pentagon have long since been swept clean— but who knows for how long?—of the anarchic dissent which, when Norman Mailer wrote of it as remarkably as he did in *Armies of the Night,* proposed so close a parallel to what was about to take place at Columbia's Low Library.

Inevitably one is moved to wonder what it was, within or outside ourselves, which in little more than a decade could this markedly alter the familiar pace of history. What I hazard as my explanation is that although the acceleration was obviously not caused by a single historical happening, the assassination of President Kennedy, it was greatly stimulated by that tragic occurrence. To be sure, the part played by television in disturbing the normal rate of national and even international development and in robbing us of the physical distance which formerly separated us from events and therefore forced us to exercise our own minds and imaginations in order to get even a first grasp on history-in-the-making, is not to be underestimated as a factor in our recent dislocation in space and time. The death of John Kennedy, however, made for a subtler and perhaps a more pervasive disturbance in our historical balance. It altered our sense of ourselves as a people; it deprived us of the promise of a future. What could more profoundly affect the motions of time?

It is for this reason that I decided to open this volume with a (much-shortened) essay which I contributed to a series of memorial pieces on the first anniversary of President Kennedy's death. The essay had appeared too late for inclusion in the American edition of *Claremont Essays* but I had reprinted it in the British edition of that volume, and now in 1976, as I re-read it in preparation for selecting the contents of the present book, it seemed to me that of all the essays I had written since November 1963, all of which had left me feeling a stranger to my previous world, this was by so much the most remote from the emotions which would make the elusive substance of a later cultural mood, that it supplied a natural point of departure for a portrait of the period to come. For how more decisively underscore the anger and emptiness of the mid- and late sixties and our American self-contempt, earned and unearned, of the early seventies than by reminding ourselves of how acute and actual had been the hope generated in us by the Kennedy presidency? Although the point is not to be pressed, it is to be made: our best educated classes would prefer to forget what they expected of Kennedy, why they expected it, and what happened to them when the expectation was taken from them. This preference is so strong, in fact, that it will be bound to encourage doubt whether mine is a truthful account of the feelings that were directed to Kennedy while he lived. But should the matter of accuracy be raised, I can only reply that no one, not a single reader of the mass circulation magazine in which the essay first appeared, ever wrote in challenge of its truth. Perhaps we have forgotten what, because it was lost, it is now too painful for us to remember.

I take the title of this volume from a projected book about Radcliffe, my old college. It is an ironic title whose source in the first stanzas of Walt Whitman's poem "Pioneers! O Pioneers!" is given at the beginning of the portion I publish: from my experience of the Radcliffe and Harvard undergraduates of 1971 I think there is ground for the possibility that it is the younger and not, to borrow from Whitman, "the elder races" who "droop and end their lesson." But here too, in the life of university students, there is no generalization to be made, no conclusion to be offered, except tentatively inasmuch as time has lost the stern definition it had in the past. Where once a new student generation was thought to arrive on the campus every twenty years, then every ten, now it is apparently the product of each new semester. My Radcliffe report must be read with the understanding that in returning to Radcliffe I was concerned to trace, through the evolution of one educational institution, a distinguished college for women, something of the general course of the American female fate— I had not undertaken to make a month by month or even year by year record of shifts in student sentiment. It turned out to be impossible to stop the spinning wheel of undergraduate change long enough to get it firmly and definitely even into one's temporary possession.

Many friends have over the years given me many different forms of support and assistance in the composition of the essays in this volume. Although this help will not be visible to my readers, I am myself deeply aware of it and forever appreciative. But I shall no more burden them with a formal acknowledgement which misses the point of the kind of relationship their help stemmed from than place upon them any responsibility for the views I express.

I mention here only my particular gratitude to Evelyn and David Riesman and to Blanche and Jerome Bruner for the encouragement they gave me to re-visit Radcliffe in 1971 and for the effort they exerted to obtain suitable living quarters for me there. I would make it as plain as possible that their opinions are at no point included with mine. I also most warmly thank the resident officers of the Radcliffe dormitories, and the Radcliffe and Harvard students who welcomed me so kindly.

D. T.

January 1977

The Assassination of President Kennedy

AS I write, it is a year since the death of President Kennedy. Another election has incredibly come and gone, and if we had supposed that with the passage of time and the interposition of a new presidential contest the pain of our loss would have notably diminished, we now know how mistaken we were. If anything, another election has deepened our sense of deprivation. We occupy ourselves with our customary concerns, no longer obsessed as we were in those first days after the assassination when suddenly we were a nation of Ancient Mariners, condemned to rehearse again and again the conditions of our grief and of our efforts to accommodate what had happened. But all at once there will be a flash of recollection: we see the name, a photograph, whatever it is that releases us from business as usual into the freedom of admitted feeling, when once more we ask ourselves if it can be true that this man who spoke to us so much of life no longer lives. To which the answer is, no. Some deaths are not possible.

"America has always taken tragedy lightly," Henry Adams comments in the *Education*. "Too busy to stop the activity of their twenty-million-horse-power society, Americans ignore tragic motives that would have overshadowed the Middle Ages." And he goes on, speaking of the deaths of Lincoln, Garfield, and McKinley: "Three hideous political murders . . . have thrown scarcely a shadow on the White House." If

3

this is historically accurate as an account of the national response—in the case of Lincoln it is perhaps open to question—Adams's generalization fails to apply in our latest tragic instance. The shadow of Kennedy's death hangs over the land, heavy, lasting. His nonpresence was a salient fact of the Democratic convention, its sole drama. For people of liberal political opinion his absence gave particular bitterness to Senator Barry Goldwater's capture of the Republican presidential nomination. Our society has not stopped its activity but it has admitted tragedy.

From the start, during the pitiless weekend which began with the news of the killing and culminated in the funeral, our response was of a kind which we usually reserve for our most intimate bereavements. People whom we wouldn't expect to cry were weeping. The nonreligious went to church or wished they could. Even among Kennedy's political opponents, or surely the majority of them, or among people who make a virtue of their political cynicism, Americans moved toward each other, groping for the connection which would dispel loneliness—I have been told that in foreign places compatriots, particularly students abroad, sought out each other as if drawn together against an unnameable enemy. As to the people I know best, the academic and literary intellectuals of New York, these had been Kennedy supporters if they are ever to be called supporters of anyone in office. The degree to which he had captivated them was made evident by the point they had to make, awkward, unconvincing, of their imperviousness to his charm. Yet even their obvious need to defend themselves against his seductiveness left them unprepared to handle their grief when he died. . . .

America, so our literature tells us, is peculiarly reluctant to renounce its dreams. Europeans accuse us, as we accuse ourselves, of the rawness which results from our unwillingness to accept the difficult actualities of life. But the interplay between idealism and realism in the American character is a complicated phenomenon, and the balance Kennedy held between them was impressive. Although the very model of American youthful heroism, and reluctant to relinquish that image of himself, he brought to the presidency a sense of the actual such as usually exists in Americans only where idealism has been sacrificed to crassness.

And yet there were the occasions when even for Kennedy the dream and the reality had but poor acquaintance with each other. The most dramatic departure from his usual deference to the plain and possible was of course the Bay of Pigs invasion, a foolhardy venture of giant proportions from which the United States emerged perhaps better than it deserved. His failure to evaluate for himself both the morality and the feasibility of an invasion of Cuba was grossest folly, of a piece with the British foray in Suez which it followed and from which it should have taken warning. The error was redeemed, insofar as it could be, only by his readiness to take blame for the adventure and by subsequent proof of how much he had learned from it. That the same person was later able to manage the Cuban missile crisis of 1962 with so much purposiveness and control testifies to Kennedy's moral strength. A lesser man would have been significantly weakened by the realization that it was in relation to Cuba that he had already gone so wrong. Perhaps—we don't know—an important part of his education in the presidency was to learn when not to move on the advice of subordinates. Certainly by the time of the second round with Castro, Kennedy had made it his crisis, his decision, and far from indulging our old belief in America's imperviousness to foreign attack, he made sternest estimate of the gravity of the threat and America's ability to withstand it, achieving a victory that presented a new picture of the United States to the world and to Americans themselves. Now it was a case not of Kennedy following the precedent of earlier administrations but of America finding a new courageous model in the deportment of Kennedy. With the Cuban missile crisis, the symbol of Kennedy, the heroic son, was invested with something of the importance of Franklin Roosevelt as symbol of the wise and benevolent father.

When the short chronicle of the Kennedy years is written, America's successful confrontation of Russia on Cuba must stand as Kennedy's major achievement in international affairs. America desperately needed a triumph of forceful principle, also a renewal of confidence in the international arena and the Cuban victory could not have been better timed to revivify the spirit of the country. Behind the Iron Curtain the admiration and even affection in which Kennedy was held was a sign of how far he had restored America to its appropriate moral rank among nations.

The effect of the Cuban episode upon American intellectuals is particularly worth comment. Virtually in a single stroke it took from under them their old ground of protest against the remote and retrograde authority of government. In England the connection between political power and the universities has always been direct and counted upon. In America the conscious intellectual has been unable to make such a ready identification with government. It was not until Kennedy's election that anything approaching the English situation came to obtain in the United States and that American intellectuals had a first sweet intimation of existing in meaningful relation to the conduct of public affairs. Kennedy took with him into government a whole group of well-known figures in the intellectual community—but so, to a degree, had FDR. Kennedy, however, by being the person he was, almost by looking as he looked, markedly closed the gap that had previously separated the life of action from the life of speculative thought. Before the Cuban crisis the American intellectual class, particularly in its radical wing, was elaborately on guard against Kennedy's pleasure in intellectual company. Was one to forfeit one's right of criticism for the sake of dinner in the White House? I think it is fair to say that it was Kennedy's handling of the Cuban confrontation, the precision with which he held the crisis to the immediate matter of hemispheric integrity, not allowing it to compromise his commitment to world peace, that chiefly disarmed criticism among that small but highly vocal part of the population which takes the moral life of nations under its special supervision. For the first time since the Second World War the American intellectual could admit the existence of an enemy other than his own government and a leadership adequate to the needs of his own nation.

And yet, curiously enough, this president who satisfied the desire of intellectuals for a government approximate to their own vision was not really an intellectual in their sense of the word. He was well educated, he read many books, he enjoyed abstract discussion, but eventually the abstract was bound to be brought under the dominion of the concrete. This set him apart from the professional intellectual community. The story is told, for example, of the time the president had a well-known New York literary critic to lunch with him in the White House to talk about the state of the nation as it was viewed by such a certified student of culture. At the end of lunch the president pressed upon his visitor the question: "Yes, but what has all of this to do with the papers waiting for me on my desk?" Miraculously, when this was reported in literary circles it was greeted with neither scorn nor irony; it was understood that Kennedy's question had intended no dismissal of the message of culture but had simply introduced into the discussion the never-to-be-ignored problem of how one goes about bringing into alignment the premises of speculative thought and the immediate demands of administration. In other words, he was not deluded that one had to disarm oneself in practical affairs in order to attain to ideality. It was thus no accident that he looked to Churchill as a model for political power in our time.

Sir Isaiah Berlin has reminded us that an essential instrument of Churchill's political strength in time of crisis was his rhetoric. This was no less true of Kennedy, although the only quality his oratory shared with Churchill's, aside from the fact that it *was* oratory rather than spoken prose, was the common touch which, whether in the speech of the political leader or the philosopher, is what comforts us that an idea is workable—this was a gift that Roosevelt had finally lacked, however convincingly he substituted for it by calling his public addresses fireside chats. Where inevitably Roosevelt was the patrician speaking on behalf of the public good, Kennedy was spokesman of the best self of his listeners. Despite his wealth and Harvard, he was never aloof from those who heard him. There was always the cadence of local American speech to take the sting of privilege out of his fluency. His literacy was shielded from the taint of ostentation by his humorousness and by the pleasure he took in his own quick wit. And if there were moments when his humor was wry, or even sharp, this too was appropriate, for his mockery was turned upon himself as often as upon others. It is a familiar American way, sometimes taken by Europeans to imply a lack of confidence but actually an expression of our deep-rooted belief in every man's ultimate insufficiency.

We have of course had modest presidents, we have also had undignified and even embarrassing presidents. But only in Kennedy have we in recent years had a president in whom dignity, pride, and modesty were so well fused. One recalls the famous Nobel Prize winners' dinner at the White House and Kennedy's speech of welcome which began with the grinning remark that probably never in the history of the White House had so much talent and genius been gathered at the president's table since Jefferson dined there alone. This was the same evening that Dr. Linus Pauling, after picketing the White House all afternoon in protest against nuclear armament of the democracies, had changed into evening dress and come down the guest line to be warmly greeted by the president with the smiling comment that little Caroline had wanted to know what her father had done wrong that people were marching around the house with placards. Humor? Graciousness? Yes, but also the behavior of a supremely serious man who granted the presidency of the United States its high place in the complex democratic structure but didn't regard it as a pinnacle of personal prestige.

And yet he was an armored man who would, one guessed, not wittingly let himself be caught out vis-à-vis other men. The shield was there to be seen even in the grace with which it could be cast aside in congenial situations. It was also not hard to suppose that he could be ruthless—in the long run this no doubt pleased the intellectuals more than it did business people. It was rumored, too, that within his family he encouraged a degree of formality which, judged superficially, disputed the casualness which was so much his public posture. Of his taste for ceremony, as distinct from formality, there is of course no question, any more than there can be doubt of his instinct for tradition. Perhaps, in fact, it was in his respect for ceremony and tradition that we discover at least one important source of his appeal to the young.

The extraordinary grief of the young at Kennedy's death cannot, I think, be accounted for merely on the ground of his youthfulness. Obviously, anyone dashing and handsome would be more attractive to young people than an older man of less fluid temperament, but it is my belief that what particularly spoke to the young in Kennedy was his ability to bring past and present together, with the hope that this offered of a continuing life in civilization—which is to say, a future. A sophisticated man in that peculiarly modern sense of having a quick relaxed acquaintance with the tastes and idiom of advanced culture—and here we cannot overlook the role of his wife in fashioning their shared availability to the new—he also revealed without apology his appreciation of the traditional. For the young he was thus more than an enlightened national leader; he represented a country which could freely move forward without forfeiting its respect for its place in history. No visitor to England can fail to be impressed by the ceremonial emphasis in British life: the panoply and parade, the reiteration of the past. Better than most who have represented America to the world, Kennedy understood, as the British seem naturally to do, that progress does not ordain a complete dumping of the old; there is always that which should be retained. By allying his unimpeachable modernity with a developed regard for tradition, for ceremony, he protected the necessary connection between generations. For the young both in his own country and abroad, he was not only the new man, he was a new kind of man for whom the acceptance of history heightened the glow of contemporaneity in which he lived.

And if we think of Kennedy as a man for whose benefit the old and the new, the traditional and the modern, worked in happiest accord, surely there can be no more useful clue to this inner balance than his relation with his family, in particular with his father. The matter is to be put baldly: to be the son of Joseph P. Kennedy and to run for elective office on a progressive platform was no light undertaking, and back in 1960 there were those of us who wondered whether Kennedy would be able to define himself for the liberal electorate with enough clarity to be rid of his father's unfortunate public image. Well, Kennedy managed it with scarcely a sign that there was any problem to manage, by refusing to entertain the possibility of guilt by association. He was his own man and continued to be when elected. Obviously he didn't flaunt his father in the face of the public; during the campaign Joseph Kennedy kept discreetly out of sight. But neither he nor the wealth he had accumulated were disclaimed. Nor did the president seem to restrict his wife's expenditure for clothes through fear of offending the less privileged sections of the population—and it turned out that rich and poor alike took pleasure in their royal lady. He even continued to make his summer residence in the family compound at Hyannis Port, the idea apparently not having occurred to him that to be a person in one's own right one must be disembarrassed of one's antecedents. Yet this is a central idea in contemporary America wherever sophistication is conscious of itself. As a matter of fact, his behavior proposed a contrary hypothesis, that a man is truly free only when he is released from the search for an unconditioned selfhood.

In the light of our current assumption that independence is a function of parentlessness, both personal and cultural, this amounts to virtually a revolutionary stance. Where else in the world does a younger generation devour its elders at the rate we do in this country, and where is progress in thought or career so consistently measured in terms of the aptitude for eliminating whatever has already been? And if we are further to understand why Kennedy was so important to the young, it is necessary to think about the extent to which they must feel themselves badly nourished on their meal of dead parents and teachers, ready for a new diet. Kennedy's family feeling was a corollary of his feeling for American history and institutions. He did not need to scorn his national and personal heritage in order to prove that he was not captive to the values of establishment.

A man, a president, who believes in history and in the continuity between past and future but who even in the view of the most intransigently young cannot be written off as a "square"; a national leader whose personal aura is one of heroism, romance, gaiety, and even a certain rakishness—and it ignores the obvious not to note the erotic element in Kennedy's charm, with what this was bound to add to his image as a champion of freedom—but who has the stern substantiality of mind and character to guide his country in international crisis and to propose new paths of domestic enlightenment; a modern who is a traditionalist; a traditionalist who is the very essence and image of the contemporary—what more could we have asked in reassurance that life was solid under our feet despite our uncertainties, and that the present was not only dread and isolation? To give us this reassurance, to dispel our loneliness: for some time now this has been the burden refused by the artist and unmet by the politician. Kennedy enlarged the political profession to provide just such an answer to the needs of the spirit. This was his gift and something of a miracle. When we mourn Kennedy it is ourselves we grieve for. We have been robbed of an enlarging vision of our nation and of ourselves as individuals.

[1964]

Celebrating
with Dr. Leary

WE had been told on what was presumably sound authority that the previous Tuesday evening, the opening night of Dr. Timothy Leary's scheduled series of Psychedelic Celebrations, the audience had been "tough" and that therefore on our evening too we must expect some element of danger, or at least of unpleasantness. But in fact it would be hard to imagine a milder scene than awaited us at the Village Barn, the small theatre in Greenwich Village to which Dr. Leary's show had suddenly been moved from the Village Theatre where it was originally booked. Here surely was nothing for fear on the score of criminality, hostility, or even bad manners. My husband and I were meeting friends; the change of theatre had made for confusion so that we arrived almost an hour before the announced curtain time. The entrance to the Barn was already jammed; no fewer than two hundred people, probably closer to three hundred, were waiting for admission and as time went on the crowd became so dense that it blocked traffic the length of the street. But the conduct of Dr. Leary's audience was exemplary. There was no sign of anxiety about getting seats, no one pushed or tried to assert territorial claim. On the other hand, I should scarcely describe it as a friendly gathering, and this despite its homogeneity.

Although most of Dr. Leary's audience seemed to be under thirty and of similar social situation—middle-class dissident,

15

above the average in education—I saw no exchange of greet-
ings, and it was not a crowd that talked or laughed. It was
even difficult to particularize couples. The group appeared to
be made up of strangely isolate young people who, if they
were acquainted with each other, were not concerned to
further the connection. Nevertheless the atmosphere was one
of almost palpable benevolence. If it is possible to speak of the
face of a gathering, this was the face of an entire, an almost
programmatic, goodwill and peaceableness. I was reminded of
the mandatory calm of recent converts to Christian Science. At
first I was surprised by this prevalence of benignity in young
people, many of whom might be assumed to be in some degree
involved in the subversive world of drug taking and who, at
any rate, were all of them dressed in the rather violent contemporary uniforms of dissent, either harshly black or, at the
other extreme, colorful in refusal of middle-class conformities
of dress—until I reminded myself that, after all, there lies at
the heart of the LSD movement, as of most contemporary
movements of youthful protest, the conviction that it is those
who accept or accommodate themselves to the values of Western society who have lost the knowledge of peace and kindliness. Then, too, LSD seems to have a gentling effect on the
personality. I have observed a curious transformation in all the
young people I know who have taken the drug; even after only
one or two trips they attain a sort of suprahumanity, as if
purged of mortal error; and as far as I can make out, this
change persists. But one must be cautious with conclusions
drawn only from personal observation. In our present highly
deficient state of scientific understanding of LSD, we know
with certainty only that its power to work alterations on the
brain is enormous: it is five thousand times more powerful
than mescaline. But the precise nature of the changes it makes
and how far they extend or how long they last we do not
know, which is of course why those who use it or who do not
oppose its use can persuade themselves that warning of its
danger is without scientific foundation.

We were fortunate to have reserved press seats for the four of us by telephone or we might not have got into Dr. Leary's show. Trying to get through the lobby to pick up our tickets, I had the encounter which stays with me as summing up the peculiar quality of transcendence that characterized this audience. A young man blocked my path. I touched his shoulder to ask if I could pass. The situation demanded no more than politeness but he turned elaborately, looked down at me from what seemed a divine height, and said, "I want you to do anything you want to do." So sublime a response surely had its reference elsewhere than where we stood. Not his words alone but his smile and bearing were clearly pointed at some sweeter moral universe than a crowded theatre lobby in Greenwich Village, New York. Yet even at so early a moment in my psychedelic evening I knew it was a mistake to regard this young man as an uncommon instance of rarification. It was his personal quality, not mine, that appeared to be the norm of the occasion: in a gathering like Dr. Leary's I had already come to feel cumbersomely earthbound, of a graceless and unloving species. Since my night among Dr. Leary's followers—and followers I must suppose the largest part of his audience to have been, judging not only by appearance and manner but by their conduct during the performance and certainly in the question-and-answer period at the end of the ceremonies—I have seen a special LSD issue of the French magazine *Crapouillot,* with excellent photographs of people at various stages of LSD intoxication. Some of the subjects appear to be having a grievously bad time but none of them, no matter in what agony, is without his smile of fine imperviousness, which bears much the same relation to our usual notions of self-containment that the smile of classical hysteria (*"la belle indifférence"*) bears to our usual imagination of pleasurable emotion.

Was I perhaps straining for consistency that I found in Dr. Leary's prose, written or spoken, a character not unlike that of his audience, the same superbness achieved at considerable cost in substance? For instance, a placard was posted in the lobby to explain the last-minute switch of Dr. Leary's show from the Village Theatre to the Village Barn. Later I copied it out:

With regard to Dr. Leary's Psychedelic Celebration at the Village Theatre: It is with regret that Dr. Leary has discovered inequities and is experiencing financial problems with the theatre. Therefore he is forced to announce that he will no longer appear at the Village Theatre. Instead, Dr. Leary will conduct a psychedelic religious celebration tonight at the Village Barn at 9:00. There will be no admission charge.

Prose like this, at once so plain and elevated, colloquial and fine, commonplace and formal, almost legalistic, is compounded of entirely familiar elements of communication. It is without shock value. But when we examine it we see that although it is offered in explanation, it explains nothing; it seduces one into the belief that one has been addressed with a familiar cogency. And so with Dr. Leary's spoken language. It creates the illusion of coherence, it seems to proceed reasonably enough, but actually it eludes comprehension. Its impossible plausibility would not appear to be consciously contrived, and in this its verbal style differs from that of more orthodox evangelists. Dr. Leary is nothing if not sincere, his language could not be less ornate or theatrical; it is indeed precisely from its naturalness that its hallucinatory quality derives. Much more than Dr. Leary's speech put me in mind of, say, a Father Divine, it reminded me of the mother of Lee Oswald, as Jean Stafford describes her in a remarkable little book, *A Mother in History,* a series of interviews between Miss Stafford and Mrs. Oswald. Reading Mrs. Oswald I longed for a stage prop or costume to assure me that this mistress of the ardently simple, utterly meaningless statement was acting out a role, not communicating a real-life condition. Just so, listening to Dr. Leary, I yearned for the honest contrivance of theatre.

But more, what particularly struck me when I returned to

Dr. Leary's notice in the lobby after I had become better acquainted with his mode of discourse was its premise of innocence. It is of course its innocence that constitutes a chief appeal of Dr. Leary's doctrine to the privileged young who, perhaps because they are the offspring of a parent generation intent on keeping no knowledge from them, now regard their elders as uniquely impure in motive and behavior. If the audience at the Village Barn was a fair sampling, as I think it was, Dr. Leary's followers are not to be associated with our ordinary image of juvenile delinquency. The class difference, involving not only differences of education but also of social assumption, significantly separates the users of LSD from the youth of street gangs and violence. The LSD phenomenon therefore represents a separate social problem located, I think, at that special place in society where cultural influences tend to supplant those social pressures which we usually have in mind when we think of economic, racial, or social inequity.

Still, nothing I learned in my evening with Dr. Leary proposed the idea that because his young followers make so urgent an option for virtue they have a special endowment of goodness, or even a notable sensitivity to ugliness. As to the first, there is no ground for belief that behind their benevolence there fail to exist our usual human angers and aggressions. As to the second, in the course of my evening at the Barn I came to suspect that if we are going to stay with the "frightened generation" explanation of the LSD phenomenon we must be precise about what we mean. Far from suggesting an extreme vulnerability to the terrors of life, these young people struck me as being markedly armored—and if this is because LSD has reduced their moral alertness, then we must regard the drug as perhaps more dehumanizing than we have yet recognized. My point could not be simpler: at the most alarming moments of the evening, such as when Dr. Leary announced that he knew no child over the age of seven who was not on drugs, or when his coadjutor, Dr. Richard Alpert, in response to a question about sixteen-, seventeen-, or eighteen-year-olds on LSD, said, "Even if they end up in a hospital or prison for a few months, it doesn't bother me," there was no slightest show of dismay from the audience. Fearful these young people may be, like the rest of us; they have a fearsome world in which to be young. But fear can present itself in a number of ways; it defines character only by the form it takes and the ends it is made to serve. To express concern for the children of Vietnam and yet remain unmoved by the idea of submitting seven-year-olds to hallucinogenic drugs is to obey the dictates of culture rather than of reliable feeling.

Dr. Leary and Dr. Alpert have both been university teachers, teaching psychologists. I daresay my own response to statements as cruelly irresponsible as these—they were spoken casually, easefully—is underscored by the importance I assign, the special importance, to their former profession. In a society as mobile as that of America and as unavailable to the ethical instruction once conveyed through established religion, the school is more than an institution for teaching the intellectual disciplines, it is the matrix of our cultural values, the chief source and guardian of our personal and social morality. What the school establishes today, it hopes that the home will have absorbed by tomorrow—we recall, for example, that the chief precepts of our present-day post-Freudian childrearing were originally promulgated in teacher-training programs. But the problem is that because America is as open-ended as it is, youth is cherished as it is, well beyond its emotional and social capacities, which means that the teacher whose task it is to instruct the young in the complexity of the social experience and in the limitations imposed upon the individual by emotional and social reality ought himself to be able to resist the seduction of rebelliousness for its own youthful sake. And this is apparently a difficult demand to make today of anyone of radical spirit and imagination. No one in the public life, certainly no one in government, has the ear of the young as do their university instructors, unless it is the advanced social and literary critics whose route to the young is of course more circuitous, so that if, as now increasingly happens, the teacher is reluctant to surrender the glamour of youthful rebelliousness and to discover in the exercise of the parental function its own grave satisfactions, he leaves his students in the position of children who have been robbed of the definition they achieve only when those who train them, and whom they naturally rebel against, have a firm authority of their own; they face emptiness, a universe without walls. I am not suggesting that the tide of nihilism in which the young appear to be more and more caught up takes its sole or primary force from the school. But if anything is to be done to stem it, this will have to be undertaken by the same class of people who did such a successful job of bringing the failure of the modern world to our educated consciousness. Dr. Leary was dismissed, as Dr. Alpert was too, from his Harvard post for engaging his students in experiments with drugs. I doubt, however, that he would have reached the young as he has were it not for this earlier professional certification.

But at our evening in the Barn Dr. Leary was not resting with his pedagogic function. He also made it a religious occasion, and thus drew on the shared fund of recollected churchgoing his audience, even his young audience, might be supposed to have brought to the celebration. (Dr. Leary, we must remember, is under indictment for illegal possession of drugs and if he is to plead freedom of religion under the First Amendment, he does well to put public emphasis on a religious purpose.) His show our night was called "The Incarnation of Christ"; he also does an "Illumination of the Buddha." The ceremonies had been advertised on the theatre rather than the religious pages of the newspapers, with Dr. Leary "IN PERSON" as the attraction. Despite the stardom, the religious note was kept dominant. In addition to the film-and-dance portion of the program, itself ritualistic, there was a sermon, there were prayers by Dr. Leary, and even a moment of silent prayer on the part of the "congregation." Early in the performance Dr. Leary reminded us that while we were gathered

here in New York for these ceremonies our opposite numbers
in India were enjoying their religious ecstasy on the shore of
the Ganges, and in Mexico they were attaining their exaltation
with peyote. Of ecstasy and exaltation there might actually be
none, either in Dr. Leary's performance or his audience, but
unmistakably a spirit of devoutness permeated the auditorium.
The religious emotions of Dr. Leary were nevertheless considerably interfered with by the strains and temptations of
showmanship. And he was very tired; one could see his fatigue
when he took his place on the platform in the darkened hall;
he might have been managing a hangover. This was a weary
impresario, a weary pedagogue, a weary Messiah. The multiplication of roles that Dr. Leary now assumes is his burden as
the leader of a movement which he could not have guessed
would grow so fast.

We had been shown to our seats at a press table: amusingly,
not unexpectably, a disproportionate space in the small auditorium had been set aside for those who would give the movement yet more of the publicity it has already had in
abundance. Although it was legitimate enough that the four of
us should present ourselves as members of the press, it added
to the self-consciousness I had felt ever since arriving at the
hall. It is always uncomfortable to sight-see in other peoples'
emotional universe; and after all it had come only as an after-
thought, when we were already seated, that perhaps I would
write about the occasion and therefore should take notes.
Some days later I was to read a review of our evening in the
New York Times by a reporter who apparently spotted us for
the tourists we were. She got us by name, described us as
"initiates of the older cults of politics and psychoanalysis." We
were likened, in uncommonly vivid reporting for the *Times* to
"atheists attending a religious ritual out of sociological interest, . . . our expressions faintly tinged with boredom and distaste." Well, the sociological posture was unquestionably
readiest to hand. But I am afraid I was unprotected by scientific distance from my objects of study. I looked at this

strangely subdued and isolate audience and I was painfully aware of the chasm that stretched between the world of these young people and mine at their age, of the difference between their dedication and the political dedication of the Marxist '30s when I and my friends had come to maturity. We too had been aware of the wrongness or insufficiencies of those in power. My contemporaries had similarly set themselves to make the "revolution." But our dedication had been social and political. Now the very concept of society was inoperative. And looking back today, how much justification have we for stern judgment upon those who lack an ideology of social involvement? To be sure, it was not our social emphasis which had led to the present blockage of hope. But the blockage of hope had nevertheless ensued for the young to cope with. And we had not had the atomic bomb. And there had been no such limitlessness in our world as there was now, no such vacuum as now passes for the structure of life. One need find no particular emotional vulnerability in Dr. Leary's followers to recognize that they had sufficient ground for confusion and despair, more by a good deal than even we had had when we rejected our society as given.

My unease was somewhat relieved when Allen Ginsberg came to sit at my side, and surely this is not the least interesting aspect of the evening, that by some marvelous transmutation of things as we think them to be, the fact that Ginsberg sat next to me through most of the performance was more than a comfort, it provided my chief link with sanity. We had seen him entering the hall and had waved. He had come over to say hello and just then the performance began. To avoid disturbance, Ginsberg sat down at my side. His beard was by far the most lavish in this well-bearded audience; were it still not a blackest black, he should be called the good gray poet of the psychedelic movement, such is his air of venerableness and wisdom, such the authority with which he now seems vested. Time had passed—seven years, eight years?—since I had last seen him. Then, too, it had been a public evening of which I had also tried (not with notable public success, as it turned out; but then, one has not the right to ask self-consciousness of one's readers, only of oneself) to report the inevitable reciprocity between the observed and the observer. It was very little later that Dr. Leary mentioned, in all mildness, the presence in the hall of agents from the Narcotics Squad. For a bad instant, as I looked around and saw no one who met the description, I supposed it must be the four of us Dr. Leary referred to—except, of course, we had Allen Ginsberg to vouch for us; he was our security in this alien territory. Throughout the ceremonies, speaking in a low steady voice, precise, in firm control of knowledge it pleased him to share, this former student of my husband's gave me the assurance I needed of my own identity, unchallenged, in no subtlest degree suborned. The adroitness with which Ginsberg made his aesthetic and critical removal from what was happening onstage, while keeping intact his old ties of theoretical and even practical approval of the drug-taking enterprise, was something of a triumph. Everything about him indeed, his weight of purpose no less than his canniness, freshly pressed upon me the importance, in the psychedelic universe as elsewhere, of the wish for fame and immortality, that most traditional impulse of the gifted. For what is it, finally, other than the force of this desire, that has sustained Ginsberg, regulated the degree of his involvement in dangerous personal experiment, urged him beyond the anonymousness implicit in the pursuit of selfhood through drugs?

Is Dr. Leary, as well, an exception to the harsh rule of self-eradication in drugs? I doubt it. Drug promotion is now giving Dr. Leary a rare celebrity. And by the evidence of these religious ceremonies he courts immortality in the largest possible way by identification with immortal principles and personages. But succeed as he may in making converts to his religion, as a self he wears the pale but indelible marks of doom: you see it as soon as he invites the spotlight. As a self, he has the invincible anonymousness of a television master of ceremonies, than which surely nothing could be more stricken from the immortal rolls. Dr. Leary looks to be in his mid-forties; he is tall, slim, with a suggestion of willowiness. He is, if you will, handsome, with something of the consciousness of the professional charmer, and I should suppose he is especially comfortable in his stage costume of white trousers and open-necked white shirt. The family background seems to be a little vague: apparently it is Irish Catholic, middle-western; one reads of an army father and that he himself went to West Point, but this is not the impression he creates—in appearance and voice he is only "sensitive" deteriorated Harvard, throwing away some considerable advantages of birth. He is fair-haired and tousled, wears a necklace, and performs in bare feet. When he takes the microphone in hand, one feels it is a natural extension of his infatuate ego and that it will more and more become his staff and his rod, his auxiliary drug, his surrogate selfhood. As the evening wore on, with Dr. Leary up there on the platform and Allen Ginsberg at my side, I had the sense of an entertaining ambiguity in the relation of these two psychedelic figures. At least before friends like ourselves from an earlier period in his career Ginsberg seemed to me to make a point of his poetic pride, of his superiority to the leader, even of his superior scholarship, but I may have misread him. At any rate, in the course of the ceremonies he several times alluded to the need for humor in dealing with the LSD subject. For the poverty of Dr. Leary's show as art he was carefully and courteously apologetic.

There was, first, the darkening of the hall and Dr. Leary's entrance into the spotlight, behind him a white and still-empty screen. From the wings of this makeshift theatre came the soft strumming of a guitar, and immediately the audience was churchy-still—except that the comparison is absurd: church is where people cough and rustle and squirm and there was no coughing or rustling or squirming in the Barn, unless on the part of four unlicensed sociologists. Through the next two hours (I guess the show lasted) Dr. Leary had his audience in entire control; he could be envied by the professionals.

With his opening remarks Dr. Leary effectively formulated, if one can put it so, the incoherence through which I would try to grope for the remainder of the evening. I have a friend who shares his apartment with a painter; one day my friend's mother (this is a Jewish story) came to see him, examined the paintings on his walls, and turned to her son with the question, "Who authorized these pictures?" It was the question I would have put to Dr. Leary: Who, or what, had authorized this particular conglomerate of pageant, preachment, classroom, revival meeting, dance, movie, and amateur night? Where had this performance come from, what was the source of its inspiration? How much was it the psychedelic experience itself being reproduced for us, how much an "artistic" derivation? How much was Dr. Leary improvising a gospel, and how much was he bearing witness to the accepted doctrine? Where did the play end and pedagogy begin, where did pedagogy end and the play begin? Had Dr. Leary and his co-performers recently taken LSD and was the drug present in the talk that accompanied the film, or had there been the intention of artistic detachment from the actual drugged state? A few years ago it was reported of the then-censored movie *Flaming Creatures*, whether accurately or not I have no way of knowing, that its actors were all of them under drugs when it was made; this one could credit from the loose automatism of their movements and their dispersed sexuality. Dr. Leary's film and the sporadic miming that took place in front of the screen and the words Dr. Leary himself spoke and those that were intoned antiphonally by the male pantomimist and a woman at the side of the stage were sufficiently lifeless to suggest some similar interference with normal process. Still, I realize that what looked like blocked transmission in Dr. Leary's show may simply have been amateurishness. "You have to go out of your mind to come to your senses." "We don't pray to anyone up there but to what is inside ourselves." Even announcing his best-shaped slogans, Dr. Leary himself, in spite of his naturalness and sincerity, failed to take significant shape except in a form already made iconographic by nightclub and television "personalities." The essential quality he conveyed was that of a schoolmaster acting the master of ceremonies in a school show, a good-looking, tired, essentially vulgar, still-boyish teacher, histrionic, equally pleased with his popularity among his students and with the privileges of office which he could exercise as occasion demanded.

He stayed in the spotlight, quite alone, for rather a while. I had no sense it was too long for his audience. His lecture-preachment-patter covered a general territory already well known from repeated accounts of the doctrine. What one had not been sufficiently prepared for was the vagrancy of Dr. Leary's thought, its bold (however weary), bald carelessness of the ordinary rules of reasonableness, of intelligible discourse. For the occasion of ceremony everything was spoken with the cadence of ceremony, something between a croon and a subdued exhortation. *We pray we are not hung up and that you will have a good trip* (did he mean in our next LSD session, or only metaphorically, here in the theatre?). . . . *The voyage is always the same* (did he mean reliable or was he remarking the singleness of the indicated path?). . . . *We renew and reenact the ancient myths* (this could refer to the play but it could also refer to the sacred journey to which we were being urged). . . . *We pass on what we* (an editorialized Dr. Leary, psychologist?) *have learned in ten years of hard work.* . . . *We* (Dr. Leary and his audience? Dr. Leary and others under the influence of LSD?) *meet in our retinas, we meet on the screen in the vibrating beams of light, also we meet in the liquid canals of the ear; then we move within to resurrect the body, rediscover the timepiece of the universe: the heartbeat.* . . . *Then we breathe together.* . . . *You should not take a trip without a road map.* . . . *Myths are cellular.* . . . *The myth is a blueprint.* . . . *Tonight we invite you to relive the myth of Jesus Christ. . . . The resurrection of Jesus Christ has been a rough trip for all of us* (Dr. Leary and his co-authors? All of us in the twentieth century who are the inheritors of the Christian tradition?).

First we ran into Christian backlash, second the backlash from Jews and atheists. . . . The Christian myth means, once there was a man who took all the guilts, the shoulds and shouldn'ts, on his own shoulders and wiped them out. If you experience this myth (before you take the drug? afterward?) *you are free. . . . Go back and free the world from good and evil. . . . The tolling of the bell at Millbrook* (here the clanging of a loud bell presumably took us to Dr. Leary's "institute") *takes us on a voyage of discovery. You have to have a guide in the person who has been there before you: an old witch or a frog or a hunchback. Today, your teenage child. . . . They have the key to the voyage and it always involves a chemical tick.* (Trick?) *This is the Chalice, the Holy Communion, and always the Last Supper: good-bye to all back there. . . . I welcome you in the name of the Father, the Son, and the Holy Ghost. . . . Give thanks as we take the Chalice and let our thanks ascend. Drink. This is my flesh, bone, and blood. . . . As often as you do this, do this in memory of me.*

Lights had now begun to flash on the screen and Dr. Leary moved to the side of the stage. His voice rose in intensity. *Open the naked eye, find the center.* Great circles of light appear on the screen, and the show complicates itself:

GIRL'S VOICE. *Can you float through the universe of your body and not lose your way?*

No one directly answers the question. Mushroomlike patterns form on the screen. In front of the screen a man in black trousers, bare above the waist, sways slowly, it would seem painfully, his arms weaving and reaching in the familiar dance idiom of tortured quest.

GIRL'S VOICE. *What is happening?*

DR. LEARY. *Float to the center.*

MAN'S VOICE. *I am drowning in blood. . . . Help. . . . Please make it stop. . . . No, no, don't make it stop.*

GIRL'S VOICE. *Blood to death. . . . Out. . . . Out. . . . Blood to death. . . . Life. . . . Life. . . . Life. . . . Scarlet. . . .*

MAN'S VOICE. *So warm. . . . Drifting down. . . . Melting. . . . Breathing. . . . Breath of life. . . .*

Here my notes indicate a certain amount of groaning on the stage but not who is the sufferer. Unfortunately, I have no shorthand. But if at first I am troubled by my inability to catch every word being spoken on the stage, soon enough, as I catch the drift, I realize that the drift is all. It is said of LSD that it taps the unconscious in order to add to the store of the conscious; this is indeed its first much-vaunted value, that it is supposed to augment consciousness. But surely to call the LSD experience consciousness-enhancing is to merge two meanings of the word "consciousness"—that which we oppose to *un*consciousness and by which we mean those activities of the mind which we can take note of as they proceed, and, second, the honorific meaning, that of active and useful awareness. If one is to judge the LSD state by Dr. Leary's representation or elaboration of it in his ceremonies or by anything one has so far read of it, what happens under LSD may very well be a flooding of the mind with images or emotions from which it is otherwise closed off. But what the mind does with this new material speaks not at all of a significantly enhanced mental activity such as we usually adduce in our appreciation of awareness. The problem is, of course, an old one in aesthetics. It is not without interest that the new Coleridge scholarship demonstrates with some persuasiveness that "Kubla Khan" was not actually an opium dream and that Coleridge offered it as such only in polemic, as a defense of the role of nonreason in the writing of poetry. But it is not solely an aesthetic problem, it is also a scientific problem and a vexing one: how define what we mean by consciousness, especially in the creative process?

The dialogue between male and female voice now peters out and Dr. Leary relinquishes the spotlight so that the full attention of the audience can be focused on the screen. The pictures that appear look to me like magnified blood cells or other organic matter. Then gradually they become more complex, "social," sometimes fleetingly identifiable. Also, the background music now rises in volume, becomes more assertive—Ginsberg whispers to me, "The *Missa Luba,* a Congo version of the Catholic mass," and obediently I hear what could perhaps be the *Kyrie Eleison.* He whispers "Verdi's *Requiem*" and, more reluctantly, I hear that as well. Without my having quite noted, the guitar has eliminated itself, been replaced by a sound track to accompany what is apparently intended as an evocation of the evolutionary process, a kind of psychedelic March of Time. Ginsberg mentions a word that sounds like *straboscopia,* which I take to derive from the same root as *strabismus:* "Med. A disorder of the eye in which the optic axes cannot be directed to the same object because of incoordination of the muscles of the eyeballs. . . ." In later dictionary consultation I realize he said *stroboscopic,* pertaining to "an instrument for observing the successive phases of a periodic motion by means of light periodically interrupted." But the difference is only objective. The camera's wish to catch the speed of psychedelic imagery affects me like a sickness of the eye. From my press table I no longer see Dr. Leary. I assume he is seated stage right. His voice resumes the incantation:

Let's return to the twentieth century and reincarnate Jesus Christ. Let's do it everyone of us right now. . . . You have to take on all the guilt, sin, and wretchedness of the world. . . . You have to do this for everyone so that there won't be any more. . . . Then we're all through with the good-evil thing and you will be reborn. . . . All-embracing, Dr. Leary invites the police and the narcotics agents to join in the rebirth, and for the first and only time in the evening his audience is vocally responsive. "You're right," come several voices from the audience, soft, devout.

My notes do not say if Dr. Leary is now once more stage center, in full spotlight, but I recollect him to be. The film has now run its spotty course, from our unicellular origins to our modern metropolitan mediocrity, and we can have the sermon. It is in fullest stage center that Dr. Leary makes his biggest pitch of the evening, inviting someone to come up from the audience to the platform, take off his clothes, and be nailed to the cross. *Let's look in the bag. There are some nails here and a crown of thorns.* The audience remains unmoving. Dr. Leary is apparently not surprised, he had expected no volunteers; one wonders, in fact, what he would do if a too-eager listener proffered his services. He repeats: *Will anyone volunteer to be nailed to the cross if we guarantee you there will be no more evil in the world?* He dissipates the reverential hush, or at least lifts it a fraction, with a prepared comment: Dr. Leary confides to us that he had been warned that if he made such a proposal in this setting, "four hundred and ninety-seven exhibitionists, sado-masochists and faggots would storm the platform." There is no laughter. *No, we must not do it that way, we must do it with our clothes on, or even our uniforms. . . . But let's do it.*

There follows the more formal sermon, wholly Dr. Leary's show and, like all sermons, lengthy. Its text, Dr. Leary announces, is from William Blake *who had been in our profession a couple of hundred years ago.* (Sic). . . . *He who is a fool persists in his folly.* (Sic). . . . We must start a new religion, says Dr. Leary, and start a new country. *We have been working six years*—it had been ten, I recall, a few minutes back—*to work out a plan to turn on this country and this planet. . . . Starting a new religion is like starting a new business. Or a garden. There are inevitable sequences. . . . A series of ordeals or tests. . . . We have no paranoia or hostility about our opposition, it's a rough business starting a new religion. It's a rough business but highly stylized, more classic than baseball or football. . . . We must turn on, tune in, and drop out. . . . Turn off your mind and go within. . . . You need a sacrament and today it is a chemical. The chemicals we use are ancient. . . . Treat these sacraments with the respect they deserve. Before you turn on you must be in a state of grace. You must look into yourself and see where you have sinned. On your own chessboard. You are the only one who can forgive yourself. You look in your mirror, in your retina is the history. You confess to yourself. If you don't go to confession before you take a sacrament you may writhe, suffer, call for a doctor. . . . Once you turn on, then you tune in, show others what has been shown to you.* Dr. Leary calls on Rudi and Jackie, assistants, to come forward and testify. They have apparently helped to put the show together, now they will help us tune in.

DR. LEARY.   *Rudi, where are we now and where are we going?*

RUDI (thinking).   *We are working from a core which is a circle of love. A very beautiful and pure thing.*

DR. LEARY.   *Jackie, where are we?*

JACKIE (who is a girl).   *We are here and happy to be here. And we are going from here out, to turn on the world.*

DR. LEARY.   *We have to work with the young, the artists, the underground groups for a new breakthrough. Artists change consciousness and the change lasts. . . . We work to change family life. . . . Encourage husbands and wives to take LSD together. . . . I can't imagine a husband being turned on without wanting to turn on his wife. I can't imagine parents being turned on without wanting to turn on their children. I know no child over the age of seven who hasn't been given drugs and I know many of them. The parents turn on the children.*

Dr. Leary has a practiced device of irony. He echoes his outrage of decency in the voice of outraged respectability: *Imagine turning on children!*

There is a pregnant pause, and Dr. Leary recapitulates:

The psychedelic experience is one you want to share with those you care most about.`. . . Inconceivable that parents would take LSD and not want their children to share the experience.

The audience continues to be dead still: no one stamps, hisses, rises to object. No one leaves the theatre. (And no reporter, to my knowledge, undertakes to report what we all of us at Dr. Leary's press tables so clearly heard.) From this point forward, the rest of Dr. Leary's sermon is bound to be anticlimax:

We are now in a legal and political phase. . . . Several million Americans are taking LSD, more taking marijuana, for serious purposes. . . . They need an institution. . . . We are working with the courts to license small groups to take LSD. . . . After you tune in you drop out. It happens so gracefully. . . . A detachment from old ambitions and drives. . . . What we meet and work for is what you want and know is possible. . . . We need and invite your comments and questions.

The comments and questions that comprise the remainder of the program may be what Dr. Leary invites, they cannot be what he needs. But then, what speaker ever gets the questions he needs, and these were at least not intended to provoke or challenge: Dr. Leary fares better than most public speakers when they finish a talk and discover to whom they have been speaking and what they are thought to have said. A man rises from the audience to say that he has confronted the beast: Is this what Dr. Leary meant by confrontation with the wolf? Myself, I had heard no mention of wolves, singular or plural. I wonder if the questioner has in mind the beast one confronts in the mirror when one confesses to oneself, or merely an encounter on the psychedelic journey. Dr. Leary is perhaps himself confused. At any rate, he chooses this moment to call to the stage "his well-known colleague" Dr. Richard Alpert, recently returned from California. Together, Dr. Leary and Dr. Alpert respond to the question that has been asked by explaining the uterine recapitulation of man's long slow evolution. *Memory cards flash through your brain when you take LSD, so it doesn't fit your tidy twentieth-century mind.* I conclude from this that when you take LSD you return to the womb and relive the prenatal development.

The second questioner is a priest; he is recognized by Dr. Leary and Dr. Alpert as a friend. The priest wants to know whether after many trips you could not have the same experience without taking the drug. It is Dr. Alpert who undertakes to reply: *After a trip you get depressed by your new sense of your daily life. After enough of this, you stay high all the time because you have revised your life. . . . LSD is not a substitute for the conscious effort of digging here and now. . . . LSD is a constant reminder of our divinity. We mustn't stop because we are too busy. . . . Find someone not on LSD and find out how he and I are us.* This is the point at which I recall, with a certain syntactical confusion, the priest in Ilf and Petrov's wonderful *Little Golden Calf* of whom the verb "befuddle" is used as an active verb of expression: "Yes," befuddled the priest; "No," befuddled the priest. But of course this was in another country. . . . The priest sits down; he is apparently satisfied with the answer that has been given him.

And now the master of ceremonies introduces Allen Ginsberg from among the audience, calls him to the stage. Ginsberg rises modestly but readily—had he been forewarned?—to join the circle on the platform. While he is threading his way through the audience, Dr. Leary intersperses some remarks on electrons, heightens the scientific authority of the occasion. He also addresses himself to the subject of people killing themselves under the effects of LSD: the percentage is negligible, he assures us, and anyway these are the people who failed to go to confession and expunge their guilts. Dr. Leary gives the nod to the next questioner.

This time the question, although manifestly not intended to give offense, does suggest criticism; it is carefully larded with apology. It seems that although the questioner himself understands the moral nature of the LSD enterprise, there are people of his acquaintance who take the drug just for kicks. Would Dr. Leary comment on this? From the other side of the theatre, I have no trouble hearing the question. But Dr. Leary seems to have difficulty; he turns to his coadjutors in appeal but getting no help he invites his interrogator to the stage. But on his way, this young man is checked by another member of the audience who rises to protest that such a question can only come from someone caught "in the game"—which is to say, someone under the influence of this-worldly, nonpsychedelic values. A moment of tension develops between the two men at the foot of the platform—it represents something of a relief amidst all this benignity—and then Allen Ginsberg intervenes: *You're taking it too seriously, keep some humor.* The questioner addresses the stage in self-defense: *But I want a successful revolution.* To which Leary responds soothingly: *Tell us why, how are we sliding back from the center?* The questioner identifies himself as an instructor in a college in South Jersey. Grievingly he explains that some of his students fail to understand the moral purpose of LSD, they take it for the sensation, they are not *serious*. (He hits the word as I have not heard a word hit since the days when the comrades would accuse each other of being *subjective*.) *And I want you to win, I want a revolution like you do.* The troubled comrade from South Jersey is at last disposed of by Dr. Alpert, judiciously: *It doesn't matter from what motive these kids of sixteen, seventeen, or eighteen take LSD, if they turn on for thirty seconds the experience is so profound. Even if they end up in a hospital or prison for a few months, it doesn't bother me. . . . The confusion is the greatest kind of confusion for these*

*kids, at any age. It opens the door and makes a mensch of
them.* The audience is relieved and ready for the catharsis of
humor after such unblessed controversy.

The necessary humorous relief is supplied by a Negro, a
solid and comely man who rises at the rear of the hall and
announces in a big resonant voice that he has only a single
question to ask: *What is LSD?* Although he has produced
through the hall the only titter of the evening, he meets a wall
of impenetrable silence on the stage. The questioner repeats
his question, once, twice, a third time. He becomes insistent:
*I'm just asking a single question. I hear you all talking about
LSD. What I want to know is, what is LSD?* After what seems
forever—the audience is becoming restive—someone onstage
has the presence of mind to answer firmly: *It is a chemical.*
And the subject is closed: the questioner sits down. Dr. Leary
makes a few remarks about his League for Spiritual Discovery,
much in the spirit of a preacher before the plate is passed; no
plate is passed, the evening has been an expense to no one. *We
in the League are working, at risk, to legalize marijuana and
LSD. . . . It is an intimate family thing we're doing.* Allen
Ginsberg steps forward and announces an antiwar rally on the
following Saturday—no, not an antiwar rally, a "peaceable
march, a transcendence over anger." The meeting is at an
end.

There is again no elbowing or pressing as the crowd begins
to leave the hall. Now, as not before the performance started, I
begin to see couples, pairs of boys and girls holding hands,
much as married couples leave funerals or weddings with
clasped hands, bound in the intimacy of shared emotion. (Dr.
Leary, incidentally, could not be more pious than he is about
coupling: approaching the sexual subject, he speaks only of
"making love to your wife.") It also becomes possible, here
and there, to particularize other sight-seers among the dedicated: the slowed-down man in his late thirties who wears the
mark of yearning, of loneliness, of the failed artist; the dykish,
tight-lipped girl who belongs at the side of the swimming-pool

of a women's "Y"; the bookkeeper, as I am certain, who stands out in the crowd for her excruciating neatness and spinsterishness no less than for her advanced years—it is she whom I overhear greeting an acquaintance: "What did you think of it? Weren't you *impressed?*" These are the wanderers between worlds.

But for the most part the audience is as one had first perceived it: young, "with-it," middle-class, good contemporary faces of the kind one wants to trust, the faces of people to whom intellectual leadership might be thought appropriate except that they had made another choice and the signal of it is in their eyes. The four of us appeal to each other: Is it only the gifted who go in for this sort of thing? Are these the best, the brightest, of their generation? We of course haven't the answer, any more than we have the answer to a corollary question, How can any enlightened person of whatever age take this psychedelic leader with intellectual seriousness, assent in an ideology so barren of ideas, so lacking even in simplest coherence? As we move to the street, away from the theatre—unregenerate, we are looking for a beer—this becomes, in fact, the nub of our anxiety. For us, Dr. Leary's religious ceremony had been ridiculous when it had not been despicable, but we had been surrounded by young people of good education who not only could take Dr. Leary's drug and this celebration of it but had also somehow managed to issue to the whole subject of LSD a safe-conduct which exempted it from rational inspection, creating—or perhaps only responding to?—an atmosphere in which whoever would put it to adverse question is automatically taken to be repressive, retrograde, lacking in imagination, deficient in scientific open-mindedness.

But Dr. Leary's epiphany gave rise to even bleaker thoughts than these. In the past month I had heard of four more young people, four adolescent children of friends, who had broken down as a result of LSD—two college boys and a college girl who had had to be hospitalized, a high school boy who, on the edge of psychosis, had had to be withdrawn from school. This made, so far, seven LSD casualties within my own small circle of acquaintance. Of course some or all of them may have been predisposed to mental breakdown. And we had no figures to tell whether they were in any way representative of what could happen to Dr. Leary's followers. This being so, how long were we to wait for the statistics to accumulate and be got in order?

For Dr. Alpert there were surely no such anxieties. "These kids" were simply casualties of the new dispensation, eggs that had to be broken to make Dr. Leary's omelette. But I could no more shrug off this concern, retreat into "scientific" or ironic detachment, than I could muster "objectivity" to meet the destruction of the young for the sake of some new Jerusalem of the political imagination. The destruction of a person's mental powers is *actual,* like hunger, poverty, death. It happens in actual life; it entails actual anguish. No, the nub of my anxiety as I left Dr. Leary's show was not that his audience could give credence to the nonsense he spoke—clever as so many of his young followers are, they have no doubt already learned to trust the LSD tale rather than its teller—but the recognition that the direction we take from our present belief that whatever is new and dissident is good in itself, no matter what its form, may very well lose for us the basic everyday knowledge of human identity, including the knowledge that the human mind in all its weakness and error is not to be so lightly tampered with.

[1967]

Two
Symposiums

1. Liberal
Anti-Communism Revisited

THE QUESTIONS

1. It has recently been charged that the anti-Communism of the Left was in some measure responsible for, or helped to create a climate of opinion favorable to, the war in Vietnam. What justification, if any, do you find in that charge? As someone whose name has been associated with the anti-Communist Left, do you feel in any way responsible for American policies in Vietnam?

2. Would you call yourself an anti-Communist today? If so, are you still willing to support a policy of containing the spread of Communism? If not, why have you changed? Assuming that you once supported containment because you were opposed on moral rather than narrowly political grounds to the spread of a totalitarian system, why do you think it wrong to apply the same principle to Vietnam?

3. Do the recent revelations concerning covert CIA backing of projects, some of which you probably sympathized with, or may perhaps have been involved in yourself, prove that liberal anti-Communism has been a dupe of, or a slave to, the darker impulses of American foreign policy?

We Must March My Darlings

[Since the publication of this symposium in 1967 the issues which
come within its orbit have continued to divide the intellectual community with ever-increasing acuteness, albeit with always–diminish-
ing intellectual force. The most recent document of this division is
Lillian Hellman's *Scoundrel Time*, published in 1976, in which
both my husband, Lionel Trilling, and I are singled out for mention:
we are described as "old, respected friends" of whom Miss Hellman
wonders how we "could have come out of the same age and time
with such different political and social views" from her own. Although the context of this inquiry is scarcely a happy one, Miss
Hellman writes of us with manifest courtesy. She has also given me
the welcome assurance that it was not her intention to imply that
my husband and I are among her "scoundrels." And indeed her
puzzlement about my husband's or my views would not be of public
consequence were it not for the unusually wide audience her book
has reached and the almost universally uncritical reception it has
received as historical statement. A narrative that should have com-
manded attention as a work of autobiography, one among several
volumes in which Miss Hellman, an imaginative writer of established gift, looks back upon her past, is being read as a political
revelation innocent of bias. And in fact *Scoundrel Time* carries a
foreword by Mr. Garry Wills whose purpose is to provide historical
validation. Among readers who have no historical knowledge to
bring to bear on the political preferences which determined Miss
Hellman's life in the period with which she is dealing, the confidence
this inspires in the objectivity of *Scoundrel Time* is likely to tran-
scend Miss Hellman's own disclaimer that she is offering us merely
a personal story and it demands, it seems to me, at least some small
effort of historical reconstruction by those of different political
opinion from hers. Then too, Miss Hellman's expression of honest
puzzlement about my husband's and my politics is difficult for me
to ignore since I have myself for so many years lived with a be-
wilderment, the obverse of hers but similarly burdensome, about
the many friends and acquaintances who—in all conscience, I prefer
to assume—have held political views not inconsistent with Miss Hellman's and therefore alien to mine.

Lionel Trilling is now dead—I would point out that Miss Hellman
could have had no knowledge of his fatal illness when she wrote as

she did—and cannot make his own response to her inquiry, and I do not presume to reply for him. Nor can I suppose this necessary inasmuch as his answer is everywhere in his writings, most explicitly in *The Liberal Imagination,* in his introduction to the stories of Isaac Babel, in his introduction to a volume of Polish stories in translation called *The Broken Mirror,* in his introduction to George Orwell's *Homage to Catalonia,* in his introduction to the reissue of his novel *The Middle of the Journey,* and in that novel itself. On his behalf I do, however, venture here a small addendum to his characterization of Whittaker Chambers as "a man of honor" in the new foreword to *The Middle of the Journey:* this is referred to in *Scoundrel Time.* My husband first employed the phrase when a lawyer for Hiss came to see him, as a Columbia College classmate of Chambers, in the hope of gaining information which would damage Chambers's credibility. What my husband meant by it was simple: he had little liking for Chambers but he didn't believe him capable of bearing false witness; and this continued to be his judgment of Chambers vis-à-vis Alger Hiss. It is perhaps worth remarking that people who know Hiss even less well than my husband knew Chambers, or who don't know him at all but think him innocent of the charges brought against him, are of course proceeding on much the same judgment of Hiss, which must make them, for those of different view, similar targets for scorn and incredulity.

It is on my own part that I take the opportunity of the present volume to reply to Miss Hellman's wonder about my politics by expanding my response to the questions asked in this *Commentary* symposium: while the other pieces in the volume which were previously published remain essentially unaltered except for minor changes in the interest of more precise formulation, this piece has been extensively rewritten in 1976 in the interest of political clarification, although even with this expansion it is palpably inadequate to the complex historical material to which it addresses itself. If, as is inevitable, the reader will be uncertain which portions of my reply were written in 1967 and which in 1976, I am afraid that the only help I can offer, other than referring him back to my original contribution of 1967, is to say that the answer which first appeared stayed almost wholly with the evolution and results of the anti–anti-Communist position, as it had come to be called. I am aware, however, that even expanded as it now is, my answer to this questionnaire is unlikely to persuade those of either the Left or the Right to amend their views or better understand mine. In the category of the Left I include Miss Hellman herself, who has been able to countenance all the atrocities of Communist power since she and I came of political age in the thirties and who even today, in *Scoundrel Time,* feels that the error in her long unwavering acquiescence in Stalinism is disposed of in a phrase such as "and there were plenty of sins [in "Stalin Communism"] and plenty that for a long time I mistakenly denied." On the Right I place those anti-Communists who, though they share my opposition to Communism, do not share its premise in liberalism as traditionally defined.

One further introductory word: For a new generation of readers the very idea of writing in 1976 about something called "anti-Communism" is bound to seem strange. They don't know any Communists, not in the America in which they grew up, nor do I. As to a division, and an ever-sharpening one, between the anti-Communist "position" and the anti–anti-Communist "position" such as I write about in this symposium, it can only strike them as bizarre—what factions are these and who are their members? I must seem to speak not only of a world they never made but of a world they don't inhabit, for theirs is a political culture in which the exercise of choice, if choice it eventually is, refers only, dismally, to the Democratic and Republican parties and not to opposing views of Stalinism—Stalin died more than twenty years ago, and what has developed in the Soviet Union since then has to do with a struggle not among American intellectuals but between two giant Communist forces, Russia and China, with other significant if less momentous contests pressing in upon this major conflict. Particularly for those who grew up in the sixties, it is the Vietnam War that made their testing ground of conscience. It was by the decision whether they were for or against the Vietnam War that they charted their political direction. The imperialist issue, the racial issue, both of which they rightly or wrongly related to our American intervention—I happen to think wrongly, but the situation was presented to them in these terms—were their issues.

Yet this generation reads a book like *Scoundrel Time* and says to itself, "See, this is how it was even thirty years ago in this country; you couldn't act in a movie that showed Russians smiling," and while they properly look upon the congressional investigations and McCarthyism as dangerous phenomena in our country's past, they fail to understand the political situation of that period, or the political and cultural conditions to which they were a reaction, conditions which had their origin in an intense Communist partisanship among our ostensibly most conscientious and enlightened classes. Or if they read established, respected periodicals such as the *New York Review of Books* or even the *New York Times Book Review*, it rarely occurs to them to ask how, other than perhaps in response to advertising pressures, their editors determine which book is worth notice, or on what principle its reviewer is selected, and how the prominence or lack of prominence given a review is decided upon: are there considerations other than those of interest and merit? And not alone for this younger generation of readers but for most of their parent generation as well, the possibility that these decisions reflect, as they so often do, present-day political choices which, in turn, sometimes directly and consciously, sometimes indirectly and automatically, refer to the divisions of as much as thirty or forty years ago on the Communist issue, is virtually inconceivable.

Well, Napoleon said that history is destiny. The history of the last forty or more years is the destiny not only of the Solzhenitsyns of our present era, it is the destiny of everyone everywhere. The destiny of people who hadn't yet been born when partisanship with or opposition to Communism made the great intellectual rift in this country, was shaped, and continues to be shaped, by the history of the period Miss Hellman writes about and, yet more importantly, by the political attitudes established in the crucial years which preceded it.]*

* In September 1976 I was informed by the publishers with whom I was originally under contract for this volume that unless I removed my critical references to Miss Hellman, author of *Scoundrel Time* and one of their best-selling writers, they would not publish my book. Four passages were specified for deletion, two in this prefatory statement and two in the text that follows; when I refused to make the deletions, my contract was terminated. In the ensuing burst of publicity—I had nothing to do with its initiation—Miss Hellman maintained the position that she didn't know what I had written about her in my book and didn't wish to know, but she was quoted in the *New York Times* (Sept. 29, 1976) as saying, " 'I was told that it contained a hysterical personal attack on me.' " And my

Not merely as preamble but because it is central to my reply to these questions, I wish to comment on your untroubled use of the word "liberal" and of the phrase "of the Left" in association with the anti-Communist view. In 1976 it is hard to re-

---

quondam editor was quoted in *Time* magazine (Oct. 11, 1976) as saying, " 'I know what the hell's in the goddam manuscript,' " implying horrors not yet revealed.

The nature of the "hysterical personal attack" and of yet-unrevealed assaults is now made public: *the references to Miss Hellman which I was asked to remove appear here unaltered.* Anyone who expected a cannonade is bound to be disappointed; and I am disappointed as well because in keeping my statements about Miss Hellman intact so that readers might judge for themselves what justification there was for the action of her publishers I have sacrificed the opportunity to make detailed reply to a book which has been widely, but mistakenly, received as a reliable history of the McCarthy period and as the record of a virtually unique personal heroism in the midst of almost universal cowardice.

Obviously even a very long footnote cannot cover the ground which needs to be covered in response to *Scoundrel Time.* There are nevertheless a few points which I think should be isolated for mention if Miss Hellman's narrative is to be properly assessed as historical reporting. Although several of them have already appeared in various periodicals, there may be usefulness in summarizing them and bringing them together in one place.

1. The fact that McCarthy used the Communist issue wholly for opportunistic purposes does not mean that Communism didn't exist as a danger in the world or that the murderous Soviet regime lacked active powerful support in America, particularly in the entertainment industry. As to the House Un-American Activities Committee, it was a duly constituted Congressional committee and the fact that it often showed itself poorly equipped to make the difficult necessary discriminations between protecting democracy and weakening it or, as would develop, that it included members of bad character cannot be taken as indication that whoever it put under scrutiny was thereby certified to be innocent.

2. As Mr. Hilton Kramer, the distinguished art critic, made plain in a long piece in the *New York Times* (Oct. 3, 1976) about the blacklisting of Communists in the theatre and Hollywood in the McCarthy period, this was no one-way street. To be sure, the infringement of the right of anti-Communists to be heard wasn't as dramatic as the Hollywood action against Communists; it didn't always rise even to the level of overtness of the recent effort of Miss Hellman's publishers to protect Miss Hellman against criticism. But not only in the past but even today, when actual Communist partisanship hardly exists in this country, we still live with the cultural detritus of Communist fellow-travelling, and

member that in 1967, a short nine years ago when this symposium was printed, it was still possible to make such easy conjunction between the liberal or left-wing position and anti-Communism. Today the connection would be impermissible for

---

highly volatile it is, whatever the form it now takes. Especially in the advanced literary community, and despite certain notable exceptions, liberal anti-Communism was not, and still is not, the recommended path to professional success.

3. In the sentence in *Scoundrel Time* which follows Miss Hellman's reference to Lionel Trilling and myself as "old, respected friends" whose political evolution she finds it difficult to comprehend, she writes: "Facts are facts—and one of them is that a pumpkin, in which Chambers claimed to have hidden the damaging evidence against Hiss, deteriorates—and there never had been a chance that, as Trilling continues to claim in the *New York Review*, Chambers was a man of honor." Facts are indeed facts—and the papers which helped to convict Hiss were never near the pumpkin. There were *no* papers among the so-called pumpkin papers, and no one acquainted with the facts had ever, as Lillian Hellman's report in *Scoundrel Time* might be taken to suggest, proposed that there were. There was a handful of microfilms, some undeveloped and even uncapped, which Chambers hurriedly took from documents he had hidden elsewhere. And these films stayed in the pumpkin for only *a single day,* outdoors, before being turned over to the authorities.

4. Readers of *Scoundrel Time,* for whom the chief value of Miss Hellman's book lies in its attestation to American "witch-hunting"—apparently we live in a world of political sanctity in which this country is to be singled out for its intolerance of dissent!—make light of the importance which was ever to be attached to Communist fellow-travelling. In this they differ from the Soviet Union which never made light of the good press it could hope to gain from those whose sympathy it trusted. Evidence of this is provided both in *Scoundrel Time* and in Miss Hellman's earlier *An Unfinished Woman* by Miss Hellman herself: as a visitor in Russia in World War II she was not only permitted the rare privilege of mingling freely with the Red Army on the Polish front and accompanying it to Warsaw and on to Berlin if she wished, but even offered an interview with Stalin.

5. Miss Hellman reports that during the presidential campaign of Henry Wallace in 1948, Mr. Wallace asked her one day if it was true—how naive can one be?—that Communists were supporting him. Miss Hellman answered that this was indeed the case and Mr. Wallace seemed less than happy. Through an unnamed friend of whose politics Miss Hellman says she was ignorant, she requested and was at once granted a private meeting with top officials of the Communist Party of the United States to inform them of Mr. Wallace's displeasure.

those who oppose themselves to anti-Communism; and an increasing number of anti-Communists would reject it as well. The passage of less than a decade has produced an extraordinary rigidification among those who commandeered the word "liberal" for views which often have their primary source in a reluctance to speak out against Communism and, among opponents of Communism, a growing movement toward, if not an explicitly right-wing position, an increased political conservatism.

I am of neither faction. I am, was, and always shall be an anti-Communist. No new look which Communism may present to the world or even to its own people frees its people from dictatorship. Therefore there can be no thaw—or detente—which can persuade me that totalitarianism is anything but an

---

6. The First Amendment protects free speech and thought. When those who were first called before the HUAC pleaded the First, they were protesting the right of the Committee to delve into their political beliefs. But if the Committee overrode this protest and demanded a reply to its questions and a witness still refused to answer, he could be cited for contempt and sentenced to jail. The Fifth Amendment protects a witness from giving testimony which might be self-incriminating. In taking the Fifth, which many of the people called before the HUAC did, they of course laid themselves open to the imputation of guilt but, not in contempt of Congress, they stayed out of jail. Much of Miss Hellman's book is the story of her stern determination to tell the truth about herself without implicating other people in her answers to the HUAC. This is the personal history which has won her such wide acclaim for courage where courage was presumably in short supply. But she too pleaded the Fifth to avoid jail. The sole difference between her response to the HUAC and that of others who took the Fifth was a public-relations strategy originated for her by Abe Fortas and developed with her by Joseph Rauh: before appearing before the HUAC she wrote her now-famous letter about not cutting her conscience to fit this year's fashions in which she offered to answer questions about herself but not about others. It was a masterpiece of moral showmanship but its offer was of course not accepted—and like everyone else who didn't want to go to jail Miss Hellman then pleaded the Fifth Amendment. Her letter, however, was released to the press at her hearing, an action which not only effectively obscured the fact that she had taken the Fifth but won for Miss Hellman the permanent celebration of a moral fortitude which in actuality she did not implement.

oppression and one to which I oppose myself unequivocally. I also know nothing in my record as a private person or a writer, other than during some instructive months in the early thirties when I was a Communist fellow-traveler and experienced at first hand the lies and chicanery by which the Soviet Union ensnared its foreign supporters, which is not in consonance with liberalism in its traditional meaning. Though liberalism came to us from the remote universe of the nineteenth century and has now, I think, to be rigorously reassessed to see how it can be made to apply to the social and technological circumstances of contemporary life, certain liberal tenets must necessarily persist so long as the word is in use. Chief among them, surely, is the refusal to countenance the abrogation of basic human and civic rights. In simplest logic it is impossible, in my opinion, for anyone of liberal commitment, and particularly in the name of liberalism, to tolerate any system of government, whatever its professed idealistic goals, which deprives its people of the elementary freedom of self-government, speech, travel, cultural expression, and—more—which implements this authoritarianism by mass murder and mass enslavement of dissidents. More people have been killed by the Soviet Union because of their opinions or even because of the circumstances of their birth—"liquidated" was the word for it—than were murdered by Hitler; and this and related facts have for long years been available to anyone concerned to know them. Not all anti-Communists are liberals, but in my view no one can call himself a liberal who is not an anti-Communist.*

* For a short time in the late forties and early fifties, as Miss Hellman's *Scoundrel Time* informs those of her readers who are without their own knowledge of the period, American "dissidents"—which is to say, Americans of some public note who gave indication of possible Communist sympathy—were under ugly attack, first by the House Un-American Activities Committee and then by Senator Joseph McCarthy. In some of the universities loyalty oaths were demanded of teachers, and in certain spheres of work, chiefly in the movies, people accused of left-wing sympathies were blacklisted and unable to continue their employment. Dashiell Hammett, for long close both to Miss Hellman and to the Communist party, who, loyal to his personal code of honor, refused to

You ask whether, as a liberal anti-Communist, I feel that I have a responsibility for the war in Vietnam. To this my answer is yes, probably I do have a responsibility for its inception, not for its continuation, as I suppose must anyone, whatever his present view, who ever at any time spoke in criticism of Communism. But before I continue on this point I think the unnamed inspiration of this symposium should be identified: Mr. Jason Epstein's "The CIA and the Intellectuals" (*The New York Review of Books*, April 20, 1967). Mr. Epstein's article is not without its place in the evolving anti–anti-Communism of several decades: it was the first (to my knowledge) statement of the idea that all opponents of Communism, even those of the Left, are of the retrograde order, and also the first (to my knowledge) to use the 1967 revelation that the CIA had subsidized anti-Communist cultural organizations to discredit not only these organizations but also anti-Communist opinion wherever it might be located on the political spectrum.

The term "anti–anti-Communism" came into being in the fifties, during the McCarthy years, when the once-unified anti-Communist faction of left-wing intellectuals, in an orgy of either/or-ism, split on the question of which was *the* enemy of democratic safety and decency, Communism or McCarthyism. Among those who took the position that Communism was the sole danger, many gave McCarthy their support. On the other

---

give the HUAC a list of names asked of him, went to jail. The actions of the HUAC and of McCarthy were plainly antiliberal. But this is not to say that everyone who came under their attack was thereby redeemed of responsibility for his own acceptance of the destruction of liberty by Communism: it takes more than victimization by illiberalism to certify one's liberalism. And even in those dark years of violation of civil rights, the only punishment of these "dissidents" was loss of very high-paid jobs or, at worst, which was indeed bad enough, a short jail term; no one was put to death for exercising his right of free speech. It is the part of intellectual seriousness to take facts like these into account in pursuing a comparison between the realities of even a very faulty democracy and the "sins" of Communism.

side were those who believed that since the Communist party of the United States was virtually nonexistent, it was McCarthyism which posed the only threat in our political life and that to be concerned about Communism was to give aid and comfort to American reaction. For this faction anti-McCarthyism, together with the rejection of anti-Communism, was what validated its liberalism. Those who held this latter view became known as "anti–anti-Communists"—this was to distinguish them from pro-Communists, which the largest number of them clearly were not.

I cannot stress too strongly my own refusal, then and still, of these simplistic choices. I saw in the McCarthy period and see today no contradiction, only an entire consistency, in having been opposed to *both* Communism and McCarthyism. The anti–anti-Communists were of course correct that in the fifties there was no longer an official Communist movement of any size, nor even an active pro-Communist sentiment, in the United States. But Communism nevertheless *was,* and on the international scene it was steadily gaining in strength. Senator McCarthy was in fact the greatest gift the United States could have given the Soviet Union (and it looks like a gift of permanent value); after him, an American Communist party was no longer required and, short of the capacity to create a revolution in the United States, would have been a liability to the Communist cause. Small as was the scope of the actual power of the junior senator from Wisconsin, it was dramatic in its ugliness. He had to be fought and it remains a blot on this country's record that Congress was as slow as it was in moving against him.

But to exaggerate McCarthy's influence in American life, as the anti–anti-Communists did, was to foster the idea that American democracy was in such bad state that as between our political system and the Communist system there could be no meaningful preference. Abroad this "neutralism" for some time did America grave disservice; it seriously reduced our power in the world. And at home it turned the

American progressive intellectual's taste for self-pity cum lacerating criticism of anything pertaining to his own country into an attitude which still persists in the seventies and which has effectively prevented the growth of any useful movement of liberal political dissent.

But although the term "anti–anti-Communism" dates from the fifties and specifically refers to the split among left-wing intellectuals on the McCarthy issue and what has followed from it, the concept was in preparation as far back as the thirties when, with the rise of Nazism in Germany and with the Spanish Civil War, the newly radicalized intellectuals in the democracies were so successful in capturing the antifascist cause and identifying it with the Communist cause. Put most summarily, what happened was that throughout the thirties the Communist party with great energy and skill organized "innocents" groups, people committed to certain presumed goals of the party but not party members or necessarily even fellow-travelers, into movements against war and fascism, a maneuver by which Communism became intimately associated in the minds of people of progressive political impulse with these dedications. As a consequence of this maneuver, whoever put himself in opposition to Communism came to be regarded as of the Right or even as an "objective fascist." To be sure, in the thirties and certainly throughout the forties there were pockets of fierce and highly knowing resistance to this prefigurement of the anti–anti-Communist spirit—*Partisan Review, Commentary,* the "back pages" of the *Nation* were the most impressive of the journals of left-wing intellectual anti-Communism. But despite this firm anti-Communist alignment, which also happened to have in its guardianship the best strength of the advanced movements in the arts, excuse was found and implemented for what were such patent violations of socialist principle as Stalin's willingness to let Hitler triumph in Germany in order to weaken, indeed destroy, the German Social Democrats, the Moscow trials and purges, the knifing in the back of the POUM and other nonparty elements among the Spanish

Loyalists. Perhaps the outstanding example of how tolerance of whatever furthered the Soviet cause became subsumed in our cultural criteria—that is, in our specifically literary as well as in our political criteria—producing judgments which lingered into the sixties and still obtain today, is the career of George Orwell, a writer of stature who went to Spain in the Spanish Civil War as a Communist sympathizer but who, because of what he learned in that country, left it a radical anti-Communist, which is what he continued to be, and whose reputation has never been allowed to recover.

Such, then, was anti–anti-Communism at its birth in the thirties and such was the anti–anti-Communism which made us able to sustain even our disappointment over the Nazi-Soviet pact and to become so unsuspicious a wartime ally of Russia. And such, as well, was the anti–anti-Communism which, while it would not be given this name until the fifties, was already so well prepared in the late forties to mount battle against President Truman's foreign policy and which was brought up to date in Mr. Epstein's article of 1967.* Just

---

* In his introduction to Miss Hellman's *Scoundrel Time*, it is upon President Truman's "cold war mentality" that Mr. Garry Wills lays most direct blame for Miss Hellman's sufferings. The choice of Mr. Wills to make this historical point must stand as one of the remarkable events of our intellectual times inasmuch as, until 1970, Mr. Wills was a steady writer for the undisguisedly right-wing *National Review*; indeed, between 1957, when William Buckley, editor of the *National Review*, mourned the death of McCarthy by writing of him as the kind of man "who fires a whole people's resolution," and 1970, Mr. Wills contributed no fewer than 150 signed reviews or articles to that periodical. The temptation to quote from these pieces which Mr. Wills wrote for the *National Review* is not lightly checked, for how resist reporting of so righteously condemnatory a chronicler of the past what he was himself saying in his past? I limit myself, however, to but a few samples from a single contribution of Mr. Wills's to that periodical, an article called "Principles and Heresies: Nero in our Camp," which appear in the *National Review* of September 12, 1959:

> Mass war has marked the modern age not because it has been a military age; but because it has not been. Hitler grew like a mushroom, Russia has grown like an evil fungus, because of the

as it was the widely held assumption of these earlier decades that only by refusing to oppose Communism could one accurately measure one's dedication to freedom, just so the underlying premise of Mr. Epstein's foray upon the anti-Communism of the Left is that whatever opposes Communism cooperates in the broad reactionary tendencies of America. There is no change in purpose, that is to say. Only the field of combat has changed, from politics to culture.

In 1967, we discover from Mr. Epstein's piece, we are no longer required, as in the antifascist days, to understand that different systems of government and different economic structures pertain to a discussion of our relation to Communism and

---

pale atmosphere of cowardice everywhere. Fear does not prevent war; it merely fosters bullies.

Our dealings with our allies reflect the frivolous attitude that war is impossible. . . . We are told to avoid committing ourselves, and not to exact the commitments of honorable men from those who would stand with us. . . . Only such terrified sway over the mind can explain the complete inability to see in Chiang Kai-shek's little garrison a desperate romance of courage. Even those who refuse to support him, even those who do not like him or agree with him, should recognize the stature of courage when they see it. This brave little band, living on the very skirts of the giant and refusing to submit, is the stuff of epic. [Chiang Kai-shek—for those too young to remember—did indeed resist Chinese Communist imperialism. But he, in earlier life an officer of the Kuomintang under Sun Yat-sen at the time of Sun's closest alliance with Stalin, was and remained a ruthless tyrant.—D.T.]

We wrong our allies and ourselves by cowardice; but we serve our enemy. . . . If men are men, and war is war, then Khrushchev is our enemy. . . . If he gets to know us in our present mood, he will know he can strike us down like the cowards we are.

And this is the man who writes with such contempt of President Truman as a cold-warmonger? We always have, of course, the privilege of changing our minds. But in a world of moral bookkeeping—and on every page of *Scoundrel Time* both Mr. Wills and Miss Hellman are calling others to moral account—do we not have some duty to disclose the grounds of our own moral authority?

are properly involved in the diagnosis of where America has gone off the track. Where once the liberal intellectual did indeed bring considerations of culture, especially as culture presents itself to the literary intelligence, to bear upon politics —it made for that valuable hyphenated category, literary-political—Mr. Epstein makes politics and culture all but indistinguishable. The modes of thought and feeling which had usually been felt to be appropriate to the literary process now constitute the mode of political judgment.

Thus, here is Mr. Epstein discussing "the" issue, as he isolates it, which divides the intellectuals of the Left and of the Right: "The issue was deeper," Mr. Epstein writes, and by this he means deeper than that of

who should control the engines of the economy or how the wealth should be distributed. . . . It had to do not with who controlled and benefited from the exploitation of the land and the people, but with the very fact of exploitation itself. The facts are clearer now than they were ten years ago. [He would be referring to 1957.] Then it surprised us to find that the country seemed to have fallen into a frenzy of self-destruction, tearing its cities apart, fouling its landscapes, poisoning the streams and skies, trivializing the education of its children. . . . What we were experiencing was the familiar philistine expansionism (of which the Vietnamese are only the latest victims).

Even were a statement like this to appear in another context than that of Mr. Epstein's attack upon anti-Communism, there would be no need to delude ourselves that America is becoming daily more beautiful, or that our air is pure, or that our children are being properly educated, in order to appreciate how this approach to politics connects with the old anti–anti-Communist position and with the American intellectual's hostile view of his country which so frequently has companioned it. Only American life is put to the test: the diseases of the twentieth century would seem to infect us alone; life in the Communist world invites no comparable scrutiny. The air over the Soviet Union remains pure, the streams of Communism run clear and unpolluted, and obviously no one would suggest that totalitarian education is trivial.

Mr. Epstein leaves us in no doubt as to how we should arrive at our political decisions. The choice, he tells us, of whether we take our stand on the political Left or Right, or even whether we support or oppose the Vietnam War, is determined by the way in which we respond to the poisoning of our land and streams. Other than abhorrence or tolerance of rank air and desecrated landscapes, we require no guide in domestic or foreign affairs. How does it then happen, I find myself asking, that Mr. Epstein and I, both of whom equally abhor rank air and desecrated landscapes and trivializing education, are in political disagreement? And in the light of Mr. Epstein's article, how can we be surprised that in our university uprisings of the sixties, including the one I was able to follow most closely, that of Mr. Epstein's own college, Columbia, there were no political ideas, only hostile stances on the part of the insurrectionary students, adversary postures in life and particularly in relation to life in America, and that nevertheless, despite the frightening dearth of political thought, pictures of the Communist revolutionary leaders decked the occupied halls?

It is against this most cursory historical background that I return now to your question: do I, as a liberal anti-Communist feel responsible for the war in Vietnam? If the answer is, as I think it has to be, yes, my anti-Communism undoubtedly contributed to the creation of a climate of opinion favorable to intervention, then it seems to me that this reply establishes a corollary proposition, that the anti–anti-Communism of the thirties and forties carries at least as heavy a burden of responsibility for creating a climate of opinion favorable to the existence of the House Un-American Activities Committee and McCarthy. For, as I wrote on several occasions during the McCarthy years, had the left-wing intellectuals of this country confronted the truth of Stalinist oppression and murder instead of measuring their liberalism by their sympathy with, or at least silence about, Soviet dictatorship, the HUAC and Mc-Carthy would never have had the field they had for their incursions upon democratic freedom. McCarthy himself was a man of no principle, he was an undisguised opportunist; but he had no trouble setting up the platform for his reactionary and demagogic anti-Communism where the progressive intellectuals had neglected to do their own principled job of intellectual housecleaning.

And if we are to continue in the unhappy business of blame, I now add yet another count to this not inconsiderable indictment. People of radical opinion in what are supposed to be the intellectual professions love to denigrate their power. In much the same way as they thought of the Soviet Union as a poor embattled minority even while it constituted one-sixth of the world, they think of themselves as without a voice in the democratic process even while as teachers, writers, journalists, artists they exercise an immeasurable influence as opinion formers. As long ago as 1838, in *Home as Found*, James Fenimore Cooper could write: "Men quarrel about opinion here, because opinion rules. It is but one mode of struggling for power."

Because of Roosevelt's far-reaching liberal domestic programs and the by-now classic inability of some of our best-trained minds to encompass more than one mental process at a time, the makers and recorders of the history of recent decades prefer not to recall that our "enlightened" acquiescence in Stalinism carried well into the White House, to the point where there were occasions during the Second World War in which Roosevelt was more on guard against Churchill than against his Soviet ally and, when the war ended, despite America's overwhelming military ascendancy, trusted Stalin's assurances at Yalta and yielded to the Soviet Union what should never have been countenanced: millions upon millions of Poles, Hungarians, Rumanians, Bulgarians, and ultimately Czechs and Germans too, were permitted to come under the domination of a brute alien force and many of them were consigned to slave-labor camps and death. The Soviet empire was doubled in size. Without greater strain than Mr. Epstein puts upon the principle of political causation, surely a grim case can be made for a counterconclusion to his, namely that had our opinion-forming class not for so many years blindly played the Soviet Union's game, Russia would not only not have achieved her present strength in Europe; she might not have been able to back North Vietnam as she did and there would have been no Vietnam War for us to have become engaged in as unwisely as we did.

In short, on both sides, that favorable to Communism and that opposed, positions were taken and inevitably exerted their influence. And on both sides there followed in their wake actions which were not necessarily foreseen or desired. As an anti-Communist I feel no more accountable, say, for the way in which the war went forward in Vietnam or for the kind of regimes with which we cooperated in South Vietnam than the anti–anti-Communists undertake to feel for the strengthening of Arab power against Israel or for the variety of money interests which exploit this preference of ritualized progressivism.

For our continuing policy in Vietnam, in fact, I feel no responsibility whatever—from the spring of 1965 I increasingly came to believe that our Vietnamese involvement was a tragic mistake. But I did not travel the usual moral-intellectual path to this conclusion; I did not come to regard our presence in Vietnam as yet another proof of the unique greed and rapacity of the United States, compared to which the armies of the North and their Soviet backers stood forth in all their brilliant heroism and virtue. My political thinking begins in the assumption that nations are power entities, and when I consider the absolute power which corrupts absolutely I find my best examples in totalitarian societies which exist under absolutist systems of government. Within a capitalist society like our own, whose form of government is democratic, it is capitalism

indeed any kind of deception or manipulation in the intellectual life. But I find I do not have to look to the CIA or other such certifiedly patriotic enterprises for my sole instances of thought manipulation. I have lived for a long time with the manipulation of mind to which those who generally share Miss Hellman's political view or Mr. Epstein's dedicate their idealism.

In 1967 when Mr. Epstein suggested that, via the CIA, liberal anti-Communism was a slave to the darker impulses of American foreign policy, he chiefly referred to the then-recent disclosures about CIA support of various cultural undertakings, especially the Congress for Cultural Freedom. The CCF was a CIA-supported activity with which I had some acquaintance: I was a member, then an officer, of the American Committee for Cultural Freedom, an independent affiliate of the international organization. Even before I came onto the Executive Board of the American Committee, I was aware, and it was my clear impression that everyone else on the board was also in some measure aware, that the international body with which we were associated was probably funded by the government. I do not say that we had hard evidence to this effect, of a sort to which one swears in a court of law, but we strongly suspected that the Farfield Foundation, which we were told supported the congress, was a filter for State Department or CIA money. What made the CIA appear to be the more likely source was the fact that, alone among the national committees, ours in America got no financial help. Since it was known that the CIA was not allowed to spend money within the United States, we concluded that it must be the CIA which funded the various programs of the congress throughout the free world, including its magazines in many countries. And this was often a subject of discussion between myself and my friends: the editors of *Partisan Review*, for instance, felt handicapped in terms of foreign circulation by lack of a subsidy such as was given *Encounter*, the intellectual journal which the congress supported in England. Finally our speculation that the CIA was the source of the congress funds became certainty for the members of the American Executive Board who happened to be present at a meeting when its then-chairman, Mr. Norman Thomas, many times Socialist candidate for the presidency of the United States and a man whose personal integrity and record in defense of civil liberties is not open to question, reported that, chronically insolvent, we now lacked money even for the next month's rent. Mr. Thomas could see but a single solution: he would "phone Allen"; he returned from the telephone to tell us that a check for a thousand dollars would be in the mail the next morning. None of us could fail to know that the "Allen" who tided us over was Allen Dulles, head of the CIA, and that in the strictest sense it was even a breach of legality for him to give us help. But none of us, myself included, protested.

And why, indeed, should we have? The response of American intellectuals to their own country and government in the mid-fifties and into the Kennedy years was not what it has since become. When the CIA was regarded at all, it was by and large associated with the highly respected wartime OSS and accepted as a necessary adjunct to our national security. At that time there was no hint of its dangerous usurpation of authority. In 1976 we know a great deal more, some of it extremely troubling, about certain activities of the CIA than we knew even when Mr. Epstein wrote in 1967. The Congress for Cultural Freedom was founded in 1950. What kind of war, I would now ask Mr. Epstein and others of his political view, does *he*, do *they*, think we should have waged in 1950 against the destruction of freedom in Europe and in the East? The hot war of which Mr. Mills, today a featured writer for the *New York Review of Books*, was so ardent a proponent in the second half of the fifties? Or a war of ideas? Or should we perhaps have done nothing except sit by and applaud the build-up of Communist agit-prop since it spoke for such a beneficent alternative to democracy? When the Congress for Cultural Freedom was formed and for the next decade and a half, Europeans who didn't live at our comfortable American remove from Communist power, people of the intellectual caliber and personal integrity of Ignazio Silone or Nicola Chiaromonte, not to speak of endangered libertarians in the Asian and African countries, had nothing to look to in encouragement of their battle for freedom except efforts like those of the Congress for Cultural Freedom. How frivolous can we be to suggest that they should have come over here, sniffed our foul air, and learned where they must *not* look for protection?

Was I "duped" by the hidden funding of the congress? Obviously, insofar as I was deceived I was duped. Whoever is deceived is duped. It has not, for instance, been a good experience to learn, as I did as recently as 1975, that a particular undertaking of the early sixties which I had thought was entirely under the aegis of a private foundation had in reality been a project of the CCF. But my disturbance at this discovery has much more to do with the idea of deception itself—among the rights I cherish is the right to reach my decisions on the basis of fact, not fabrication—and with my disagreement with some of the procedures of the Congress for Cultural Freedom than with the source of its money. And let me put it on record here that far fewer people were in fact deceived about the financial connection between the congress and the American government than was made to appear in the ignoble scurrying for cover which followed the 1967 revelations about the cultural activities of the CIA. Those who time and time again traveled around the world to participate in various projects of the congress had plainest reason to know that their excursions were being paid for by the United States government—or plainest reason not to let themselves know.

Inasmuch as I never heard of anyone, not a single person, who did anything in connection with the undertakings of the Congress for Cultural Freedom which wasn't entirely consonant with his beliefs, it seems to me that in any final assessment of the activities of that organization it is rather more important to ask what was the purpose of its ventures and how were they pursued than to stress the source of its funds. The word "independent"—an independent affiliate of the Congress for Cultural Freedom—was introduced on the stationery of the American Committee not from the belief that to touch American government money is to be defiled but because there were those of us on the Executive Board of the American Committee who felt that the congress compromised itself and us by some of the attitudes it took in the cultural battle against Communism. My own most dramatic instance of disagreement with the congress concerned the conduct of Bertrand Russell, a top officer of the international organization, who had publicly described America as a fascist country, a statement which had been of course happily picked up by the press of the world. In my view this was irresponsible, indeed vicious, untruth. The American Committee, adding to other criticisms it had of the congress, took a strong stand against the dissemination of this malign fantasy of Russell's in the name of an organization to which we were presumed to be related. Our position was defeated; the Executive Board of the international body in Paris thought the purposes of the congress in Asia and Africa were best served by not countering Russell's anti-Americanism. Today, I find ironic amusement in the fact that among anti–anti-Communists this same Congress for Cultural Freedom, which in many of its practices though not in basic principle was often even to the left of usual liberal opinion, should have become so stirring a symbol of illiberalism!

And perhaps it is because I have this acquaintance with the actual workings of the CIA-funded Congress for Cultural Freedom that I find no great incongruousness in the recent revelation that William Sloane Coffin, Jr., a notable leader in the antiwar movement of the sixties, was earlier in his career an agent of the CIA—I now learn that it was in 1949, a year before the formation of the congress, that Mr. Coffin graduated from Yale and entered upon his "contentious" later life which included service in this secret agency.* There is no anomaly for me in Mr. Coffin's having been employed by the CIA and yet having also been opposed to the Vietnam War: the CIA has been turned to chauvinist uses and worse, but this is not how it always was. But to my mind it does make for profound moral contradiction that a former CIA agent should be willing to demonstrate against the war under a Viet Cong flag—and I myself never saw a demonstration against the Vietnam War in which this emblem failed to be visible or even to dominate the scene. I should also find it morally reassuring,

---

* For this information, as also for the word I quote, I am indebted—again—to Mr. Garry Wills who carefully provides both in an essay called "The CIA from Beginning to End" (*New York Review of Books*, January 22, 1976). Mr. Wills's article is very long, taking up a substantial part of an issue of the *New York Review*, and eventually it gets a good deal that is not very comforting said about the CIA. But only its opening paragraph—seventeen lines in all—makes mention of Mr. Coffin, and this paragraph contains no slightest touch of criticism of Mr. Coffin for having been a government agent. On the contrary, "Bill Coffin" enters and leaves Mr. Wills's article amid the well-earned applause of the Yale student body. The rest of Mr. Wills's protracted and knowing study of the history of the CIA deals at some length with another public figure, Mr. William Buckley, who, it turns out, was also a CIA agent at much the same time as Mr. Coffin although, so we must understand, he was of course of quite different stripe. It seems that Mr. Buckley, having written a novel, *Saving the Queen,* about a CIA spy, has provided Mr. Wills with the material for understanding Mr. Buckley's own real-life activities as an agent—these include, we suppose, the signal accomplishment of having gone to bed with the Queen of England! Indeed, so curiously uneven is Mr. Wills's estimate of Mr. Coffin *qua* CIA man and Mr. Buckley *qua* CIA man that I wonder if Mr. Wills ever heard the story of the two Jewish mothers who meet after several years of not having seen each other and undertake to catch up on the well-being of each other's children. First Mrs. Gold's old friend inquires about Mrs. Gold's son, and Mrs. Gold laments: "Oh, my poor son! That lazy no-good he married, nothing's enough for her! Breakfast in bed every morning, two maids, two cars, two fur coats. . . ." Her friend sympathizes with Mrs. Gold, then inquires about Mrs. Gold's daughter. Mrs. Gold beams: "Oh, my daughter! Is that a lucky girl! Such a husband, nothing's too much for her. Breakfast in bed every morning, two maids, two cars, two fur coats. . . ."

in Mr. Coffin's as in Mr. Wills's instance, if not only the politics of his past but also the bridge between his political past and his political present had been defined for those who looked to him for leadership. Not but that I am aware of what the effort would have cost Mr. Coffin in influence on the young: I clearly recall the occasion during the strike which followed the Columbia sit-in of 1968 when Mr. Noam Chomsky, also a leader of the antiwar movement, spoke at a Columbia panel discussion of how he felt in relation to the government–sponsored Institute for Defense Analyses. Although the presence of the IDA on the Columbia campus was presumed to be an issue in the uprising—actually it was no issue at all, as was later admitted*—Mr. Chomsky had the courage to say that he had no objection to the IDA on the campus of M.I.T. where he taught: it was out in the open and the money it brought M.I.T. from the government helped pay his salary. More, M.I.T. had never, because of the IDA, interfered with his freedom of speech. For this display of honesty Mr. Chomsky was jeered and booed by the same student generation which, as Mr. Wills is at pains to let us know, showed nothing but approval of Mr. Coffin.

Only one further point: I write at this length chiefly in response to what calls itself liberal opinion but which I less honorifically prefer to call progressivism: as I have tried to make clear, the word "liberal" is one I do not readily cede to those whom I consider but poor custodians of the values it has traditionally stood for. Yet, as I have also indicated, it is my belief that at our present stage of social and technological development liberalism must be rethought if it is to be a useful guide to social and political decision. In situation after situation, to examine a liberal accomplishment of our century is to be confronted with the grave problem which it has produced or at least which has followed from it: the right of labor to bargain collectively has not only created a polity within the polity but spurred inflation and unemployment; the

* See footnote, page 102.

gains of feminism have been lost in the nuclear family; programs of public welfare issue in corruption and bankruptcy; universal compulsory education has produced mass subliteracy; and so on.

If we indeed have a working liberal-intellectual class and not merely an intellectual lobby for moral self-certification, it seems to me that these are matters to which it should be giving itself. Instead, the greater part of the hard work of dealing with our difficult public problems is today being done not on the Left but at the Center or often on the Right. For the Left, other issues are deemed more worthwhile, indeed exclusively worthy of attention. I take it for granted that all activities of government, including that of our intelligence services, demand our vigilance. But for the CIA, today in 1976, to be such an all-absorbing object of left-wing concern as it is, overshadowing even the problems of government organization and supervision revealed in the Watergate scandal, fills me with dismay about the present relation of our enlightened classes to politics.

[1967/1976]

2. What's Happening to America?

THE QUESTIONS

1. Does it matter who is in the White House? Or is there something in our system which would force any president to act as Johnson is acting?

2. How serious is the problem of inflation? The problem of poverty?

3. What is the meaning of the split between the administration and the American intellectuals?

4. Is white America committed to granting equality to the American Negro?

5. Where do you think our foreign policies are likely to lead us?

6. What, in general, do you think is likely to happen in America?

7. Do you think any promise is to be found in the activities of young people today?

Before addressing myself to the substance of your questionnaire I should like to pause over the formulation of your first question. You ask whether or not it matters who is in the White House. In general your questions have the virtue of directing this symposium to political actualities. But not this question. If you are speaking of the actual conduct of affairs, how can it conceivably *not* matter who is in the White House? Would you seriously suggest that there is no basis for choice among presidents, that Harding and Franklin Roosevelt were for all practical purposes interchangeable; that Kennedy's handling of the Cuban confrontation was so natural and inevitable, given our system, that we must suppose that Eisenhower or Johnson would have performed no differently? In the phrasing of such a question you express, I think, the special hopelessness into which intellectuals seem to have fallen, their taste for absolutes, even for ultimates. One understands of course that the purpose of your question is to bring under examination the democratic process itself, to inquire whether there are forces in American life, inherent either in capitalism or in the complex democratic organization, which are so powerful and so remote from our control as individual citizens that they are inescapably determining, a negation of the democratic possibility. But the extravagance with which you open this pertinent inquiry surely derives from the continuing wish of intellectuals, ever since the ideological thirties, to reconstitute a "scientific"—that is, an entirely coherent, rationalized, and invulnerable—structure for political life and thought such as Marxism was once thought to be; only the state as it is conceived by Marxism proposes the idea (which in reality it contradicts) that it makes no difference who its officers are: the system is all. But in addition your disregard for political actuality points to the reliance of present-day intellectuals upon sensibility as a mode of political comprehension. The formulation, "Does it matter who is in the White House?" pertains not to an intellectual life in which we define ourselves by our manifest responsibility to reason and to the consequences of thought, but to a world in which we validate our sensibility by our apocalypticism.

The most primitive expression of our current politics of sensibility is the application of criteria of personal style to the making of political judgments. I am not implying that there is no truth to be arrived at by this mode of judgment. But such truth is limited in its usefulness, sometimes misleading, and likely to paralyze discourse. And when sensibility takes over the entire work of reasoned argument, when—say—the acute issues involved in the Vietnam War are let disappear in observations upon Johnson's personal style, intellect has deserted politics. We are properly contemptuous of an administration unable to make a cogent statement of its Vietnam position. But has the intellectual opposition done better? The fact is that the American intellectual has for so long lived at such a far remove from power that he has developed a peculiarly grim imagination of power, to which he can relate himself only in angry passivity. This hostile separation from government has no doubt played its part in creating our famed American rigorousness in matters of culture; indeed the degree to which we exclude from our respected world of mind anyone who participates in public affairs can be understood as an aspect of this rigorousness. We reserve for culture and deny to politics our best energies of discrimination, now more than ever necessary if we are to shape reliable political judgments.

In particular they are needed as we direct ourselves to the difficult problem of democracy itself, and especially as we bring to bear upon it recent developments in the civil rights movement. Obviously were the whole of white America committed to Negro equality, equality would long since have been achieved. (The truism is not to be avoided if your Question 4 is to be noticed.) What we now see rather more dramatically than we have before is that even when an administration commits itself to equality, it can be defeated by opposition from certain sections of the population. Does this represent a failure of the democratic system? Yes, certainly it represents a failure. But *a* failure of democracy, grave as it may be, does not represent *the* failure of democracy, unless by democracy we mean a system of government—and when has there ever been one—which guarantees the achievement of all our best social goals.

I can see no reason for Negroes themselves to be patient with the small progress that has been made in racial equality in this country. Their moderation up to now has been phenomenal. But those of us whose anger at racial injustice is supposed to be in the control of reason—that is, held in check by our understanding of the many conflicting forces involved in racial bias and by our commitment to the national interest as a whole—have not the privilege of desperation; we have the onerous duty of patience. By patience I most distinctly do not mean retreat or the countenancing of any diminution of governmental effort. Building on what gains in civil rights have already been made, and they are considerable, we must force new efforts in legislation and education, new programs for economic and social betterment. Except the intellectual is prepared to name and commit his energies to the system with which he proposes to replace a faulty democracy, his despair can only make itself felt in regression or as inertia.

Myself, I know nothing better to substitute for a faulty democracy. I wish I did, and not merely because ours is a system which has not eradicated racial inequity or even because it offers us so little connection with government but because of my extreme distaste for the dominant American culture. (Yet, obviously, to ascribe our culture to the American "system" is to ignore the similar movement in culture everywhere in the modern industrialized world, including the Communist countries.) One term, but one term only, of American democracy is capitalism. Socialism as an alternative to capitalism would, one could hope, go some distance toward removing the economic motive in racial inequality but important as this undoubtedly would be, it still would leave unaltered many other factors involved in racial bias, including original sin. Too, we need to keep it in mind that socialism is an alternative to capitalism, it is not an alternative to democracy. If by socialism we mean democratic socialism we have to realize that in a vast and complex country like ours it would take more than a reorganization of the economy to put the individual citizen in a closer, more responsive relationship with government. Only an enormous decentralization could accomplish this—which would create its own problems, not least a grave divisiveness in the national life. There is no easy answer to the questions pressed upon us by what has happened in the civil rights movement; we have to rate our values in the order of their importance to us. And at the top of the scale, for me, are the prerogatives of democracy: a multiparty system, the right to vote, work, speak and move about as I will, all the benefits Americans can afford to belittle because they have them. Or at any rate, some of us have all of them, all of us have some of them. It makes poor sense, it seems to me, to be bitter over the fact that Negroes are deprived of rights which we ourselves hold cheap.

As to our foreign policies. I have found it extraordinary, the ease and speed with which most intellectuals have come to their stands on the Vietnam War; I should have thought that decision between support of, or opposition to, the war could be this quick only for the conscientious objector to all war. It has been extremely difficult for me to come to a "position," when there has been such substantial argument to marshal on both sides of the question. And if, finally, I am opposed to our Vietnam engagement, it is not because of an ingrained distrust of American motive or even of Johnson's motive, and certainly not because I am indifferent to the spread of Communism, but because I have come to the opinion that the best interests of America and of democracy are not served by the kind of war we are fighting. I think that there were other better ways to help the South Vietnamese resist Communist aggression—with money, technical assistance, arms—without our proclaiming ourselves, as we have, the far-reaching nation of the sword, and without our overt support of a regime of our choice, and a corrupt one at that. The overt military stance seriously injures us with those very elements in the non-Communist world— democratic, liberal, socialist—which we have most to count on if the independent nations are to develop programs of internal health which are yet resistant to Communism; I have in mind

Latin American democrats, liberals, socialists, no less than those of Asia. The Russians fight wars all over the world without such self-exposure. In addition, I don't see how we could implement a military victory even if we attained it.

Now, writing shortly after the Manila conference, my worry about the Vietnam War is immeasurably increased by the promise of its possible multiplication. America has in these last days been committed to a most active future role in Asia, and one in which we apparently mean to bypass our European allies. At least, such was the position Johnson described. (And how was I supposed to vote against *this* at the polls? Let us not deceive ourselves that the option for democracy makes life simple!) Johnson's position at Manila was as if designed to intensify the already all-too-eagerly grasped-at image of America as an imperialism, to be feared equally with Communist imperialism. Although in some quarters his statements were greeted as a triumph of statesmanship, I regard them as quite the opposite: an insult to our European allies and a vaunt of military power in a political situation which calls for endless strategies, of a sort that are substantially hampered, if not finally frustrated, by military threat. I am of course acquainted with the argument which says that it is the presence of our troops in Vietnam which encouraged the overthrow of Communism in Indonesia. This is conjecture, there is no proof, and I am not convinced; at any rate, I offer the counterargument that the presence of American troops ninety miles from Cuba has not brought about the overthrow of Castro because Cuba is not internally prepared to make this overthrow; for a country to *be* ready, as Indonesia must have been, there must exist an internal opposition of sufficient scope to promise success without external intervention. I am also not convinced that Johnson's statements on Asia were required or useful as a deterrent to China or even as an encouragement to the independent Asian countries. The possession of military strength is obviously an adjunct of political strength. The proclamation of military intention is something else again and dangerously fixes us in a position which I think abets the Communist powers in their political war against us, with an eventual increase in the possibility of military recourse. And this is not to speak of the damage Johnson's extreme and unnecessary overtness has done to the very concept of the United Nations.

Your remaining questions. Concrete economic problems like that of inflation are not within the competence of any literary intellectual I know, certainly not within mine. I'd only be communicating my ignorant alarm. I also have no competence in prophecy. I could wish, though, that I had saved space for comment upon the activities of young people today beyond merely stating my belief that there are few aspects of the contemporary disturbances of youth in which the parent generation fails to conspire, whether in manifest or hidden ways. It is the forms taken by their idealism that are more likely to be their own, and of course more significant and interesting for that reason.

[1967]

On the Steps of Low Library

promised to be undisturbed; the air held no portents. But by afternoon my telephone was jangling with news of the seizure of Columbia's Hamilton Hall, the building which houses most of the offices and classrooms of the undergraduate College, by white student members of the Students for a Democratic Society (SDS) and black student members of the Students' Afro-American Society (SAS) and of the imprisonment of Acting Dean Coleman of the College. And in the course of the next sleepless night, the first of many, word came that the black students had expelled the white students from "their" hall and that the white students had now moved into Low Library and occupied the president's offices. Columbia is my husband's university which he first came to as a freshman of sixteen and never left except for a distant year at Wisconsin and a recent year at Oxford, and I live close to the campus. An uprising at the University could be no minor episode in our lives: inevitably, like much else that mattered in accustomed existence, Mailer's book went into the discard, not to be picked up again until mid-June when the school year at last staggered to its close and I was able to put the space of an ocean between me and what had been happening on Morningside Heights.

And yet Mailer's Pentagon story was seldom out of my mind; how could it be when its cultural and political message was so much the same as was being dinned into my ears by the event on my doorstep? To be sure, the march on the Pentagon was organized as a protest of the Vietnam War whereas the war was all but invisible as an issue in the University uprising. The Washington occasion, taken as a whole, also permitted a broader representation of political view than was manifest in the early stages of the University disruption: it was only as time went on that various shades of moderate opinion came to the side of the Columbia demonstrators, and this is just the opposite of the Pentagon march, where moderate opinion gradually dropped away, leaving the field to the extremists. But these differences are of minor importance compared to the similar philosophies and tactics of the two events.

Both were acts of civil disobedience initiated by people who
regard the law as the arm of a despised form of social organization—the fact that in the months which intervened between
the assault on the Pentagon and the Columbia sit-in the New
Left learned to refuse the concept of civil disobedience on the
ground that it grants an unwarranted authority to the established power represents a sophistication of argument but
doesn't alter the illegal character of either the Pentagon assault
or the University sit-in. Both events dramatized drastically opposed ideas of what is meant by social responsibility and both
had the intention of forcing on us a new examination of the
workings of democracy: the discrepancy between democratic
theory and practice. Both proceeded by, or at least began in,
outrage of the conventions of educated speech and behavior.
And both events faced us, whether or not we were prepared to
look at what was being shown, with the capacity for hatred
and violence which many of the educationally privileged left-
wing young share with those they most condemn on the score
of their hatred and violence. This is no small likeness. The two
occasions, indeed, can significantly be separated only in terms
of their practical outcome and the emotions consequent on
their differing capacity for effectiveness.

At the height of the Columbia disorders Mailer was quoted
as approving the University uprising because it was "existential." Whoever is familiar with his work will recognize this as
his criterion of the worthwhile; Mailer has for some years
served faithfully at the ceremonies of experience. But the word
"existential" is also in fairly general use to describe the improvisational character of our contemporary revolution, its dis-
dain of ideology and program, and its appeal as an instrument
of personal definition, and in this accepted sense Mailer's
honorific designation is an accurate one. The Columbia revolution was nothing if not improvisational, scornful of systematic
political thought, especially of systematic planning for the
future, dependent for its attractiveness to the young on the
immediate gratifications to be discovered in the release of so-

cial bitterness and rage. In fact, so urgent were the responses invoked by the Columbia revolution that they quite precluded involvement in the subjective emotions which are the heart of Mailer's Washington report—one's own existential moment yields to no other. Even at my remove from direct participation in the affairs of the campus, the Columbia disorders became throughout their duration my entire and overwhelming absorption simply because I was in their orbit. In the light of what was taking place on the steps of Low Library or, more grimly, within its walls, "On the Steps of the Pentagon" was like a case study of last year's illness intruded into today's sickroom.

But even apart from the ability to empathize with another person's experience when one has one's own acute concerns, Mailer's Washington story was bound to be lacking in emotional relevance to the Columbia disturbances. Existential the two occasions might be, and morally and politically continuous with each other, but the march on the Pentagon was a wholly symbolic enterprise whereas the University uprising, while not without its large symbolic impulse, was shatteringly actual. The Washington demonstration was a protest of the Vietnam War and as such was logically directed against the building which houses the Department of Defense. But no one supposed the Pentagon could be occupied or its work halted. The University uprising made a different situation. For the present-day revolution all universities are representative of their societies, which is why they are under assault. But here the relation between reality and symbolic action asks for examination. Touch with hostile hands the building which houses the Department of Defense and you perhaps flick the soul of your nation but the building and your nation remain intact. You have made a statement but you have not delivered death or necessarily even its premonition. Touch a university with hostile hands and the blood you draw is prompt, copious, and real. There may be disagreement on the quality of the blood, it may be good blood or bad blood, pure or impure blood, but as to the actuality of the wound you have inflicted there can be no question.

Too, the operation at the Pentagon, even for its most radical participants, had a built-in finiteness not present in the University occasion. The demonstrators, including Mailer, would move upon the giant structure, capture a step or two, conceivably some small corner of a remote corridor, create a disruption, provoke a confrontation—sanctified contemporary word! —with the police or military, and plainly announce to the world the distance in thought and feeling between those who carry on the war and those who most actively oppose it. A plan like this requires that whatever momentum is generated in the event must be expended on the spot within the period of time allotted to it. It puts distinct boundaries to the enterprise, both objectively and subjectively, not only limiting the range of decision but altering the quality of feeling which was brought to the situation or produced in it.

It was not necessary for anyone to put his life on the line in the Pentagon march unless, like Mailer, in private measure of a manhood he could as well have tested, and has as well tested (Hemingway before him), in the prize ring or in casual or bar encounters. No career or old commitment or old loyalty or even old friendship was at stake. But the University event continued for long weeks and it involved daily, hourly decisions of men whose professional lives are inextricably interwoven. I am not suggesting that the Washington demonstration was free of personal challenge or danger. There was the possibility that the marchers might be clubbed or that tear gas or Mace might be used against them—this gave what Mailer would no doubt call the cutting edge to the mood. And some of this bad possibility was indeed realized for the hippies in the contingent who, perhaps because they are already so far gone in their self-created universe of metaphor that the line between the real and the fancied is forever blurred, stayed around to offer always larger and more ingenious provocations, chiefly of a sexual sort, to the military guarding the building. Nevertheless, once a demonstrator had joined the march, he had only to decide how much discomfort he wished to take in countermeasures by the police, or in arrest and jailing, before he could be free of involvement. And whatever the choice, whether to go for an extra bonus of excitement, get a bloodied head, refuse or invite arrest, and, if the latter, delay his return home, there was still home to return to when the march was over. His protest accomplished, he hadn't the distance between civilizations to retrieve. The same assumptions and world the demonstrators had left at the start of their Washington weekend awaited them unchanged at its end.

Mailer's Washington occasion was thus of a different existential order from the Columbia uprising. Its bearing on the Columbia disturbances is moral, political, cultural, but not, in final analysis, experiential. For me, in fact, there was less emotional connection between these two man-made occasions than between the Columbia disruption and an upheaval in nature that I experienced some years ago, a hurricane followed by flood at the Connecticut shore. Although the black students who held Hamilton Hall might refuse to regard the uprisings as a revolutionary act and insist, as we are told they did, that it was no more than a demonstration, the white insurrectionary students didn't make this distinction, nor did other members of the University who suffered its force. In the flood at the seashore the emotions experienced by the residents conformed to an occasion which, even apart from its possible threat to life, was bound to alter our familiar landscape, perhaps permanently, and so it was at Columbia too: the emotions of everyone connected with the University, whether as student, teacher, administrator, or only faculty wife, were appropriate to an event which, although the University might sustain it, could leave no assumption or loyalty or familiar occupation as it had previously been—they were appropriate, that is, to a revolution. Many new and important loyalties were no doubt formed in the Columbia disorders, and not merely for the students brought into uncommon intimacy in the sit-in but for their teachers as well, suddenly exposed to the unaccustomed tensions of University emergency. As in the flood at the seashore, people were brought into quick necessary connection who before this had lived in only formal or casual association. And even old friends revealed new aspects of character—generosities one might not have looked for, courage, flexibility of mind of which one had not been as aware as one might have been. Recording his Pentagon occasion Mailer is not a novelist in depth; he has no need to be. His imaginativeness makes a sufficient arc over the wide flat field laid out for inspection. The novelist of the Columbia revolution has not appeared and probably never will, but the material available to him was of another dimension.

Out of his rich literary resources Mailer undertakes to create the depth and multifacetedness which the Pentagon march actually lacked. Illegitimately he makes a tragic confrontation out of what was in substance only a nervous foray. He asks for our pity and terror in a situation where the protagonist of the story invited what might happen to him—after all, if one exceeds one's permit for a peaceful march and assaults a federal building, one is at the mercy not of autonomous forces but of forces which one has oneself and deliberately set in motion. This confusion that Mailer makes between victimization by fate and self-victimization, or at least self-implication, robs his book of more than political authority, it deprives it of moral stature as well: its grandeur is only (but what an only) that of literary invention and virtuosity. Inevitably self-pity presides over—no, this is perhaps too strong: inevitably self-pity haunts—a story which demanded sterner emotions.

Documents of the Columbia disturbances now also have begun to appear and they too, while making no claim like Mailer's to cross-fertilizing fiction and history, reveal the curious confusion the contemporary revolution makes between external and internal reality. In *Evergreen Review* one reads, for instance, Dotson Rader's report of the sit-in and is bound to be struck by the ease with which it transforms a self-created battle into a brutal social coercion—even in the act of provoking the authorities the demonstrator portrays himself as their innocent victim. In any revolution, no matter how circumscribed, we assume that its rationale lies in the fact that it is a response to an external aggressive force. But usually revolution is ready to take responsibility for what it sets going in counteractivity. What is interesting both in Mailer and in the Columbia writer is their stance of blamelessness. At their most threatening they see themselves as inert recipients of a social fate. For both the SDS and the SAS this nonculpability was the stated premise of insurrectionary action. The University alone bore blame for the uprising; those who rose against it had no responsibility for what they did or its consequences. A premise like this makes thought unnecessary and one searches Rader's memoir or that of another Columbia demonstrator, James Kunen, in *New York* magazine, without finding a vestige of idea, let alone of revolutionary ideology. Indeed, the presence of political intellection in Mailer's book seems somehow incongruous with its prevailing mood of nonresponsibility for the action it reports on, a paradox, a reassuring leftover from the radicalism of an earlier generation.

For the students in the occupied buildings, as for Mailer, the emotions of heroism experienced in the demonstration stemmed chiefly from the conquest of personal fear, in particular fear of countermeasures by the police of a more extreme sort, even, than were actually employed when the police were finally called into action in the early morning of April 30. And these first-hand accounts make plain what someone like myself who, until their publication, would have been reluctant to put into words: my suspicion of the extent to which the fantasy of imminent police brutality provided the emotional motive of revolutionary intransigence. So central to Mr. Rader's appreciation of his revolutionary action is his fear of being manhandled by the police that one is impelled to conjecture that had he been given absolute assurance that no hand would be laid on him he might well have deserted the whole insurrectionary enterprise. It was not that the prospect of suspension from the University was absent from the minds of those engaged in the sit-in, or that they were unworried about arrest and going to jail, but simply that these did not inhabit their minds with anything like the vividness with which they imagined beatings, gas, Mace—especially the beatings. The fantasy of beatings by the police was of course to be made all too real on the morning of April 30, and the careful instruction the demonstrators had received in the correct fetal position to assume in self-defense would turn out to be small protection: they would be picked up and thrown from the buildings, punched and kicked and knocked about the head with billies. But at least chemicals would not be used; this had to wait for a non-university occasion several months later, the demonstrations in Chicago. At Columbia the students' preparation against gas was chiefly useful in evidence of the existence of large supply lines between the occupants of the buildings and outside sympathizers. WKCR, Columbia's deservedly celebrated student radio, had reporters everywhere on the campus throughout the disturbances, on window ledges and on rooftops, sometimes, so it seemed, in the very crevices of the walls. Listening to their broadcasts like an idiot addict, especially alone at night when my husband was still at the University doing whatever it was that the faculty was then doing, or trying to do, I learned of the regular visits to the occupied halls of friendly doctors and nurses and the frequent delivery of medical supplies, with emphasis on large quantities of Vaseline and plastic bags for use against burns.

But for those not inside the captured buildings there also was fear, whose source was other than the law. Columbia and its immediate vicinity, where many of the faculty live, has for some years now been a constantly shrinking white island. This is not something that is much talked about among the faculty but it can be perceived in their steady migration to the suburbs; and among those who continue to live in the University-owned apartment houses on Claremont Avenue and Riverside Drive, west of the campus, or in the Amsterdam–Morningside Drive area to the east, it plays a not inconsiderable part in curtailing the freedom of movement of the residents and in the venturesomeness permitted their children. It is the proximity of Harlem to Columbia that made the student uprising of this spring much more than a mere campus manifestation, both bigger and more delicate to handle, and warrantedly or unwarrantedly frightening to the neighborhood as no disturbance confined only to an educational institution would have been. In fact, judgment on the conduct of the Columbia administration which assumes that it had only a student outbreak to manage and fails to appreciate the credence which everyone involved in the University emergency gave to the possibility of a move against Columbia by a supposedly inflamed Negro ghetto rather misses the point of an insurrection in which the first building to be taken, Hamilton Hall, was within a few hours held wholly by black militant students. That President Kirk and his coadjutors were unequal to the demands made on them in the revolt, and in ways that showed not only a grave deficiency of statesmanship but also a perilously poor reading of present-day student emotion, is, I think, unquestionable. But even if their understanding of the changes that have taken place in the attitudes of the young over recent years had been entirely adequate, they would still have been effectively paralyzed once Hamilton Hall had been taken by black students. Mayor John Lindsay vests much of his political future in his sympathy with the young and in the trust placed in him by the black population of New York but, called on for advice by the University, he had little counsel to offer. Nor were his experts in Harlem affairs, some of them themselves Negro, able to be more helpful.

It would probably go too far to say that the reason it was at Columbia that we had this campus offensive against society, the first in a major private American university, was its closeness to Harlem. Although a Columbia demonstration had been planned some months earlier, there was a considerable element of accident in the start of the uprising; even the occupation of Hamilton Hall had not been formulated in advance, and the expulsion of the white students seems to have been an ad hoc decision though one with precedent in recent black militant action. But unmistakably the physical closeness of Columbia to a region of disquiet and racial grievance made Columbia infinitely more vulnerable than universities normally are, which is vulnerable enough. Even without the danger of invasion from Harlem there was sufficient in the Columbia disturbance to suggest a catastrophe in nature. With Harlem on its borders a measurable catastrophe might have become an immeasurable disaster—the University might be overrun or burned down.

And all through the last week of April and throughout the month of May this was the potential horror which hung over our island. At night, my husband on the campus, I, like (I suppose) all wives of faculty, obeyed our instruction to stay behind bolted doors. But sleep was impossible for everyone in the vicinity—the most decorous of us had no hesitation in phoning each other at whatever hour of the night, two o'clock, four o'clock, when the lonely waiting got to be more than we could bear. That first night I myself sat through the endless hours playing Canfield, an unopened book on my lap, the unceasing campus radio at my side, straining for the unfamiliar sound on the street beneath my shaded windows, the tramp or rush or scuffle of invasion.

Had Harlem risen as in our exacerbated anxiety we thought it would, obviously more than the life of a university would have been lost. At no point, however, did the black population outside Columbia make more than a token contribution to the revolt. This was through no lack of effort on the part of the revolutionary students who launched the uprising and continued to have it in their charge. For some time before the April outbreak the organized radical activists on the campus, members of the SDS and SAS, had been focusing hostility to the

University "establishment" on the issue of the new gymnasium which Columbia planned to build in Morningside Park to serve not only Columbia's own students but the residents of Harlem on the other side of this small little-used stretch of open land. A project once gratefully approved by a wide range of Harlem civic organizations—but this was in the long-ago days of the late fifties, when Negroes and whites were joined in the civil rights movement—had recently given rise to the charge of racism against Columbia. Racist it was felt to be that the facilities of the building were not to be used jointly but severally by Harlem and the University, although this arrangement, insofar as it could be said to be discriminatory, constituted a division between town and gown rather than a color line—the black students of Columbia would of course swim and play with their white schoolmates. Racist it was also said to be that the new building would have two entrances, a "front" door on Morningside Drive, the University side of the park, and a "back" entrance in the park itself for nonmembers of the University. But actually the land in the park slopes sharply so that were the people from Harlem made to enter from Morningside Drive they would have had reason for complaint about the distance they had to walk and the hill they had to climb. Too, the fact that the University was able to acquire an inexpensive long-term lease on a parcel of public property confirmed the revolutionary students in the belief that there was a conspiracy between the University and the city against the interests and just claims of the black population. But of course these interests and claims announce themselves differently at different times, according to changes in political climate.

The charges of Columbia racism and Columbia economic privilege had been agitated in a series of demonstrations at the site of the proposed gymnasium to which militant groups in Harlem had sometimes sent participants. Harlem had even made anti-gymnasium demonstrations of its own though they were unimpressive. But once the first buildings at Columbia were seized, one of them by black students who now held it alone, it was understandable that the revolutionaries should hope that black dissatisfaction with Columbia, not alone due to the gymnasium but also because Columbia had engendered a considerable enmity as landlord of buildings chiefly tenanted by Negroes and Puerto Ricans, or only because it was a powerful white institution bordering the black ghetto, might be triggered into a significant black assault. Probably there is no single explanation of why this hope was disappointed other than that Harlem is not as widely roused to militant action as we have been led to believe. The people of Harlem, apart from their revolutionary leaders, apparently care less than we have been led to suppose about the construction of an only semi-public facility in a public park which until now has had no recreational facilities at all and which for years has been consecrated to the use of small-time criminals making their getaway after purse-snatchings on Morningside Drive: in long years of residence on Morningside Heights I myself have never known anyone, black or white, who dared use the park even for a shortcut, let alone for relaxation. In addition, the people of Harlem look upon their black children studying at Columbia as particularly fortunate of their kind, the beneficiaries of an advantage they want to see multiplied, not sacrificed. The existential revolution of our day clearly has its populist bent but so far it seems to be more apt at subverting the intelligence and self-interest of our better-educated than our less-educated classes.

At any rate, Harlem was not delivered; this which was the most awful of the fears attending the Columbia disturbances turned out to be baseless. Charles 37X Kenyatta, Stokeley Carmichael, and H. Rap Brown all came to the campus; it was no doubt necessary for the militant record or perhaps they looked for a tie-in of their programs with that of the students. But the single palpable effect of their appearance was to keep the University aware of possibly yet-unleashed black furies and, in fact, for some of us their presence on the scene, if threatening, was more appropriate than that of other non-University visitors to Morningside Heights, the sight-seers for whom the disruption of a great university represented the newest fun spectacle in our famous fun city, or the literary-intellectual fellow-travelers of the revolutionary young. The militant Harlem leaders had at least a demonstrable political motive based in the genuine grievances of their race and class: could one say as much for the white tourists, for—say—Robert Lowell, Dwight Macdonald, Paul Goodman? Is the University an appropriate symbol of the hated white authority for such as these? I mention only the people who also appear in Mailer's report of the Washington march, the busy "notables" about whom Mailer writes so winningly in *The Armies of the Night*. There were of course many others.

But on the early morning of April 24 when the SDS were being expelled from Hamilton Hall by those they presume to call their black brothers, an act of black racism in which the white students had to accede in deference to the rule of the New Left that the dictate of one's black comrades is not to be disputed or resisted—and then too, that first day, the blacks were said to have guns and gasoline—the reluctance of Harlem to add its fuel to the fire this time was not yet known; indeed throughout this first week, while increasing numbers of students joined the original occupants of Low Library and even added three more buildings to those taken in the first day of the outbreak and while the faculty quickly organized itself into something it called the Ad Hoc Faculty Group, meeting around the clock to try to negotiate the conflict and persuade the students to terminate the sit-in, it was Harlem which was the ace in the hole of the insurrectionary forces. Those who occupied the buildings were adamant in their refusal of any peace plan offered them—when Mark Rudd, chairman of the SDS and now its best-publicized character, left his headquarters in Ferris Booth Hall to hear the latest proposal of the faculty, he greeted their offer with a stunning economy: "Bullshit."

The occupation lasted the longest week in memory. Despite the insistence of the Ad Hoc Faculty Group that the police not be used until every conceivable recourse of mediation had been exhausted and despite their pledge physically to interpose themselves between the sitters-in and the police should their peaceable principle not be respected, on April 30 the administration ordered the buildings entered and cleared. By this time it was of course manifest that the students had no intention of leaving the buildings of their own accord and the Ad Hoc Faculty Group had been reduced to such unlikely expedients as calling on Governor Rockefeller or Mayor Lindsay for personal intervention. But in calling upon the police without the consent of the Ad Hoc Group the administration opened a deep chasm between itself and the faculty. No force was required against Hamilton Hall: the removal of the black students was negotiated through Professor Kenneth Clark, the eminent Negro psychologist—the fact that he had a son in the building must have made his undertaking a peculiarly subtle one. The black students quietly evacuated their stronghold and got themselves booked by the police; they then joined the strike which was to halt classes for the rest of the term. Throughout the strike, however, Columbia's alleged depredations against the "community" continued to be the focal issue of the University revolution and the proximity of Harlem to the campus continued to be the most explosive potential of the uprising.

I put "community" in the quotation marks which should have been around it whenever the word was spoken at Columbia, which was incessantly. At Columbia "community" has now come to mean but one thing, Harlem, the black community to the east and northeast of the campus, though when necessary it is also made to include anyone in the University vicinity who could be antagonistic to it. "Community" is thus to be distinguished from neighborhood, by which one means those in the Columbia vicinity, residents or storekeepers, for whom the University is a neutral presence or comfortably inte-

gral to their lives. Expanding, as all universities must if they
are to fulfill their programs of new educational opportunity in
the democracies, but with no space for growth, Columbia decided several years ago that not only its own needs but the
public welfare too would be served if the University bought
the derelict apartment buildings in the surrounding streets: by
tearing down or improving these shabby dwellings, they
would eventually improve the area. The question the University failed to consider, or certainly failed to answer to the
satisfaction of the many long-time inhabitants of these deteriorated buildings, most of them poor, many with no tie to the
world except their physical roots in their own houses and
streets, was whether they desired an improvement in which
they were unlikely to share and which robbed them of what
small sense of place they had. The University, that is, let itself
remain unaware not only of the dismays of displacement from
one's familiar surroundings but also of the always-mounting
hostility of present-day progressive thought to unilateral social
actions *de haut en bas*. In an earlier day, when the plan was
conceived, it had been thought civic-minded and notably
forward-looking.

I have no breakdown of the subjects being studied by the
students who either sat-in at Columbia or urgently joined the
strike that all but paralyzed the campus throughout the month
of May. It is my impression that most of the student radicals
major in history, political science, government, anthropology,
sociology, architecture, city planning: subjects which directly
involve them in public affairs and in the problems of society.
Moving in on what it perhaps plausibly but, in reality, wrongly
anticipated would be fertile soil for more than mere campus
protest—the unfriendliness of the "community" for the University—the SDS concentrated its agitational energies on non-
academic issues: the construction of the gymnasium in
Morningside Park, the behavior of the University as landlord,
the University's character as a power structure within the
larger power structure of the State. It was interesting that in

this social-political effort the word "capitalism," with its reference to specific injustice rooted in the economic organization of the society, was never mentioned—for someone who had been inducted into politics in the Marxist thirties, the omission was glaring. At Columbia, as in France, the student revolution had its mysterious intangible references to the superiority of the Communist system but it had no reference at all to the programmatic doctrine of Marx and Lenin or even of Mao, only, vaguely, to what is regarded as the more directly human and certainly the more romantic Communism of Castro, particularly of Che Guevara: here as abroad the red flag hung along with the black flag of anarchism; the commonest decoration of disorder was, however, pictures of Che. In fact, it was Che far more than Professor Herbert Marcuse, prime ideologue of the non-ideological revolution of our time, whose spirit presided over the boiling campus, and this is no doubt explained by the unwillingness of Marcuse, a product of the German professorial tradition, to encourage the application of his revolutionary teachings to the universities. In New York at the time of the uprising and invited to Morningside Heights to view what he had wrought, he stayed disapprovingly away from an insurrection wholly consonant with his understanding of what makes for a sound and vital democratic process.

If one is to be an urban guerrilla—and along with such improvisations as Arabic Belly Dancing and Liberated Genetics, guerrilla warfare both urban and rural stood high in the curriculum through the weeks of the strike when the University was said to have been "liberated" and classes were being held anywhere but in classrooms—one needs streets to fight in and it was not surprising that it was to the meaner streets of the vicinity that the SDS beamed its message. For as long as the strike continued, the appeal to "community" was tireless: through microphones and bullhorns, written, typewritten, xeroxed, mimeographed, posted on placards on the now barred gates of the University through which one supposedly entered the campus only on presentation of an ID card. And in the meanwhile one's friendly neighborhood suffered in its own existential fashion, unnoticed except by those—they have not the makings of revolutionaries—for whom it happened to be their familiar defining community.

At the Connecticut shore during the hurricane it was "my" neighborhood that was flooded, "my" community which suffered the insult of nature: child, kittens, manuscripts held high in the air, we had pressed through the rising water—but we had swum in it every day, how could it turn on us so fiercely?—until a better-situated house than our own had given us refuge. From its roof we had had at last the fine safe funny spectacle of summer beach-life swirling beneath us, deck chairs and beach umbrellas, beach balls, swings, grills, beer bottles and boats and picnic baskets bobbing under our eyes in a wild prepsychedelic canvas of random association. The swirl of a campus in convulsion brought to the level of perception no such amusing conjunction of the frivolous and banal. Nevertheless it too made its accidental work of art, of all-too-familiar design, its form that of sullen and agitated crowds, its elements the fearfulness of desecrated buildings and raging young faces and voices, overturned police barricades or, worse, police barricades in dead alignment, police in their uniforms, police horses, police cars, sidewalks thick with the casual throwaways of persuasion: pamphlets, leaflets, posters, printed or stenciled demands and protests, bulletins, denunciations, exhortations. There was no business as usual for the Columbia neighborhood, I suppose there never is in the neighborhood of revolution. One was everywhere pressed upon by the disorder, unable to be clear of it. It was like being among the audience at *Marat/Sade:* between oneself and a demented world there was no curtain. The teaching of modern subjects in our universities, especially literature, proceeds on some unadmitted assumption of a drastic discontinuity between art and life. It is as if the professor who sanctions the revolutionary content of the contemporary literary works which he teaches were still speaking from the platform of a hundred years ago, when art was outside the stream of "real" life, outside the world of action and political choice, its influence upon public affairs a matter of some slow unfathomable penetration of the public consciousness by a remote mysterious object called culture. Among the many assumptions undermined by the attack on Columbia, not the least important was the illusion that contemporary art is an academic subject like any other, adequately dealt with without doctrinal commitment. Only the blindest eye could fail to see the extent to which the revolutionary scene at the University represented the moral substance of contemporary art translated into actuality; indeed the triumph of culture over politics.

The detritus of communal compassion piling up at their doors, the Columbia shopkeepers studied a confused and embarrassed stoicism. What was it all about, they would inquire shyly of their old University friends, and when would it end? But how did one explain to the grocer, badly disappointed that his son, instead of becoming a doctor or lawyer, had elected to carry on in the family store, that his hopes for his boy had been socially retrograde and that the University was a power elite fashioned in the image of the malign State, bent on its own greedy self-perpetuation? The shops, excepting the butcher's and Takome, local emporium of the hero sandwich, were bleakly empty: the one thing people don't do in the neighborhood of a revolution is buy Pyrex bowls or asparagus or early lilac. On the other hand, of the buying of sandwiches by the young—it seems that the girl students in the occupied halls had refused the order of their male comrades that they be the cooks of revolution—or of hamburger by faculty wives, there was no discernible end. A faculty wife became short-order chef at any hour of the day or night for her husband and his exhausted colleagues working without rest to protect, not the abstract idea of a university—abstract speculation on the nature of the university had to await the panel discussions which were initiated when the strike had begun to lose some

of its fervor and the less excited students were ready to return
to thought—but the living University which must be sustained
against a saner day.

Wherever liberal people gather—and if I speak of the consciously liberal, it turns out that I speak of the radical since for
more than thirty years the two sections of political opinion
have been intimately, unsoundly allied—the current outbreaks
in the universities of the world are being welcomed. It is felt
that they must be justified because they constitute change,
movement; and whatever changes, moves, is assumed to be
progress. In part this strange idea is accounted for by the fear
under which people of conscience now live of being thought
opposed to useful social renovation. But this fear, in turn,
must be accounted for, and it is generously explained only by
the bad condition of modern democratic life. Virtually no one
of developed imagination now approves of life in the democracies. True, we have all the proof anyone needs that conditions in the Communist countries are worse by any proper
liberal test. But liberalism has long had the habit of exempting
Communism even from sharing in the nonpartisan shortcomings of industrial modernity, and of replacing criticism of
totalitarianism with democratic self-criticism, for is it not democracy in which we have our citizenship? By what right do
we accuse others when our own house is in such disorder? In
fact, under the pressures of recent years, especially since the
Vietnam War, even people critical of the abrogation of civil
freedom under Communism would seem to find it difficult
to distinguish between the social and political, if not the
strictly libertarian, outcomes of the two systems, the democratic and the Communist. What good, they ask, is there in
representative government if we cannot halt a war we hate or
use the money spent on it to help our multiplying poor and
relieve the blight on our cities?

Well, our universities are presumably the place where our
best wisdom resides. They are our founts of learning, the

guardians of our humane tradition. If life in our society is this unsatisfactory, is it not reasonable to find the universities at fault and to conclude that the lesson they teach is wrong or insufficient? Do they not need to be shaken out of their self-approval, cleansed of the error they tolerate or even nurture? Perhaps there is still hope for a world whose students refuse to comply in complacency and cooperate in error but, instead, take a stand against the wrong in their educational institutions.

Reasoning like this is of the essence of progressive thought and does some credit to conscience. Who even of soundest liberal persuasion would not welcome a movement of the young directed to the revitalization of the democratic ideal? (It was the miracle we thought Eugene McCarthy had produced until he lost sight of his own best goal.) If the young do not reform us, who will, and if we are not reformed, what future do we face?

The first and eminently sensible question put to one, then, by conscientious people outside of Columbia is, What are the student demands and will they be met? The question clearly intends to ask what deep-rooted mistake the University perpetuates which, corrected, would promise an improvement in American life insofar as it is within the power of our students to extend the benefits of their schooling. And more specifically the question has reference to those unhappy aspects of contemporary life to which liberals and progressives are now most alert: its inequity and harshness, its depersonalization, the alienation of the individual from his fellow man and government, the loss of personal identity, affectlessness nourished in lack of concern for those less fortunate than oneself.

The question, taken on its highest level of intention, could not be more difficult to answer because inevitably the answer is circular. Is there, has there been, that in the condition of Columbia which reflects the bad condition of our society? Obviously, yes. How could it be otherwise, since Columbia, like any institution in society, is part of its society. We cannot imagine a school in any country which would not mirror the condition of that country, or anywhere in the modern world which would not be shaped by the condition of the modern world. It is therefore in the degree that one is dissatisfied with the state of one's country and world that one will necessarily be dissatisfied with its institutions of learning. There can be no doubt that just as the sense of the individual's alienation from his fellow citizens and his government has so markedly increased throughout America in recent decades, our students' sense of alienation from their educational institutions has similarly increased, and from much the same primary cause: the growth of populations. But what is overlooked is the fact that our enlightened effort to correct our modern troubles is also involved in their spread. In the desire to enhance the individual and collective well-being of our citizens we have undertaken to provide higher education for as many people as want it. We would consider it retrograde to cut back on the number of people we educate in order to achieve a more personal relation between student and student, or student and teacher. What is both right and wrong with America and with much of the present-day democratic world is therefore what is both right and wrong with our universities: they have a dream of progress, a sweet dream of the good, but haven't solved the problems of modernity. And thus in important measure any student uprising is not so much a rebellion against the particular institution as against the century.

Still, even while we accept a generalization such as this, we all of us know that schools, like nations, vary in their problems; one university may offer solider reason for student complaint than the next. What then was particularly wrong with Columbia that the uprising took hold as it did, to the point where a revolt that had begun with a handful of students was able to win to its side, in the space of a week, not only a large portion of the student body but even a considerable part of the faculty?

I admit a possible bias. One marries into a university much as one once married into one's husband's family: there develops a not insignificant attachment and a perhaps distorting intimacy. The university commonly talks of itself as a family, and when dissension arises there is much to remind one of family angers: one speaks of insufficient respect for this or that member of the group, failures of tenderness or trust, the wrong distribution or use of authority, even misapplication of funds. Still, with all allowance for subjectivity, I find myself unable to locate a sufficient cause for revolution at Columbia —reason for complaint, certainly; reason for protest, yes, especially in the graduate schools which are the more crowded and anonymous sections of the University, but no reason, no reasonable reason, to tear the place to pieces. Columbia is not the Sorbonne, where nothing less than a major assault could hope to blast the authorities into awareness that the institution exists to educate students and not merely to honor the abstract idea of learning. It is not Berkeley. Absurd as it may be for its dissenting students to call Berkeley a "totalitarian think-factory," it was justifiable to call it a factory, it was so gigantic and dehumanized. But even in the Columbia graduate schools, where the classes are often too large, they are smaller than in many undergraduate courses elsewhere, notably at Harvard. Any lecture courses for as many as a hundred students are uncommon and in the undergraduate school I have heard bitter faculty complaint against classes of forty: the College is indeed celebrated for its insistence on keeping its classes small. In the graduate faculties, again, there had long been warranted complaint against the lack of close student guidance in the writing of dissertations, and the absence of easy association between professors and students. But there was at no time ground for this complaint in the undergraduate school where the most one heard was criticism of the curriculum, inspired by political partisanship: there must be more courses in African history, African literature, African art. And even this demand, evidence of the presence in the College of a group of students committed to a preference for the black as against the white cultural heritage, was not sufficiently widespread to have prepared anyone for imminent revolt on the campus.

Genuine intimations of trouble had come only from that small group of radicals whose sights were fixed elsewhere than on campus concerns, and from this quarter there had been substantial warnings. The president of the University having promulgated a rule against indoor demonstrations, this minority defied the order by gathering in Low Library to protest Columbia's membership in the Institute for Defense Analyses, a consortium of some dozen or more universities which supervises the distribution of government contracts for university research projects. There were six demonstrators, five of them undergraduates, one a graduate student, who came to be known as the IDA Six. They had been identified and asked to report to their deans for discipline, which meant probation. They refused the order; one of them demanded that instead of their appearing before the deans of their schools, the vice-president of the University should come to meet them. It was these IDA Six and their supporters whose rally at the sundial at noon on April 23 launched the disturbances of the next weeks. Vice-President Truman did not come to meet them as demanded but he sent the group a letter saying he would meet with them in Columbia's McMillin Theater. The group found this unacceptable and attempted another demonstration inside Low; prevented in this attempt, they moved to the site of the proposed new gymnasium and tore down the fence surrounding the newly started excavation. Scattered by the police—one of them was arrested—they then reformed at the sundial and came to the decision to hold an indoor demonstration in Hamilton Hall at the office of Acting Dean Coleman, before whom five of their number had been supposed to appear for disciplinary action. They imprisoned the dean and announced their occupation of the building.

The issue the SDS and SAS were making in this series of actions was an ultimate one: they were challenging the basis

and nature of the University authority just as they would continue to do in their demand for amnesty—the use of a word
associated in most people's minds with the exercise of executive charity would become confused in a situation in which
what the white insurrectionary students meant by amnesty
was the acknowledgment that the government of the institution had no right to exercise authority of any sort and in which
what the black insurrectionary students meant by amnesty was
the acknowledgment that the white government of the institution was racist and therefore solely to blame for the uprising.
The SDS and SAS were certainly not making any mere "protest," even of Columbia's membership in the IDA or of the
plan for the gymnasium. By customary standards no one could
accuse the University of excessive disciplinary severity, nor
was this a point made by the students. Rather, the position of
the SDS was that the University, like the State, has no legitimate power such as it claims. The protest of Columbia's membership in the IDA was therefore but one useful means of
defying the University's "illegitimate" authority, and even
more useful as a ground for defiance was the plan for the
gymnasium, for here one brought the University into confrontation with the "community." As to the occupation of Hamilton
Hall by the black students, this served two simultaneous, even
inseparable, purposes: it put the University authority under
question, though not precisely the same question it was being
put under by the SDS, and it gave the rebellion the wider
social and political reference it would have lacked if the
demonstration had stayed only with academic concerns. In
fact—and this is perhaps the chief point about the Columbia
revolution—academic concerns *followed* the occupation of the
buildings or, rather, appeared during the strike after the police
action; they had no part in the original outbreak. They were
not the incentive of the revolution, they surfaced in its current.
The uprising had the declared intention of large social destructiveness, the largest. In an open letter to President Grayson Kirk on April 22, Mark Rudd wrote: "We will destroy your

world, your corporation, your University." Although he reverses the obvious schedule, his purpose is plain. Of course, so extreme an intention didn't motivate everyone who took part in the occupation. But the uprising is not properly understood unless this avowed goal of its leadership is held firmly in view.*

Like the liberal public, a significant part of the University population failed, however, to grasp this fact. This is not to say that there was broad campus approval for the action of the radical minority in seizing the University buildings. On the contrary, at the outset of the disturbances the methods of the SDS aroused strong opposition on the campus. But as the days went by, many even stern opponents of the SDS, both students and faculty, went over in some measure to its side or, at any rate, to the side of protest, bringing with them the academic issues which had been missing at the start and thus changing the face that the rebellion would otherwise have shown the world. Now, to be sure, academic complaints were grafted on to the original non-academic demands. Just as in Chicago several months later a demonstration whose ruling intention was anarchic was able, because of the violence with which it was met, to mobilize the sympathies of people who would have wanted no part of its actual purpose, just so at Columbia the way in which the occupation was handled by the administration, or perhaps just the fact that it could take place and throw the University off balance as it did, made it possible for the SDS to activate a campus which hadn't previously realized there was anything spectacularly wrong with it.

---

* In the fall, in a speech made in Boston and reported in the *Boston Globe* (October 1, 1968), Mr. Rudd said of the Columbia uprising: "We manufactured the issues. The Institute for Defense Analyses is nothing at Columbia. Just three professors." And he continued in the same vein of belated truth. "And the gym issue is bull. It doesn't mean anything to anybody. I had never been to the gym site before the demonstrations began. I didn't even know how to get there." Mr. Rudd has never, to my knowledge, disavowed these statements.

Primarily, the wide disaffection from the University after the buildings were evacuated by the police on April 30 and during the strike following the police action was a response to the use of police on the campus. The brutality of the police on the morning of April 30 outraged virtually everyone who saw or heard about it. Not content with releasing their week-old hatred for the students who held the buildings, the police swung wildly at whatever head there was to hit, not alone in the halls but even outside the buildings. Hordes of innocent spectators had come to the campus as word spread of a bust, students who had no love of the sit-in: these bystanders too were ridden down, assaulted, pressed to the edges of the campus from which they couldn't escape. True to their pledge to interpose themselves between the occupied buildings and the police until they should themselves decide that the police must be called, the faculty tried to hold the steps of Low, Fayerweather, Avery, Mathematics: they were similarly brutalized. It was easy in such a situation to forget that were it not for student lawlessness the law would never have been called to the campus. Not only a good portion of the student body but many members of the Ad Hoc Faculty Group which had agreed in principle to the use of police, insisting only that this be postponed until every conceivable avenue of peace was explored, now forgot who had brought rage and disorder to the University and turned on the administration for its brutality to its students. In other words, everyone—students, faculty, the public—blamed the University for the ugliness of the police. The SDS could not have hoped for a greater victory.

But if this was the chief cause of the swing in campus sentiment, disaffection from the University had another source too: the conduct of the administration during the crisis. The inability of the president and vice-president to address the campus except in the language of traditional authority, in self-defense and defense of established procedures, had revealed a gulf, which had previously been scarcely noticed, between the will of the administration and the will of students and teachers. Few members of the Columbia faculty had ever to my knowledge felt that they had too little voice in the running of the University or their departments. On the contrary, the departments were democratic enough and the faculty was glad to have administrative details taken off its hands so it could get on with its own work. And only in the last year, under the SDS slogan of "participatory democracy," had the students come to think that it would improve their educations to be involved in the direct management of the institution, and even now what they had sought was much more a channel for student opinion than actual "student power." But when administrative power showed itself to be so inadequate in crisis, faults in the institutional structure which had previously gone unmarked took on importance. This is of course what the SDS and indeed the whole of the New Left has in mind when it undertakes to "politicize" the unpolitical: put enough pressure on an institution or government, offer it enough provocation, and the sad likelihood is that it will reveal its worst face and thus confirm the radical assumption of its unsoundness and corruption.

And, finally, subtly but most forcefully, disaffection from the University represented the disaffection from modern society and its authorities of people everywhere today. When the moderate students of Columbia were outraged by the police action of April 30, they were responding not merely to an isolated act of ugliness. What the overt brutal conduct of the police symbolized for them was some less readily visible brutality of modern democracy. It was as if there had now been fully disclosed to them something in the American condition to which they had let themselves be blind while those of radical persuasion had seen it for what it really was. They came to regard their moderation as a self-deception, a propitiation of evil, of which they were suddenly ashamed and for which they had need to atone by some radical action of their own. Clearly this sense of wakening to the true state of affairs wouldn't have been possible had there not existed, though perhaps not at the level of full consciousness, a generalized suspicion of their society. Even in the moderate young this suspicion had been already well implanted, however, and not simply by their mass culture but by what must be called their classical modern culture, those major statements of modern art which precisely intend to subvert confidence in the values of the past.

Nor, of course, is it only the young who have learnt disgust with the given of society. A Columbia faculty sympathetic to the strike was sympathetic not to the political motive and strategies of the uprising but to the idea of necessary revolt of some kind against a social force which, by its nature or perhaps merely by its existence, disappoints our best expectations from life, for this is the idea that now binds together the cultural generations, gives them a shared moral premise for social action, keeps full the reservoir of guilt when action is taken by others and not by oneself. The ugliness of the police made many of the faculty feel morally laggard in not having matched the certitude with which their radical students had perceived the connection between power and force. "Even you would have become a revolutionary," said an old faculty friend speaking to me of the behavior of the police; yet only a few days before he had retreated to the country, sickened by the violence of the demonstrators. And even faculty who didn't respond simplistically, who were perhaps less susceptible to social guilt and therefore better able to see the moral double-dealing which underlies the absoluteness of the judgment the contemporary revolution passes on our society, were bound to respect some new seriousness on the part of the students in the wake of the police action. The day after the bust, when the strike was called, far from a majority of the faculty supported it. But as the days passed and the professors began to talk with their students, fewer and fewer found it possible to make the break with them which would have been the consequence of their insisting that classes be held in the struck buildings. These newly politicized students were too genuine in their commitment to the strike, too impressive in their new gravity.

Thus when people now ask, will the student demands be met, will the University reform itself, one must be sure what is meant by the question. If it means, will dissatisfaction and anger disappear from the campus, one can answer only with a question of one's own: Is a happier consciousness about to be given us in our country? But if they are asking the more immediate practical question, will there be useful reform at Columbia, will the students be given participation in decisions of curriculum and departmental management, and will the University be restored to its peaceful functioning as an educational institution, then the reply must be that no part of the question, let alone its whole, can be answered with certainty. In fact, to group together all of these inquiries as if they were one implies that student "demands," whatever their character, are necessarily useful and, more, that the future good of Columbia depends on the readiness of the University to concede their worth. Even before the spring term ended, machinery was put in motion to explore the possibilities of alteration in the structure of the University, and over the summer, under the guidance of various faculty-student committees, much progress has been made toward achieving greater student and faculty representation in University procedure and decision. Too, the resignation of President Kirk and the appointment of Andrew Cordier as acting president of Columbia promises a new administrative responsiveness. But none of these moves provides a firm assurance that the University will be restored to peace or even, if it is peaceful, that it will be the better educational institution for what will have been changed because of the uprising. While social progressivism suggests that the more that students and teachers participate in the decisions of a school, the better the school will serve their needs, this may prove to be the opposite of the case. Some of the changes proposed by the students are on their face perilous to democratic education—for instance, a plan formulated by graduate students in political science that there be substituted for the traditional Ph.D. something called an "action Ph.D." in which the candidate, instead of writing a dissertation, chooses a street in a disadvantaged New York area and organizes the residents for social-political activity; patently a proposal like this, far from freeing the University from old academic bonds, is asking for academic dictatorship, for how else, except by dictate, would one determine the correct social and political activity into which the poor of the city should be inducted? As to peace on the campus, finally this has little to do with reform of the University. It depends on what happens to the SDS and other campus extremists in the next months and years.

For while it is fairly plain that without University change, or at least an expression on the part of the administration of availability to change, the SDS will have an open field for its activities because of student restiveness, even the best administrative will is no guarantee against continued SDS subversion. The leadership of the revolution has not abandoned its original purpose. The rebellion having started in the wish to "shove" our society—as a sympathizer from outside the University has put it—with the University serving as simply one immediate object of a wider revolutionary impulse, it is hard to suppose that the insurrectionary minority will now quietly withdraw in favor of a movement for University reform. Virtually in the measure that campus reform is accomplished, the revolutionary leadership may put itself to the stimulation of fresh disorders and to the forcing of fresh confrontations, preferably of the sort that invite the use of police. It doesn't take many people to create a provocation of authority, and if their action goes unchecked, authority is threatened; certainly it is weakened in the minds of those who look to its command. Yet if law is invoked, this means police, and by now, with not only the campus busts but the Chicago experience behind us, we know what to count on from the police in excess and from the public in reaction to such excess. Even in the eight months between the march on the Pentagon and the move against Columbia and the fewer months that have elapsed between the outbreak at the University and my present time of writing, the white revolutionary movement in this country has made large gains in confidence and much advanced its techniques of disruption. It begins, not without justice, to feel that it has the society as a whole and not merely a single university considerably at its mercy. What more could it ask, for instance, than that on the largest public front, that of the nation, it should have managed to contribute so substantially to the discrediting of one of our two major political parties? It may be that what will save our universities will be the decision of the New Left to concentrate on larger social disruption and leave the universities to their own devices.

So those who welcome the Columbia uprising as a strenuous but nonetheless necessary occasion in the reform of our universities perhaps cling to liberal hopes that have no basis in political reality. The Columbia revolution wasn't a reformist or liberal revolution. It was not even a radical revolution in any sense for which we have been prepared in the political history of this century, which has taught us how to overthrow the unloved State and replace it with another. No new and better form of government, either for the university or the nation, has been described by this revolution. It is not even properly understood as a university revolution, though it took place at a university, badly hurt a university, even (eventually) may have produced some good for a university. It was an event in contemporary life, an event in the culture of our time, a revolution in and of modern culture.

And of that aspect of the cultural upheaval of our time presented to us at Columbia in the spring of 1968, surely Norman Mailer's *Armies of the Night* is the best—and a really superb—document. While it perhaps wasn't a book to read during the disturbances themselves, when one had one's own consciousness to tune to circumstance, it is not possible to comprehend our general revolutionary situation as we should without studying it now in all its wisdom and folly, complexity and oversimplification, reasonableness and unthinkingness, vision and blindness, idealism and disgust, love and rage, amiability and fierceness, self-aggrandizement and humility, exaggeration and precision, absolutism and accommodation. It is a work of staggering ambiguities, of which the author himself openly proposes the one we can most readily comprehend: politically, Mailer tells us, but he also means culturally, for the cultural and political are symbiotic in him and even undistinguishable from each other, he is a Conservative Radical. *The Armies of the Night* is also something close to Tolstoyan, and strikingly unfamiliar, in its wish to find resolution of ambiguity in the teachings of Christianity about which, naturally enough, Mailer is also ambiguous. In sufficient humility but also in full exulting consciousness of himself as player of a star public role, a person of many-faceted "image" for those young people who are most irreverent of the past and distrustful of the present, Mailer joined the march on the Pentagon in protest of a war which he feels is the worst and most unjust in American history, a proof of the near-total moral sickness of a society that once had at least an intuition of God. What made the march a commanding act of conscience for him, rather than yet another among many all-too-wearisome and doomed exercises in political conscientiousness, was the plan to extend a legal demonstration into an act of civil disobedience, even of overt (though limited) insurrection. If one overstepped the boundaries of protest designated by the police, one could get oneself arrested, and the story that a "notable" had been arrested, perhaps beaten by the police, would make the headlines and the TV screens. The line that separates merely dull liberal opposition to the war from radical opposition to the war would be made clear.

As it turned out, it was not as easy as Mailer had supposed to get oneself arrested at the Pentagon. Equally eager but less skilled than Mailer on the field of battle, Robert Lowell and Dwight Macdonald never managed it; Mailer is gentle with their failure. And even the hippies, who remained longest on the scene and who can usually activate the police simply by the way they dress and wear their hair, had to exercise a degree of ingenuity to excite the full terror they attribute to the civic or national power—the hippie girls bared their breasts outside the Pentagon to tease the soldiers guarding the steps, many of them young boys, into direct assault. But throughout the Washington weekend Mailer found himself placed where reputation and temperament could best meet in service to the cause of peace. There were rallies, and Mailer likes to speak to big audiences. Unlike many left-wing intellectuals, he has always preferred to address the still-unresolved many rather than the predisposed few; he stretches to exhibition like a professional athlete. He happily accepted the invitation to speak to a meeting on the eve of the march.

One had read about this speech in *Time:* how the famous author, drunk, traded obscenities (not to be mentioned by *Time*) with his audience. Mailer, to whom nothing in his own humanity is alien, gives an unedited report of the occasion. The speaker, it seems, had not prepared his speech; he prefers not to. His "fuck yous" and "bullshits" were ad hoc, like the politics to which he now gives his approval. It must have been a sudden providence—no, that is not right, it is not providence, certainly not Mailer's Christian providence, to which the existential revolution looks for guidance in its program of programlessness, but some intuitive knowledge of the fitness of things, of need and the fitting response to need—it must have been his nicest intuition of fitness, then, that suggested to Mailer the possibilities of political persuasion in his need to go to the bathroom and evacuate his bowels. Earlier in the evening, a pint of bourbon tormenting his bladder, he had missed the urinal in the men's room of the meeting hall; it had created a trenchant moment of struggle between the radical and the conservative in him, and this too Mailer now recounted to his audience.

On the platform with Mailer, Lowell and Macdonald were discomfited: the author of *The Armies of the Night* shows them to be more traditional characters than himself. They were the friends of the drunken orator, having to handle him in public without compromising their own acquiescence in the radical culture of our time. Lowell, Mailer tells us, sat sternly aloof at the side of the stage: if you are put out of countenance, you avert your countenance, you look only within yourself, as a poet should. Macdonald, a critic and therefore less the private man than Lowell, made stumbling moves of public responsibility; they were calculated not to offend but to get Mailer off the platform. The situation must have been painful for both Lowell and Macdonald: one wonders in what light it presented itself to them afterward, when they were going to bed that night, or, more soberly, shaving the next morning. But Mailer, describing it, manages not only to seal, as between himself and them, a political comradeship immune to such fortuitous violations; he also communicates his belief—and is it not ours as well? Is it not the belief of all of us whose advanced politics are indissolubly joined to the advanced culture of our time?—that he himself stands an important few paces forward of these more cautious friends of his in the march toward freedom, the march that must continue beyond the shared Washington target. The scene is wonderfully written, no one now writing could match it. It is worth isolating from *The Armies of the Night* for its bearing on the outbreak at Columbia, the parallel it proposes between the cultural styles, the political styles, the moral styles, the life styles of the two events, that in Washington and that on Morningside Heights.

At Columbia it was Mark Rudd—but he encompasses, one knows, none of Mailer's ambiguities; he will never be a novelist—who launched the University insurrection with his letter to President Grayson Kirk. Addressed "Dear Grayson," it announced, as I say, the intention of the SDS to destroy President Kirk's world, corporation, University. The letter concludes with the words of LeRoi Jones, "Up against the wall, motherfucker, this is a stick-up." Such was the opening volley in a barrage of violent and abusive language and behavior which continued throughout the disturbances. It was not alone President Kirk who was addressed as a motherfucker. Vice-President Truman was a motherfucker, Acting Dean Coleman was a motherfucker, the police were—naturally—motherfuckers, any disapproved member of the faculty was a motherfucker. Rudd's response to the mediating efforts of his faculty was "bullshit." In a Mediterranean importation, the revolutionary students spat at people they disliked, including senior faculty members. An old couple crossing the campus was shouted at: "Go home and die, you old people." A law professor, a neighbor of mine on Claremont Avenue, walking with his wife near the campus gates, was gratuitously punched in the stomach by a passing student wearing the red armband of his militancy. President Kirk's occupied offices were ransacked, his personal correspondence photostated for campus broadcast. His wastebasket was urinated in, the windows of his office were urinated out of. At a tense moment on the steps of Low Library a Barnard girl-demonstrator jumped up and down in front of the faculty line—the faculty were wearing their white armbands of peace—compulsively shouting, "Shit, shit, shit, shit." In the police bust another girl-demonstrator bit a policeman in the stomach. A professor's papers were taken from his office files—they represented ten years of research—and burned: he was an opponent of the revolution. During the occupation of Mathematics Hall, it was debated whether or not its library should be destroyed; although this plan was decided against, quantities of notes and other personal papers were taken from various of the faculty offices in the building and scattered around the stairwell; later, in preparation for the expected bust, liquid soap was spread on the stairs to deter the police, hoses had to be used, and these papers became an irretrievable mash. The day after the strike began, a member of the faculty who had helped persuade the president of the need for student participation in matters of campus discipline learned that the students were erroneously being led to believe that the membership of their new tripartite disciplinary committee was self-perpetuating; when he then went to a strike meeting of students and faculty to explain how in future the disciplinary board would actually be elected, his request for the platform was refused; he was told by the chairman, a faculty colleague, that he could "not take responsibility for the physical safety of anyone who came with such a message." The most gravely injured person in the two police actions at Columbia was not a student but a policeman who was permanently paralyzed when a student jumped down on him from above. On a terrace overlooking the campus some students managed to lift a potted tree which they crashed down over the side of the terrace—this was in the bust of May 22, when the second student attempt was made to seize Hamilton Hall; by good luck no one was killed.

A press which could not have been more diligent in covering the happenings at Columbia, or less capable of understanding the situation or even trying to, reported little of this to the public. Certainly it reported none of the obscenities: decent American newspapers don't print such language. But one has to ask what decent Americans our media have in mind when they exercise such censorship? Where do they locate the propriety they are so intent on protecting? The phenomenon being reported on was not of the gutter. This violence and nastiness took place at an Ivy League university. The speech and acts which our newspapers and television withheld from the public were the speech and acts of young people who supposedly represent the American educated middle classes in their most ardent desire to rid us of the indecencies of our present society, and one discovered that a decent proportion of the decent American middle-class mothers and fathers of these young people, as well as other energetic spokesmen for progress, supported their offspring. Mr. (Lt. Col.) Rudd, father of Mark, strode the campus boasting his paternity; Mrs. Rudd, mother of Mark, gave the proudest and tenderest of interviews to the *Times* about how her-son-the-rebel plants tulips in their suburban garden. Some two hundred or so mothers and fathers of students at Columbia banded into a Committee of Concerned Columbia Parents to back their children and further harry the administration. Dwight Macdonald, who is supposed to loathe all violence, wrote his friends a letter of appeal for funds for the SDS and considered my letter of refusal the joke of a lifetime. And the Columbia clergy, with the exception of its Catholic officer, threw themselves with hearts bleeding and souls aflame into this newest movement of youthful idealism—it was the Reverend Starr, counselor to Protestant students and the most muscular of campus Christians (there was much for the Pentagon reporter to admire in him, appreciative as Mailer had been in Washington of the Reverend Coffin's split-second furious reflex* when an officer of the law dared place the lightest of hands on the clerical arm) who manned the barred gates of Columbia one evening during the strike, exhorting the "community" to join Columbia's liberation classes and make the campus its own, while the adjacent streets blackened with rank after newly formed rank of police. And in a parallel though less athletic manifestation it was Rabbi Goldman, counselor to Jewish students, black patch over an eye—it was injured not by the police but by a dissenting parent at a Concerned Parents' meeting—who stood on the sidewalk that same threatening May evening sighing heavily and regarding with his one free eye, not his colleague the Reverend Starr and Starr's student-followers trying to incite the "community," but only and woefully the malign civic power. One of course had heard much of

---

* I didn't of course know of Coffin's earlier CIA involvement, now revealed by Garry Wills in the *New York Review of Books* (Jan. 22, 1976), when I wrote this passage. (See footnote, page 64.)

the Reverend Starr. It was he who had read a wedding service for a pair of demonstrators in occupied Fayerweather: "I pronounce you children of the new age." Tonight he was too well surrounded with student militants to be recklessly approached at his post, but it was to her enlightened co-religionist, the rabbi, that a faculty wife, quite lost to humor, issued her invitation—no, I guess it too was an exhortation—that the rabbi sit down with her for a liberation class of their own, right there on the 116th Street pavement; its subject would be the history of the Weimar Republic.

It is of some significance, however, that this style of white revolution at Columbia was not the style of black revolution at Columbia. No doubt it goes too far for a critic of insurrection to isolate the black militants as the heroes of the Columbia disturbances—after all, they were well forward in the insurrectionary column, they cooperated in the imprisonment of Acting Dean Coleman, they refused negotiation of the sit-in, and they are said to have expelled the whites from Hamilton Hall for more reasons than that of black separatism, because they felt that the white students would not use guns and gasoline, that they were not ready to die for the cause. Eventually the conduct of the black occupants of Hamilton Hall was nevertheless of a different order from that of the SDS-led demonstrators. The distinction necessarily includes the fact that all blacks in our society, even the most privileged, those in the universities, have ground for revolutionary feeling such as no white college student has the right to pitch his tent on. But this is not alone what I have in mind here; I am talking of the way in which they made their existential occasion. These were serious people, these blacks, and so they comported themselves. They were frightening—all demonstrated power not of one's own election is frightening—but they were serious even in their menace, and certainly in their stance. They were not cosseted middle-class boys playing violent games whose consequences they felt no necessity to assess. For them the authority of the white world is an illegitimate authority, it is not the parental authority despised as much or more for the gifts it so prodigally gives its fortunate children as for the inequities it tolerates and for its concealed ambitions and intractability.

A day or two before the police action of April 30, an emergency meeting of the joint Morningside faculties—such meetings are unprecedented but this was the second within a week—had appointed an Executive Committee of the Faculties, ten senior professors who then co-opted to their committee two members of the nontenure staff, to examine the need for reconstruction of the University and to try to bring peace to the campus. In the next days and weeks this Executive Committee interviewed many representatives of campus opinion, including several black militants, one of whom was asked to speak about the relation between his position and that of the SDS. I had report of his remarkable response. The SDS, he said, wanted to "apply a gangrene" to American society in order to destroy it, and he was opposed to this. What his group wanted was to "test the tolerance" of the society—he meant this, he said, in a physical, not a social sense—to see how much play it allowed. The black students had occupied Hamilton Hall because they wanted to be inside a society that excluded them, but they wanted to keep the society in good condition for themselves, and this was why, if they could help it, the black students would in no way harm a building they occupied.

And indeed Hamilton Hall, unlike the buildings that were held by white students, was undefaced when it was evacuated, the refuse of the occupation was for the most part stacked in containers, no office or classroom had been disturbed, no file broken into. (The black students had also held a dance in Hamilton while they occupied it. A white passerby, hearing the music from behind the barricaded doors, could comprehend with some poignancy the emotions of exclusion for color.) It is of course possible that Professor Kenneth Clark, in his long hours of talk with these black students, had

116

spoken to them of the need for decorum and of the practical advantages to be gained if they continued in the dignity they had shown ever since they had rid the hall of the white demonstrators. But I doubt the situation required any such appeal; I suspect that early in their militant careers these black students had proposed the argument from self-respect: it has something in common with the argument from idea. In the course of the Columbia disturbances note was taken by various members of the faculty of the fact that a high percentage of all the student extremists were honor students; four, I think, were elected to Phi Beta Kappa while they sat-in. And it was commented upon by a historian that this was his first knowledge of revolutionaries on fellowships—also, for that matter, of a strike in which its salaried participants were kept on full pay. He spoke in wryness but not in bitterness, for such is the affection in which most university teachers hold their students that there was little bitterness even among conservative faculty. But except for younger teaching staff—preceptors, readers, research and lab assistants—and those few professors who automatically subscribe to any form of radical action, the faculty seemed at times to be almost as much distressed by the lack of idea in the revolution as by its methods. No one, however, accused the black militants of scorning thought. Respected for their self-respect, the black students were also held in regard for what self-respecting conduct promises in the way of thoughtful political conduct. Intransigent the black students at Columbia assuredly are, but they are concerned with racial, not personal, definition. And black definition in a white-dominated society is an enterprise of more than "existential" interest.

The blacks kept separate on Mailer's occasion too, which no doubt upset him more than he admits. The reader misses their presence in his book—it would be interesting to know whether black militant behavior frequently conforms to the Columbia pattern and how the black separatists act among themselves: how much and what kind of talk they carry on; whether their "participatory democracy" is an actuality or a form of manipulation by their leaders; how much humor they bring to their occasions. The talk in the buildings occupied by the white students at Columbia was apparently marathon; one hears of endless debate and putting-to-the-vote as the leadership reported on new developments and strategies but from information that now emerges there is reason to believe that this nonstop discussion of whether a new offer of mediation or a new proposal by the administration should or should not be accepted didn't always refer to the actual terms presented to the leadership for consideration—unquestionably as a participant in the democracy of revolution one fully exercises one's franchise, but there is question whether one exercises it on the point at issue. As to humor, one wonders if black revolution can conceivably be as humorless as present-day white revolution—in the Marxist thirties, at least among intellectuals, it was marvelously funny.

Mailer's own wit in his Pentagon report is not only abundant, it is most attractively wicked, particularly in the scenes with his fellow writers. But no one with him in Washington seems to have contributed to it. His brilliantly caustic portraits of his fellow notables introduce into contemporary literary practice something which it has signally lacked, the right to treat one's political and intellectual friends as if they were live, breathing human beings, quirky, deficient, ostentatious, vain, or redundant, inviting one's malice no less than one's comradeship, and not merely as bundles of political rectitude or its failure, to be labeled and shipped off for the moral weighings-in. But his ignorant army was apparently as humorless as the army with which it clashed, and this left a hole at the center of the Pentagon adventure which presently filled with ugliness.

It may of course be the balance that Mailer is able to hold between grimness and gaiety that accounts for his final hesitation before the revolution. At any rate, his book makes a curious ideological case for humor; he traces a connection between humor and obscenity, on the one hand, and politics on the other. "There was," he writes of himself,

no villainy in obscenity for him, just—paradoxically, characteristically his love for America: he had first come to love America when he served in the U.S. Army, not the America of course of the flag, the patriotic unendurable fix of the television programs and the newspapers, no, long before he was ever aware of the institutional oleo of the most suffocating American ideas he had come to love what editorial writers were fond of calling the democratic principle with its faith in the common man. He found that principle and that man in the Army, but what none of the editorial writers ever mentioned was that that noble common man was obscene as an old goat, and his obscenity was what saved him. The sanity of said common man was in his humor, his humor was in his obscenity.

And he adds: "And his philosophy as well—a reductive philosophy which looked to restore the hard edge of proportion to the overblown values overhanging each military existence." One wants to pause on that "unendurable fix" of television and the newspapers: does Mailer not understand that the real corruption they work on the American spirit is not that of inspiring us to a suffocating patriotism but of fixing us in false and vulgar personal and social values, to the point where even our acts of dissent such as an illegal move on the Pentagon are planned as a seduction of the media? Mailer himself admits, only well on in his book and with a disarming sheepishness, that throughout his Washington weekend he had by pre-arrangement a British TV crew at his side, recording his every pictorial possibility. But notwithstanding: No statement could more soundly than this of Mailer's describe the America Mailer got to know and love in the Army. But the armies of our present night (he would agree) represent a different America on both sides of the Pentagon steps, and on Mailer's side the battalions produced not a single moment of natural American fun, of native obscenity of the kind which, in the ideological revolution of an earlier decade, restored the hard edge of proportion to one's own enterprise. Mailer's obscenities may not have been prepared but they were calculated and similarly at Columbia the obscenity was calculated. This makes it phenomenologically different from the old-goat obscenities of Mailer's noble common man. The saving sanity of Mailer's report is distinctly not its obscenity but its complex if not always reliable intelligence, and for the complex intelligence there is nothing saving about obscenity, unless perhaps as it is used to assert a bond with the noncomplex intelligence —and this, obviously, is more often a sentimentality than a reliable bridge between classes. Reductive Mailer's or anyone else's use of obscenity can be and is, but used by educated people as a weapon in the cultural-political war, it can backfire and blow their own saving values instead of reducing the overblown values against which it is directed.

Manifestly, the rhetoric of the Columbia revolution was meant to deflate the University establishment. To call the president and the vice-president, the deans and the faculty of one's University motherfuckers is no doubt meant to restore the hard edge of proportion to the overblown values of the University authority, and of all established power. But obscenity and humor had not even a nodding acquaintance with each other at Columbia, except as an occasional much-beset professor looked to them in order to preserve his sanity—there was the well-known punster, for instance, who decided that the insurrectionary students were "Alma Materfuckers." Obscenity did, however, make the most obvious ties between cultural and political intention, or even between artistic and political intention. And it brought in its wake just such sentimentality as is proposed in Mailer's appeal to the rock-bottom Americanism shared with his beloved G.I.'s: suddenly there was much talk at Columbia about campus "fathers," how there weren't enough of the right kind, and how they should have been where they were not. If I, like so many others, had been shaken by the internationally publicized presumption of the undergraduate demonstrator who had been photographed sitting in the chair of the University's Top Authority, his feet on the desk of the Top Authority, smoking the Top Authority's cigar, I had no reluctance in voicing my contemptuous anger when this same young man, fresh out of jail after the police bust, apparently rushed to the nearest phone to demand why my writer-husband had not been present to protect the writer-student against the police. This was revolutionary scorekeeping, its own fine intimation of terror; to my ear it spoke all too reverberantly of concentration camps and the knock on the door in the night. But, not all that paradoxically, it was of course also the wail of a child coming out of tantrum, when, before he takes quieter and crueler stock of his new-found power, he makes a first ploy of family devotion. The analogy to temper tantrum is nevertheless a dangerous one; it sets up vibrations from a world of ready psychological explanation of phenomena that are not to be written off by canned reference to our culture's famous "permissiveness" in childrearing, or its affluence. No more than, say, Dr. Spock's illegal public actions against the Vietnam War are sensibly traced to a permissiveness he has himself undertaken to keep in proper dimension in his teachings on child care, or no more than the uprisings in German universities can be supposed to constitute a response to excessive permissiveness in German upbringings and schooling, do these familiar explanations of the nihilism of the insurrectionary students tell us anything useful to our understanding of the campus disruptions. To its credit, the Columbia faculty didn't retreat to these prepared psychological positions. It was the administration—and far more than this was a deficiency of human insight, it was a failure of cultural awareness—which seemed to regard the demonstration as if it were a tantrum, best handled by being ridden out with no show of parental affect.

As the chief parental figures on the campus, the Columbia administrators were fathers in an anxiety dream—uncomprehending, unyielding, present but unreachable. To the obscene and ugly rhetoric of longed-for student power they opposed the gray grinding rhetoric of established power: power threatened, power now suddenly uncertain of itself, benevolently intentioned power, but power nonetheless, and one could only be puzzled at how it had come about that these conscientious hard-working heads of what had been truly a family, a reasonably contented one too, could all at once be revealed as so remote from those they were meant to guide, so insensitive to the internal stresses to which even the most contented family is liable, so poor in the imagination of our present-day tormented culture.

From the rhetoric of President Kirk and Vice-President Truman one might have thought that what was happening at Columbia was a wholly egregious instance of unrest and social rage, that our world was only harmonious and balanced, and that the future course of the University, as set by themselves in decency and good purpose, was unavailable to question, a contract binding upon all men of honor. It is total error to ascribe "racism" to the Columbia administration: these are men of sound if old-fashioned social principle, for whom the construction of a gymnasium to be shared by the University and Harlem was embarked upon to put enlightened principle into practice. It is total error to charge them with being the instrument of a war-making government: no one was ever forced or influenced to participate in the research projects of the IDA, and the University's membership in the consortium was not allowed to interfere with the expression of antiwar opinion on the campus. When Noam Chomsky, the distinguished professor of linguistics at M.I.T. and a passionate opponent of the Vietnam War (he was one of Mailer's "notables"), came to Columbia during the month of May to take part in one of the panel discussions which followed the strike, he was booed for saying no less for the freedom of dissent permitted by his own university, also a member of the IDA. The public meeting rooms of Columbia have always been open for antiwar rallies, and a recent day-long moratorium on classes in protest of the war was fully accepted by the administration; the administration has also backed the faculty in its refusal to give the class standings of its students to the Selective Service. Again, the administration is not to be accused of wanting and inviting police brutality. It bypassed the faculty in calling the police because it believed—rightly, I think—that the faculty was making matters worse by delaying the police confrontation which the demonstrators refused to forgo, but this represented no cruel intention toward the students; the faculty had itself accepted the idea that police intervention might be unavoidable. In part the brutality of the police on April 30 was no doubt a result of administrative miscalculation: it requires four policemen to remove a person who even passively resists removal, and the administration had told the police that there were a few hundred students in the occupied halls when by that time there were more than seven hundred. The administration is not accountable, however, for the private rages of the men who enforce the law.

But neither President Kirk nor Vice-President Truman was present, observably present, on the campus when the police went into action, and although Dr. Truman explained that the police had asked them not to appear, their absence suggested their inability to look at, *see*, what was going on in their University and world. They had never perceived the need to set up an apparatus for discourse between students and administration. They seemed unaware of a difference between the students they had addressed in the past and those they address today, between the comfortable culture the University had once inhabited and our present culture of stress. It was not only that they couldn't speak persuasively to the revolutionaries—who could?—but that they couldn't properly communicate even with the uncommitted student population or the "jocks," the college athletes who, as part of the Majority Coalition, as it was called, of students opposed to the sit-in, persistently threatened to break into the buildings and remove their occupants if the University continued not to act. It was faculty and younger administration who blocked this miserable prospect, much as they circumvented the potential crisis of Kenyatta's visit to the campus and of the march on Columbia of some high school students who decided to widen a day of opposition to the war to embrace opposition to Columbia: welcoming these youngsters to the campus, the faculty managed to make a melancholy picnic of what had promised to be a freshly disturbed scene.

Even in relation to the faculty with whom it had lived on amicable terms, the administration was lamentably lacking in trust, even in respect. There was much unsuitable reference to loyalty: in a public interview the vice-president went so far as to name the professors he felt were sufficiently faithful. And faculty loyalty, which necessarily includes the recognition that the dull unrewarding endlessly detailed practical work of administering a vast institution has to be done by someone, and fortunately it isn't the professors, was in fact increasingly strained by the humiliating discovery that in the eyes of the administration it is apparently not the students and teachers who are the living core of the University but the administration itself. Tireless WKCR disseminated the statements of the administration as it did the ceaseless pronouncements of dissent or of just plain confusion; on more than one occasion the Columbia faculty was to learn that for Vice-President Truman, himself but recently a teaching colleague, the faculty had now to all effect become a paid convenience—most shattering was the time he was asked by the press what the administration would do if there were another sit-in and he replied that he really didn't know, perhaps they would have again to call the police or perhaps they would "use the faculty." The faculty had never proposed to be "used." Wise or unwise, it had acted in conscience, in independence and honor, on an initiative it felt it had the right to claim. Truman's message was inescapable: it was not alone the expression of student will that the administration undertook to deny, it was all will except its own. There were moments, that is, when even members of the faculty who were thoroughly opposed to the uprising would murmur, "Maybe the students are right."

And just as it soon became tedious to try to discriminate between the views of the president and vice-president, just so it became futile to try to figure out when these University officers were speaking in their own persons and when by direction of the trustees. No sooner had the faculty made known its own position on, say, the matter of University discipline or the problem about the new gymnasium—obviously, construction must be stopped; it's only common sense that if your gift is not acceptable you don't force it on people—and no sooner was it convinced that now at last it had the administration's agreement, than an official statement would be issued in contradiction. Day to day the official line on the gymnasium shifted— now construction would be called off, now the subject would be reinvestigated, now construction was stopped temporarily—and similarly unreliable was official acceptance of the Joint Committee on Disciplinary Affairs, a committee of seven students, seven faculty, and three members of the administration, whose formation was the first meaningful gain in campus reform as a result of the uprising. One would suppose that in a period when the young come at least to social and sexual if not to intellectual maturity so much faster than they once did, it would take little argument to persuade an administration that university students cannot be treated like children answerable to the grown-ups for their conduct. But there were statutory powers not to be quickly yielded; the president was adamant on his right to ultimate word on campus discipline. Whether this insistence on his disciplinary role represented Dr. Kirk's personal reluctance to relinquish parental authority or followed a direction of the trustees it is not possible to determine. In fact, the role of the trustees throughout the disturbances is yet to be put on record though there is ground enough for knowing that their understanding of student sentiment was surely no firmer than that of the administration. They were even more remote than the president from the actual emotions of the campus, their minds occupied with the management and financing of the institution, not with student feeling. They had never met with the faculty of the institution until its existence was forced on their notice by the disturbances, since which time a committee of trustees has frequently met with the Executive Committee of the Faculties; now they give sign of learning—it must be a stringent education—that the world they govern is not necessarily amenable to the plans they decide on for it. Their arrogance of power at the start of the troubles will not soon be lived down, however. The folly of supposing, as our campus radicals do, that a great educational institution need pay no heed to the money that builds and equips its buildings, pays its professors, takes up the slack between student fees and the actual cost of running the place, is matched only by the folly of supposing that money still speaks in our society with its old moral authority. Early in the revolution a member of the Executive Committee of the Faculties undertook to instruct the trustees of the University, those practical and powerful men of affairs, in the now long–available knowledge that just as the Industrial Revolution brought into being a conscious working class with "grievances" and "demands" and "interests," so our cultural revolution has brought into being a new class, youth, with its special demands and interests. While only a short time has elapsed since this pilot lesson, it already looks as if the trustees, who last spring at the height of the disorders could recommend the engagement of a professional public-relations man to fashion the language in which the head of the University would address the students and faculty, are no longer this disoriented. The new acting president steers a different course from President Kirk's and, so far, with no sign of conflict with the trustees.

But faculty, too, suffered its disorientation in the uprising, of a subtler and more profound kind than that of Columbia's administration and trustees. In recent decades liberals and radicals have not only lived in sufficient harmony, they have often held views indistinguishable from each other—where the two most regularly and mistakenly joined was of course in the refusal to oppose the Communist dictatorship as directly and unequivocally as liberalism sets itself against other forms of despotism. The happenings at Columbia suddenly made it clear that one had to locate political opinion, if only in relation to the goal of social revolution in America, with a new precision within the spectrum of the Left. The purpose of the Columbia uprising was not properly described even as radical; it was revolutionary. Its message was antiliberal. It was antiliberal in its lawlessness and its refusal of reasonable process, and it was antiliberal in its scorn for the liberal goodwill with which the faculty tried to meet it—as in most American universities, the Columbia faculty is largely liberal in its sympathies. Much more than Mark Rudd's "bullshit" expressed the lack of personal respect of the insurrectionary students for their teachers, it communicated the contempt of a revolution for whatever is the embodiment of liberal commitment or suggestive of reform. In the instance of both faculty and students the uprising demanded that one choose, simply, between conservatism and revolution. Some few members of the faculty might be prepared for the choice and even exult in its being forced on their less radical friends but the large majority felt they were being deprived of a definition for which they were offered no acceptable substitute and without which they had no bearings.

And in the months that have passed since the Columbia outbreak, this campus dilemma has spread across the nation. It is the undertaking of the New Left to destroy any common ground among Democrats, left-wing Republicans, liberals, and radicals. It means to polarize the country between extreme reaction and revolution; and it has been doing better than it could have dreamed before the Chicago convention. The extreme Left never actually supported Senator Eugene Mc-

Carthy; it welcomed his presence as a divisive force in the Democratic ranks and if temporarily he seemed to be return- ing the disenchanted young to legal political participation and even to be uniting certain quasi-radical elements in the popu- lation with the liberals, the New Left understood that this could not last under the best of circumstances, those of quiet defeat, and certainly not under the disruptive circumstances that they themselves had it in mind to create. In France, stu- dent disorders, while promising necessary academic reform and providing an impetus for a strike that won much-needed economic gain for the working class, restored de Gaulle to power and frustrated hope for a more liberal regime. At Columbia, liberalism suffered as much damage in the uprising as the institution itself. And before that, in Berkeley, when the New Left movement was still young, the campus disorders brought about the election of Reagan as the governor of Cali- fornia and the resignation of the liberal chancellor of the Uni- versity, Clark Kerr, a consummation in which the New Left had mightily rejoiced. Johnson would not have had to conspire as he did in his own emasculation for the New Left to know that, given enough disorder in Chicago, the Democratic party and, with it, the country would look to the eyes of the world as if it offered America only the grim choice between Nixon (or even Governor Wallace) and revolution; Mayor Daley's con- tribution to the occasion, the violence with which he met the long-planned provocations of the New Left, was only the devil's crown to an already-prepared achievement. After the police action in Chicago, the liberal McCarthy, like the liberal Columbia faculty after the police bust of April 30, was prop- erly outraged. But also like the liberal faculty, he failed to hold two ideas in his mind simultaneously and with equal force—in his public statements he condemned only Daley and the Chicago police, and failed to name the provocateurs of violence who had deliberately invited retaliation. In repudiat- ing the actions of the Democratic organization but failing at the same time to disavow the revolution, in effect he sanctioned the position of the New Left, that any liberalism which means to go forward with history, as opposed to a liberalism in thrall to the establishment, has no move except to embrace the revolution. Of course what path a vigorous ongoing liberalism should properly take in our present situation in which the democratic establishment has so plainly shown its bankruptcy is now far from easy to chart. But at least this much should be clear: if liberalism lacks the fortitude and intelligence to stand up to the New Left and deceives itself that the principles of liberalism betrayed by the present democratic establishment depend for their preservation on the contemporary revolution, it will have a major responsibility for the triumph of reaction in this country. A simple, dependable guide to liberal intelligence is available: an examination of the morality of the proffered revolution as this reveals itself in its actions and rhetoric. Surely a correction of the evils of contemporary society is no more to be found in lawlessness and licensed rage on the Left than on the Right.

Inspired in his campaign chiefly by opposition to the war, McCarthy might of course have been sounder in his assessment of the Chicago demonstration if he had known how little part the Vietnam War played in the Columbia uprising. Of all the problems that now confront America, it is the war that brings liberal teachers most into conjunction with their dissenting students. Had opposition to the war been a major issue in the Columbia protest, the Columbia campus would have looked like Central Park on May Day. But the Vietnam War, whatever its share in creating unrest among the students of this country, had as little part in the Columbia uprising as in parallel campus disturbances in countries not involved in the war: France, Germany, Italy, Mexico. Naturally, Vietnam came into the oratory of the Columbia revolution, but ritualistically; it was not a major concern. Even the demand that Columbia sever its connection with the IDA emphasized the identification between university power and government power rather than the actuality of our Vietnam engagement.

During the strike several participants in the panel discussions on the campus, Stuart Hampshire, Stephen Spender, Jean Floud, Noam Chomsky, made the point—it was received with some apathy by their audiences—that students today tend to confuse their university citizenship with their national citizenship. Because they are aware of the acute problems with which the nation deals wrongly or insufficiently, they involve themselves in actions within their universities which conflict with their interests as students and which endanger their educational institutions. The speakers were at great pains, however, to explain that they were not urging the students to forsake political activity. They particularly stressed the entire appropriateness of student protest of the war. The revolution took a different position. It was as if the war were either unreal to them or real merely as a quite minor charge in their indictment of the social authority. It had more reality than this for a faculty much worried lest suspensions of students might lead to their being drafted.

The readiest explanation of the absence of the war as a campus issue is, of course, that in the weeks just before the Columbia outbreak President Johnson had made his peace speech and the Paris Peace Talks had been initiated. Too, with Eugene McCarthy and Robert Kennedy in the field, the prospect for a peace candidate in the presidential elections was for the moment much improved. Yet the draft continued, the war continued, Americans and Vietnamese still were dying in quantity. Students who would soon graduate could have no confidence that they would be able to go on to graduate school. Something other than the hopeful turn in public affairs had to account for the relegation of the Vietnam issue to virtual obscurity—and this, one conjectures, was the reluctance of the revolution to put stress upon a cause it shared with liberalism and moderation; its refusal, that is, to join up with campus forces of the kind which in Washington had swelled the ranks of protest but then backed away from actual assault on the Pentagon or settled for peaceful arrest. The small part played by the war in the University disturbance—and most people who were themselves against the war but had no first-hand knowledge of the uprising were reluctant to believe that it wasn't the central issue—was another negative but telling way in which the revolution communicated its contempt of liberalism and added to the guilt and insecurity of a liberal faculty. If even its opposition to the war failed to validate liberalism in the eyes of the Left, then surely to be "merely" a liberal was to be retrograde to history.

The personal, moral, and intellectual offense suffered by the Columbia faculty in the uprising was indeed momentous. It is to be thought of only with pain. If Columbia has pioneered the future of the universities of this country and there are to be other insurrectionary uprisings on our campuses, it is logical to suppose that the loneliness consequent upon the rejection of our university teachers by the students to whom they have given their devotion is bound to be dispelled by multiplication, much as has happened in the instance of the rejected parents of our time. Of course it was not only the Columbia faculty that experienced insult; everyone not of the revolutionary faction suffered offense, even the nonrevolutionary students. One of the lessons taught in the uprising—it bears on the old question of why the center cannot hold—is the speed with which whatever makes its appeal to direct action achieves emotional advantage over whatever is committed to the slower and more passive (as it would appear) process of reasonableness; how to activate decency and teach it to stop feeling deficient because of its low quotient of drama is obviously one of the urgent problems of modern society. What makes the terrible near-endemic ache of contemporary parenthood, especially in enlightened homes where parental love and hope are so regularly, casually, and, in most part, inexplicably flouted by children grown to a sudden harsh scornfulness of which their parents could have no expectation, was now suddenly the experience of university professors who also had no reason to expect such an unprecedented violation of natural feeling and who in fact had supposed that they were perhaps the single remaining bridge between the dissident young and their elders. And what had built this bridge, what had made the special tenderness of the teacher for the young if not the teacher's commitment to social continuity, social improvement, to all the vaults of imagination and feeling that have tradition-ally defined the liberal enterprise? There were emotional breakdowns among the faculty due to the uprising, and sev-eral car accidents attributed to exhaustion. It is a fair guess that had the administration shown more sensitivity, if not to the demonstrators, at least to the student population in general and thus left the faculty with nothing to be angry at, nowhere to stand except at the administration's side, looking together at the chasm that had opened up between themselves and a gen-eration in such newly bitter revolt against them, the toll for the faculty might have been even more severe.

But I speak of senior faculty. Junior nontenure faculty are usually still of an age to depart their elders rather than to be departed from, to reject rather than be rejected, to ask rather than give tenderness, to demand rather than share or cede power. Not that they had been demanding power at Columbia before the uprising and been refused; the possibility of im-proving their status came to them only by student example. There is irony in the failure of political forethought involved in the welcome of junior teaching staff into the shaky councils of the Ad Hoc Faculty Group during the sit-in. Anyone had a vote in these loosely organized meetings, anyone could tie a white handkerchief around his sleeve and join the faculty cordons at the occupied buildings: the younger, the sturdier. In this sudden heady alteration of status, the nontenure staff decided that if it was deemed equal to faculty emergency, it merited equality on all scores—one form (but perhaps it is not to be generalized from) in which this particular "radicaliza-tion" announced itself was in the unsmiling question put to a senior professor by a much-junior colleague: there being a scarcity of chairs at a meeting, must the junior rise for his senior? As I write, the junior staff is busily formulating its corporate right, equal with that of senior professors, in the shaping of departmental policy and in decisions on appointments and promotions in a University to whose future they bring only such sense of responsibility as they may have as individual persons.

And yet how are we to know—the question bears in on one with an always-increasing weight—the proper character in which responsibility now announces itself, or should announce itself? How do we even know that we will recognize it when we see it, since it may show a wholly unfamiliar face? For many among the educated classes, the right aspect of responsibility has for long been centrist moderation, a cautious mature deliberation in the implementing of social ideals; it has been difficult to envisage responsibility in any other way than this, which is the liberal way. But an inescapably more pressing sense of our public dilemmas and of the extreme inequities which exist in what we call our liberal democracy makes it always less possible for us to be content with our habitual knowledge of what responsibility looks like. Almost with each passing day it becomes harder for liberalism to claim that it has been adequate to the tasks it undertook. We caution against capitulation to the revolution designed by the New Left, point to its ugly violence, warn whoever deceives himself into supposing that it represents a movement of progress that it has no program to which people committed to the reconstruction of democracy can pledge themselves, underscore its clearly announced goal of destructiveness and the methods it employs to achieve this goal, methods that inevitably give aid solely to the forces of reaction. But must we not also caution against the comfortable assumption that liberalism has only to shine up its old medals and resurrect its old rhetoric of responsibility to be equal to the responsibility that now devolves upon it? To deal only with campus problems: Would the useful changes now being instituted at Columbia, would even the change in administration, have been this quickly accomplished without the violent disruptions of the uprising? No one, I think, can honestly answer this in the affirmative; there wasn't that much quiet will for change. And here liberalism must take its share of blame for the disorders. By confusing quiet with quietism, by buttressing legality with inertia, liberalism has earned at least some part of its present poor reputation on the campus. Yet it will suffer more than disrepute, destruction, if in admitting its deficiencies it either rests with these as its cozy guilt or, in its desire for revitalization, takes the revolution as its alternative.

And so through the month of May, in dissension and anxiety and confusion, with no resolution of these terrible conflicts of the modern world which suddenly were being acted out on the campus, the University struggled to maintain a semblance of its accustomed life. But resolution of a kind—temporary, unreliable, uneasy—was of course approaching with the end of the term and graduation: Commencement was scheduled for June 4. There had been no regular classes in the College or even in some of the graduate schools since April 23—how were students to take examinations and be graded? This problem was resolved by the decision to call off final examinations and to give all students a grade of either Pass or Fail according to the work they had done before the disruptions; should a student desire a more precise grade he could arrange with his instructor for a private examination. Less encompassable was the problem of discipline. The newly formed Joint Committee on Disciplinary Affairs had had little time to construct a body of law. It was May 9 before it could make known its new rules for student government: a first student offense was punishable by probation, a second by more severe penalties—suspension or expulsion; whoever was charged with offense would be summoned to appear before the dean of his school to learn the charge that had been made against him and the punishment that the committee had assigned to it, and if the charged student denied his guilt or even stood mute before his dean, the dean could bring the case, if he had enough evidence to support it, before a tribunal of his school, composed, like the Joint Committee, of representatives from the student body, the faculty, and the administration. From the decision of this tribunal the student might again appeal to the Joint Committee itself.

There were hundreds of summonses arising from the disturbances; they could not all go out at the same time. The first of them went (unstrategically) to the leaders of the insurrection and (sensibly) to the offenders in the senior class whose graduation depended on disciplinary clearance—it had been arranged that no offender would be denied graduation; if he answered his summons he would be put on probation or suspended for the few remaining days of the term. But a great many of these students were also awaiting action against them in the police courts on charges that arose from trespass and resistance to arrest. Legal assistance and money for bail was abundantly available to the demonstrators, and for the most part they refused their disciplinary summonses. The Columbia air was suddenly thick with talk of due process, double jeopardy, indictments unsupported by evidence, although none of the students with whom I spoke had troubled to read the body of law constructed on their own demand for participation in their governance. And this agitation would continue and increase throughout the summer, abate in fact only partially when the new acting president would call on the district attorney to dismiss such charges as arose from simple trespass and grant clemency to a good proportion of the demonstrators, those charged with only a single offense. The SDS, still led by the now suspended Mark Rudd, would settle for no less than total amnesty.

Such was the heavily laden atmosphere into which the University moved with its plans for Commencement. Usually, if the weather permits, graduation exercises are held on the steps and the plaza of Low Library. The administration decided

that this year it would be unwise to have the ceremonies outdoors where they might be interfered with by the same people
who had given the police all they could handle on the morning
of May 22, when the second move had been made on Hamilton Hall in protest of the disciplinary actions stemming from
the sit-in and had provoked another fierce confrontation with
the police, with even greater brutality on the part both of the
students and the police. Instead, they transferred the graduation ceremonies to the Cathedral of St. John the Divine, four
blocks away, where in the past they have been held only in
case of rain.

Rumors at once began to fly through the neighborhood of
new and extraordinary measures being planned by the SDS to
disrupt the exercises in the cathedral: tear gas, stink bombs,
secret torments being prepared in secret basement labora-
tories. A group of campus militants, Students for a Restruc-
tured University, who had broken with the SDS leadership in
the strike because they felt that the SDS was more concerned
with off-campus than campus affairs, announced their boycott
of Commencement in the cathedral; they would hold their
own counter-Commencement in front of Low Library, its
traditional location. Various members of the faculty, speaking
for general faculty sentiment, pleaded with the administration
to call off the exercises altogether—the University was in disruption, why ask for further disorder, why not simply announce the uncelebrated end of a miserable year? But the
administration refused; letters were by now pouring in from
"loyal" alumni, demanding that the administration stand firm,
and the administration reassured alumni that it would no
longer yield to illegal pressure. However, Class Day, the most
intimate ceremony of College graduation, was called off when
the marshals of the senior class informed the dean that they
did not wish it to be held. And in recognition of the hostility
directed to him as symbol of the hated authority, President
Kirk yielded his traditional role as Commencement speaker to
a member of the faculty, Professor Richard Hofstadter, the

distinguished historian, whose acceptance of the assignment required, in the circumstances, a not inconsiderable courage.

One prayed for the rain one had always prayed against on other Commencements. The day was beautiful and full of promise. Or could it be threat? There was threat, surely, in the tight clusters of students one saw at various points of the campus that early afternoon, talking to each other all too earnestly, all too conspiratorially. And what except protection against threat could be implied by the big unfamiliar buses waiting on 114th Street at the entrance to Ferris Booth Hall and again on Morningside Drive at the entrance to the Faculty Club? The honored guests of the University, including those who were to receive honorary degrees, were lunching in Ferris Booth, their wives in the Faculty Club—the buses would transport them the few short sunny streets to the cathedral. Everywhere there were police; the control van that had been set up near the Amsterdam Avenue gates to the campus was well staffed. A faculty wife had urged on her reluctant husband and his friends their own protection in the cathedral: little pocket flasks of water in which to soak their handkerchiefs should tear gas be used. The offer was made as if in joke but the situation was no more one of fun than of morbid fantasy: one doubts there were many of the faculty who marched into the cathedral that afternoon who expected the exercises to go off without incident or even actual physical assault. I can suppose that most of them, like Mailer marching on the Pentagon, marched in fear—but here, of course, they had not themselves provoked the danger. They marched nevertheless, in what must have been larger number than ever before at a Columbia Commencement. A university lived, badly weakened: they wished to be present at the ceremony of its continuing life. For this day differences of opinion about what should or should not have been done in the previous weeks must be buried, wounds must seem to be healed, rifts closed. If one had sufficient dissent from the living University, one stayed away or even went to the counter–Commencement—some few professors made this latter choice but they were not many, nor did anyone I know go out of his way to discover who they were. The division had dignity.

Mailer, too, sees life in ceremony. He contrives ceremony out of each existential moment of his experience, his art out of their sum. But much of the ambiguousness of *The Armies of the Night* stems from the strange compound of innocence and non-innocence he took with him to the ceremonies at the Pentagon or, at any rate, brings to their report. There is innocence, one feels, in his love for America and much boldness in its statement; it is no longer easy to state one's love of country. But surely there is no innocence in his flamboyant invention— it makes a rousing little chapter in the book—of the "grand-mother with the orange hair," gone mad with lust and greed, who is made to represent an America gone mad with lust and greed, feeding dead Vietnamese babies into the slot machine of its imperial gamble. This is uncommonly gifted radical propaganda but too little complex for truth and therefore less than truth, a subversion, really, of truth. There is innocence in his love for the God of the Christian ethic, and its statement too takes courage, for it is also no longer easy to speak of one's imagination of God. But there is no innocence in suggesting a connection in the life of spirit between the Christian effort to improve the condition of man on earth and the hippie effort— Mailer describes it marvelously—to levitate the Pentagon, be-tween Christ risen and the Pentagon raised. This is befuddling literary ecumenicism. And although there is innocence in Mailer's hope of rest and peace for mankind and an end to irrational violence, there is no innocence—how can there be in so conscious an intelligence as his?—in proposing this hope in circumstances where reasonableness is flouted and impulse sanctioned. The same ambiguousness, or defect in thought, of course exists in whoever was witness to the disturbances at Columbia but could still propose that the insurrectionary undertaking was a good thing, necessary in order to shove our society toward greater reasonableness and peace.

I had no ticket to St. John the Divine but as the Commencement procession began to form I stood for a moment at the University gate on Amsterdam Avenue, listening for sounds of assault upon the march just as, six weeks earlier, I had listened for the sound of Harlem rushing upon our white island. Then I moved homeward across the campus, pausing briefly at the counter-Commencement gathering at the feet of the statue of Alma Mater on the steps of Low Library. Here the crowd was not large, smaller than I had foreseen, and it was entirely pacific, unduly quiet, in fact; not depressed exactly, or sober, but dispirited. The students looked lost or deprived, as if left over from a festivity which even at its height had been disappointing. But this festivity had not yet begun; perhaps later it would be livelier. I tried to see the notables of this occasion of protest—the counterspeakers were to be Dwight Macdonald, critic; Dr. Erich Fromm, psychoanalyst; and Harold Taylor, former president of Sarah Lawrence. I especially wanted to see Macdonald and if possible exchange a friendly word because we had had an unhappy correspondence and telephone conversation as a result of his appeal for funds for the SDS. He was not in sight—later I was to hear that he, like Chomsky at one of the panel discussions, had been booed for certain portions of his speech: perhaps he had introduced a modification of the SDS position and thus breached the solidarity that the revolution demands of its sympathizers. I decided to go home to my good old standby, WKCR.

But my radio knew the time of day better than I did. It had done its full stint and would be pushed no further: I could coax no sound from it.

Too restless to stay indoors, I walked to the Riverside Church where the overflow from the cathedral was to assemble. I don't know what I had supposed would constitute an overflow from St. John the Divine but certainly I was not

prepared for a big church filled, every seat taken in row after
sober row—here indeed were the faces of sobriety and even
pain, the faces of mothers and fathers separated (by what
distance? only the distance of a half-dozen city blocks?) from
their graduating young, having their parental epiphany, the
ceremony of their accomplished motherhood and fatherhood,
by closed-circuit radio. The loudspeaker was very clear, at
moments it ebbed in volume, then again swelled, but it was
never loud or brash: it was as if the mechanics of the occasion
were sensible of moderation, gravity. I stood at the back of the
nave and heard report of the last of the faculty and student
procession filing into St. John the Divine—what a long line it
must have been and with what measured pace it must have
moved! Then there was the invocation. The presentation of
degrees. The speech of Richard Hofstadter. He spoke with a
luminous simplicity of the meaning and purpose of a university and of how change must come to it by means which
would preserve, not destroy, the good it stood for in our
world—it might be that the good the university stood for was
the best we knew in our faulty world. And these parents who
listened to him without seeing him, these mothers in their
nicest summer dresses, these fathers who had taken off the day
so that they might see their children in this moment of fulfillment (had it been awkward for them at their work, had there
been laughter as they explained that they must be free to see
their sons graduate from Columbia? What Columbia?) listened to his speech as one must doubt they had ever before
listened in a church. The pulpit was empty, the ceremony was
an achievement of technology in our despised technological
society, but education was addressing the congregation. And
for most of us education is still sacred, for where else in this
modern universe of ours, unless to education, are we to look
for our continuing civilization, where else do we issue our
passports to enlightenment? Nothing interrupted the speech
these parents wanted to hear. When I learned, later, that just
before the Commencement address some of the graduating

students and a dozen or more of the faculty had risen in their places and walked out of St. John the Divine, away from their "illegitimate" ceremonies, I was surprised. From the broadcast in the Riverside Church one knew of no disturbance of even this token kind; there had been only silence and the calm voice of reason. The emotions of the long spring weeks finally overcame me and I began to cry.

It was a very few hours later that Senator Robert Kennedy was shot. Two assassinations framed the Columbia disturbances. Two acts of personal violence against public men bracketed the violent act against a university: the assassination of Dr. Martin Luther King and the assassination of Senator Kennedy. There had been a memorial service for Dr. King in St. Paul's Chapel, the University chapel at Columbia. The services had been interrupted by a group of SDS students who rushed the pulpit and seized the microphone from the University chaplain. They said that Columbia had no right to memorialize the civil rights leader, that it was hypocrisy for a racist institution to hold such services. Chaplain Cannon had condoned the SDS action with the explanation that anyone was free to speak in his church who spoke in the spirit of truth. But the spirit of truth, or something akin to it, something that bears upon a vision of the way life ought to be, always actuates extreme forms of political behavior and often even imputes to them some terrible impulse of the heroic. No doubt the assassins of Dr. King and Robert Kennedy also acted out of a sense of dedication to what, in their tortured minds, they took to be the right true way of life.

From the newspapers we learn that among the many who mourned the death of Robert Kennedy—whether as personal friend or public admirer, we are not told—was Tom Hayden, a revolutionary intellectual who helped found the SDS a decade ago. Though neither a student nor teacher at Columbia, Hayden had an important role in the Columbia revolution. One of the buildings seized in the uprising was Mathematics

Hall—it was not the first of the buildings to be held but it was the one held with the greatest panache. It was to the red and black flags of liberation that flew from Mathematics Hall—it backs on Broadway—that random sympathizers of the revolution, even passing motorists, offered their salute. From its windows a basket was lowered for contributions of money and food for the demonstrators, and through its windows distinguished visitors, including some of Mailer's "notables," also were lifted into the revolutionary future. Hayden was the chairman of Mathematics Hall, the leader of the nonstop discussions which kept its occupiers occupied and which outside visitors to the building took to be proof that an entire and reliable democracy was being practiced in the uprising. He was important in planning the strategies which were presented to the demonstrators for their ratification—since there was constant communication among the various leaders in the various buildings one can suppose that his influence extended well beyond his single "commune," as each building was called, and that probably far more than the undergraduate Mark Rudd, who has been so much advertised and glamourized by the "media," he is to be credited with the fierceness and intransigence of the rebellion. Some weeks after the Chicago demonstrations, where he was similarly a leader, I saw Hayden in a television interview. His dedication is implicit in his appearance—were one not to know his profession one would still know that whatever he did, he did with an extreme intensity. There is great nervousness in his face and body but it is nervousness under practiced control, almost to the point of rigidity: he occupies a chair, he doesn't rest in it; he allows himself no freedom or forgetfulness within his lean frame; his head and neck are joined with his body as if by visible cords. The face is long, thin, narrowed-eyed, tight-lipped, with little flexibility—here is someone who has gone beyond the need for ordinary human, ordinary social responsiveness; there is no charm, only intention and discipline and an overcast of hard dreariness.

The newspapers reported that late at night when Robert Kennedy's body lay in state in St. Patrick's, Hayden came to the cathedral to mourn. The cathedral was dark, empty except for the guard around the coffin. Holding in his hand the field cap which reputedly was given him by Castro, Hayden sat alone in the shadows, weeping, until someone who saw him invited him to stand a watch at the coffin, which he did, probably glad of the invitation—in moments of grief, it is helpful to be part of a ceremony. The question this newspaper report raised in my mind—and it refuses to be answered—was, how can the strong emotion which brought Hayden to St. Patrick's in the middle of the night to mourn for Robert Kennedy so totally divorce itself from the ideas which govern the SDS and Hayden as one of its chief leaders? After all, everything that Hayden most significantly lives and works for is directed to the destruction of everything that Kennedy most significantly lived and worked for. One can truly love one's political enemy, and not only in the way dictated by Christianity. But to the degree that one weeps for him alone in the night? And when the political difference is so nearly absolute? It can be put simply: Kennedy believed in the possibility of our society and Hayden believes that our society must be destroyed. These are antithetical principles. Do they not generate antithetical emotions, or at least require some distancing in personal feeling?

I speak of the ambiguousness of Mailer's Pentagon story, in particular of the ambiguousness which resides in supposing that a higher reasonableness will be reached by acts of unreason, a more reliable condition for peace by acts of violence. But perhaps more than we can readily recognize, Mailer's ambiguousness is also the ambiguousness of our apparently most single-minded insurrectionary students and their leaders, of all our intellectuals and all our enlightened population which welcomes the student revolution; the ambiguousness, in fact, of our moral and intellectual times.

[1968]

143

[After the publication of my report on the Columbia disturbances, a considerable correspondence, most of it hostile to my view of the uprising, appeared in *Commentary* magazine. I print here only the exchange of letters between Mr. Robert Lowell and myself.]

To the editor of Commentary:

A fog of rumor came to us last April of a black descent on Columbia, then the mice stood up at attention with rifles in their hands, nerved for blood, but with fingers stretched to their typewriters. Still, there's no gravy in hitting a respected, not too much on target, though a great lady, controversialist. No one can be in much disagreement with Diana Trilling's desire for more reason, sense, and seniority in our "confrontations of protest." We pray to be more conservative or radical in our gentler intuitions. What's crossed then? The fussing at thought, the patter of smear. No one thought Mrs. Trilling heaves into my thoughts lands straight. All's twisted in the current of ignorant, unseeing didacticism, in the rattled sentences of her "On the Steps of Low Library."

ROBERT LOWELL

New York City

Mrs. Trilling writes:

Although my article was not intended as a theoretical piece, I hoped it would generate some serious discussion of the problem of the future of liberalism in the democracies. I had emphasized the fact that the revolution at Columbia was no more a liberal than a Marxist revolution and that, indeed, it was a revolution *against* liberalism which in actual effect polarized the University between the radical position, as this was defined by the SDS and the revolutionary minority, on the one hand, and a conservative position, on the other. And I raised the question whether liberalism was any longer a viable political concept or whether, as a force for progress, it had been carried as far as it could go—to the point where, because it is subsumed in our present governmental establishment, it has ceased to offer any promise as a means of moving beyond the impositions of established power.

I find it disheartening that not one thoughtful word on the subject appears in these letters or, for that matter, in the correspondence which came to me directly. . . . There is no intellectual content in Mr. Lowell's grim little communication, not an argument is marshaled; there is not even a reference to political views already made public. There is only the intention to put on record Mr. Lowell's contemptuous rejection of my view of last spring's events at Columbia.

And yet, as politics go these days, it must of course be understood that Mr. Lowell is performing a political act. Mr. Lowell is a very eminent poet and he has significant influence with the young. Modern poets are no longer Shelley's unacknowledged legislators or unconscious ones either—at least Mr. Lowell is not. He is a public man who speaks to public issues with what is thought to be the wisdom of his special gifts; he has great authority with those who are responsive to his sensibility. With this letter Mr. Lowell announces where his sensibility was located during the Columbia disturbances: it is where the vastest of chasms separates the actual facts of the situation from the will to believe that the cause was just and where a concern, like mine, with the possible social and political consequences of our actions represents a retrograde refusal of necessary change and progress.

The strategy Mr. Lowell uses to protect his sensibility against the intrusion of uncomfortable fact and against concern with the possible consequences of conduct like that of the insurrectionary minority at Columbia is to say that he failed to understand my article. This I very much doubt. I think he understands me fully, quite as well as I understand him—which is more of an achievement: I was writing prose. He fully understands my report that throughout the crisis there was fear that Harlem might march on Columbia, though it may be that he questions my accuracy in the matter, in which case he might consult the mayor's office, which shared the fear, or I can now refer him, as I could not when I wrote my article, to the recently published *Up Against the Ivy Wall*, a detailed account of the happenings on the campus by the student editors of the *Columbia Spectator*. But of course my accuracy or inaccuracy is not to the point—the clear reason why Mr. Lowell writes as he does about the fear of an uprising in Harlem is that he wants to suggest that the kind of person who withholds approval of the student rebellion is also the kind of person who, in her own blood-lust and hatred, would have fantasies of black terror. I also believe that Mr. Lowell fully understands that what I was seeing in my "unseeing didacticism" was the moral character of a revolution whose moral character is the one thing he prefers not to look at. For were he to look at it, he might be deprived of the emotions of righteousness which now so regularly and automatically accrue to any attitude of the Left, armoring it against the charge of vagrancy or frivolousness.

I have no wish to deprive Mr. Lowell of his armor of radical piety if he so badly needs it. But since he has performed his kind of political act by writing of my article as he does, I now perform my kind of political act by inviting him to enter the serious discussion and share with us some of his ideas on the questions explicitly or implicitly raised in my Columbia report. And I address him not as a poet, not as a licensed sensibility, but as a powerful working member of the intellectual community, himself one of its most active controversialists, a signer of protests, a joiner of demonstrations, a writer of letters to the press, a much valued speaker at meetings and rallies.

What, for instance, does Mr. Lowell now feel about the use of violence as an instrument of social change? Does he still hold with the pacifism he professed in the past and, if so, how does he reconcile it with the violent means employed by the insurrectionary students at Columbia? Does Mr. Lowell think the time is past for rational discourse and mediation in America? Does he believe that no choice remains to us except either the anarchic disruptiveness of the New Left or compliance in establishment, or does he think that the liberal tradition is still to be drawn upon? And if the latter, what does he think must be the premises and programs of a revivified liberalism? Does Mr. Lowell think it permissible for students to occupy their university buildings and, if he does, where and on what principle would he set limits to such actions: if one may occupy a building, may one also burn the building? If not, why not? What does Mr. Lowell think will be the consequences for this country of actions such as the revolutionary students took at Columbia? What, in greatest simplicity, does Mr. Lowell think of the Columbia uprising as a moral spectacle: how does he feel about students kidnapping an officer of the University, rifling the personal files of the president and broadcasting their contents, urinating on floors, spitting at their teachers, destroying the research of one of their professors, shouting obscenities? Does he think conduct like this promises a better future for all of us? Does he think it makes for better human beings? It could be that, in straightforward reply to such elementary questions as these, Mr. Lowell might persuade me that my view of the Columbia uprising is unsound. I am as open to argument as I am resistant to unreasoned assault, no matter how morally certified.

Robert Lowell writes:

Controversy is bad for the mind and worse for the heart. I know it's rude and ludicrous for me to have entered this one, and now to follow my first "grim communication" with a second. I apologize to Mrs. Trilling the person for my attack on Mrs. Trilling the polemicist. In this game, may the opponents use its wooden swords fairly.

Mrs. Trilling's original article was so haunted with apprehension, and bristling with the professional logic of prosecution, that I did not think it of sufficient interest to "answer." My quarrel is with the part that heavily banters Dwight Macdonald and me. We were not in the picture, but perhaps the article was once planned as a sequel to Mailer's *Steps of the Pentagon,* and her plot forced her to borrow two of his supporting characters.

Her rather majestic irony about my "radical piety," and my signing petitions, appearing at rallies, seems to suggest that I act to draw applause from the young, get in fashion, or whatever. This may be consoling to her own picture of herself as some housekeeping goddess of reason, preferring the confines of her mind to experience, and pronouncing on the confusion of the crowd, unconfused herself and unpronounced on. Surely, she will not be indicted for activism. On the great day, when she meets her Maker, John Stuart Mill on his right hand and Diderot on his left, they will say, "Liberalism gave you a standard; what have you done for liberalism?" Then she will answer that her record is clear of agitation about the Vietnam War, clear of a feverish concern for the drafting of reluctant young men to fight it, free of a nervous fear about the militarization of our country. Terror of the nuclear bombs never forced her to lose hope. She seems more preoccupied with the little violence of the unarmed student uprisings than with the great violence of the nation at war. She implies that we who are horrified by napalm on human flesh are somehow indifferent to the piss on President Kirk's carpet. She wants to be sure where I stand on this. She asks me many questions.

I answer that I might wish to be a hundred percent pro-student, but the other morning, or some morning, I saw a newspaper photograph of students marching through Rome with banners showing a young Clark Gable–style Stalin and a very fat old Mao—that was a salute to the glacier. No cause is pure enough to support these faces. We are fond of saying that our students have more generosity, idealism, and freshness than any other group. Even granting this, they are only us, younger, and the violence that has betrayed our desires will also betray theirs if they trust to it.

I would like to tell Mrs. Trilling one thing very clearly. I had nothing to do with the student strike at Columbia. I was at

Columbia just once two or three weeks before the troubles. I spoke for four or five minutes against President Johnson's Vietnam War. I received tame applause. Also, I want to explain to her, finally I hope, that I have never been New Left, Old Left, or liberal. I wish to turn the clock back with every breath I draw, but I hope I have the courage to occasionally cry out against those who wrongly rule us, and wrongly lecture us.

Diana Trilling writes:

I have never thought controversy bad for either the mind or heart. And I have never found it necessary for anyone to apologize for disagreeing with my opinions. I am nevertheless glad to accept Mr. Lowell's public amends—I shall assume that he is apologizing, not for having a different view of the Columbia disturbances from the one I have, but for suggesting that my report that Columbia was fearful that Harlem would rise against the University was the product of my overheated imagination. To this play of Mr. Lowell's own imagination, I responded in quite unitary fashion: I do not admit his distinction between "person" and "polemicist," between, that is, one's private and public values. If, as a person, I accept, say, Dewey's definition of manners as small morals, which I do and which, from my acquaintance with Mr. Lowell, I should suppose he does too, then as polemicist I naturally address myself to the moral implications of students urinating on President Kirk's carpet or spitting at their teachers.

While it was never required of Mr. Lowell that he "answer" my original article, I did ask him a series of rather basic questions when I replied to his letter about my Columbia report. I am sorry he has chosen not to respond to them. One of these questions I now repeat: Does Mr. Lowell still hold with the pacifism he professed in the past and, if so, how does he reconcile it with the violent methods employed by the insurrectionary minority at Columbia? I press the point for manifest reasons. Surely pacifism doesn't permit the distinction that Mr.

Lowell makes between small and large violences any more than it countenances the use of violent means for even the best of ends. Perhaps Mr. Lowell no longer subscribes to the pacifist position; he doesn't say. Neither does he put himself on record as actually *approving* the methods of the SDS at Columbia. All he does say is that I should stop looking at the violent conduct of the insurrectionary students and give my full attention to the Vietnam War—let's wash the piss under Kirk's carpet and keep our minds on napalm.

This I am afraid I cannot do. In the first place, I am not prepared to say—is Mr. Lowell?—at what point and by what psychological alteration a violence which we had previously thought was big will come to seem small to us. I should suppose in fact that Mr. Lowell would agree with me that one of the frightening aspects of the Vietnam War is that Americans have got used to it as an act of violence and therefore don't respond to it with sufficient shock. Even changes in our manner of speech can represent a process of public accommodation to assault—take, for instance, the word "piss." Five years ago I very much doubt that Mr. Lowell would have used the word "piss" in a communication to a magazine. Certainly I know that I would not have picked it up. But the Columbia disturbances habituated me to such violent invective that my old standards of speech no longer prevail. And I am a mature woman. How much more available to this process of habituation are young people of nineteen or twenty, and not only in speech which is preparatory to action but in action itself.

Second, it happens to be true, not a befuddlement, that violence begets violence. This assumption is indeed basic in the confrontation tactics of the New Left—the idea is to force the use of police whose violence is then counted on to mobilize sympathy and support to the insurrectionary side. Thus we have a chain of mounting violence, from the "little" violence of piss on the president's carpet, or spitting at one's teachers, or seizing a building held for the public good, or destroying the researches of a professor with whom one doesn't agree, to the more substantial physical violence of the police. And parallel to this chain of mounting violence we have a chain of intensifying political reactions. When Mr. Lowell asks me to ignore the "little" violence at Columbia, in effect he is asking me to ignore the disastrous political consequences for all of us should these violences multiply in our society. If our insurrectionary minorities insist that the power of the police replace our present social authorities, there is every promise that their wish will be granted.

It would be reassuring to believe that in measuring piss against napalm Mr. Lowell is merely playing a rhetorical game. I don't think this is the case; I think that he is making serious reference to a scale of moral and political values in which quality is determined by quantity. . . . Obviously there is a hierarchy of violence. The person who shoves you in the subway in order to grab your seat is not equivalently violent with someone who holds a gun to your head. But because he is not a murderer is he immune to moral judgment? A poet reacts with moral acuteness even to assaults on language. Why not, then, to assaults on human decency, and especially when these assaults are made in the name of a more decent society in which people will live with a sweeter awareness of themselves and others? There is nothing in the conduct of the SDS to persuade me that today's piss won't be tomorrow's more lethal weapon—unless those who, like Mr. Lowell, have the power to influence the dissident young (and what a sizable power it is!) stop fooling themselves that either they or the student population represent a negligible factor in the national life and speak out against their dangerous procedures with some simplicity and courage.

But to charge Mr. Lowell with insufficient activism in protest of the war now being waged on our campuses does not, of course, constitute an adequate reply to his charge against me, of an insufficient activism in protest of the Vietnam War. As he defines activism, he is justified in this accusation—although I have written against the war whenever I could, it is a fact that

I have joined no marches or demonstrations. But this is not because the war is remote from my concern—having a son of draft age brings it home to me with quite sufficient force. Nor is it because I would be reluctant to participate in orderly demonstrations. But as is implied even in so brief a statement as Mr. Lowell's, protest of the Vietnam War has been preempted by political opinion in which I do not share, and it has been channeled in forms of action to which I cannot subscribe. In declaring my opposition to the war I cannot make a united front with the anti-Americanism which provides the overarching principle of all "active" protest of our Vietnam engagement, nor adopt its strategies. I do not regard the war as burning evidence of our national viciousness. I can talk about American stupidity or complacency or about the contradictions between American capitalism and American idealism, but I cannot talk about American genocide in Vietnam or about American imperialist greed and rapaciousness in Vietnam as if America were uniquely greedy and rapacious among nations—which means that I am without a passport to Mr. Lowell's world of political activism. Most important of all, I will not march under the flag of the Viet Cong, and where has there been a protest against American error under an American flag? I have seen none. My opposition to the war is based not on American self-hatred and preference for the government and methods of North Vietnam but on the belief that its pursuit is the gravest of political mistakes; that its continuation and escalation, not its inception, constitute a most grievous distortion of democratic purpose; that in actual effect if not by intention America is now cast in the role of an independently combatant nation, even an aggressor nation. It is on this ground that I am against the war—because it is a bad political mistake with bad moral implications for our democratic future, and not only because we use napalm. All war is hideous. The saturation bombing of Dresden in a war to which I gave my support was no less hideous than the use of napalm in a war I oppose.

These opinions I have already published and shall continue to publish wherever I have, or can make, the opportunity. But if we are to take Mr. Lowell at his word here, writing against the war does not qualify as an activity. He apparently doesn't regard thought as a form of action, even for professional intellectuals. In his view, thoughtfulness exists in *opposition* to activism: he makes it an accusation against me that I prefer the confines of my mind to experience. He even makes it an accusation that I am—as he so flatteringly puts it—unconfused. But if reason is not consonant with the life of action, are we to conclude that action is only action when it is unreasonable, when it is "agitated," "feverish," "nervous"? These are the states of being to which Mr. Lowell calls me. He goes so far, in fact, as to propose that liberalism—the liberalism of Mill and Diderot, no less—is certified only in the degree that it discards reason in favor of these distressed emotions, and he warns me of the day when I shall have to meet my Maker.

Well, rationalist that I am, this particular confrontation has not been much of a concern to me. And if I have let my mind turn to the affairs of Heaven, I must confess that it has not occurred to me to think of Mill and Diderot as seated on either side of the Heavenly Father. But should these indeed be the judges who await me, I can hardly suppose I shall be as much at a loss for words as Mr. Lowell suggests. To Mill I shall say that I did my best to see the truth, and to Diderot I shall say that I did my best to look beneath the appearance of things, especially the things which announce themselves as virtue. And surely it is not impossible that I'll get by.

[1969]

Our
Uncomplaining
Homosexuals

social idioms. Roth's protagonist is the son of a hard-working but unsuccessful insurance salesman. Anxious, inept, his spirit the slave of his recalcitrant bowels, the senior Portnoy is the familiar Jewish father-failure—we made his acquaintance a long time ago in Clifford Odets's *Awake and Sing!* Constipation is also a worry in the Ackerley family but with this coincidence all resemblance between the American and English households ends. Ackerley's father is neither anxious, inept, nor a failure. By his own efforts he has become a wealthy fruit importer, enough established to send his son to a public school and Cambridge. On the surface he appears to have always led the conventional life of his class; it is only when his son comes to maturity that he discovers that his father was an active homosexual as a young man and, later, so urgent a heterosexual that, not content to produce a single family, the one into which the writer was born, he simultaneously and secretly fathered a second of equal size. As to the mothers in the two stories, the difference is even more striking. Where Mrs. Portnoy is a Jewish mother of the sort which is now so dear to the mythic imaginings of their sons, a woman of wild humors and pulverizing energies, all of them preternaturally concentrated on molding her male offspring to her notions of a proper Jewish-American son and man, Ackerley's mother was once an aspiring actress who steadily retreated into isolated eccentricity. She is offstage through most of her son's history.

But there are books which ask to be brought together exactly because of the divergence in their approach to a common subject matter. Both Roth's book and Ackerley's are sexual "confessions." In both, sexual honesty is a first command: presumably, if we are honest about our sexual selves, we cannot be false to any man or woman and we are on the way to saying something useful about the general life of feeling, perhaps even about the general life of humankind. But it turns out that strangely different enterprises can proceed from the same premise. Portnoy, full of complaint because of his sexual fate, is bent on tracking down the source of his grievances. In need of a culprit, he finds it, or them. The "myself" of *My Father and Myself* has complaint against no one. He is innocent of impulse to place blame for his sexual situation—unlike Portnoy, who thinks his parents took the id out of Yid, it never occurs to Ackerley to accuse his parents of putting the oy in Goy. And we follow his example: finally it doesn't occur to his readers to assign blame for Ackerley's fate though the force of contemporary culture presses us toward Roth's "position."

And a "position" the author of *Portnoy's Complaint* is indeed fortifying: here is farce with a thesis. The burden of Portnoy's fiercely funny self-revelation is that all his sexual difficulty derives from the guilt imposed on him in his upbringing. It is guilt that made Portnoy the athletic and ingenious masturbator that Roth shows him to have been in his boyhood, and guilt that makes him impotent with all except Gentile girls when he comes to manhood—after various sexual adventures among the Wasps, his author leads Portnoy to amorous disaster in Israel. The chief purveyor of this guilt is, naturally, his Jewish mother: she has ladled out injunction and precept, sometimes at the point of a knife, with each mouthful of nourishment she has forced upon her defenseless child; Portnoy's father is indictable largely as an example of the capitulation of the Jewish male to the Jewish female. The clue to Portnoy's rage at the pass to which he has been brought lies in the word "imposed." Just as we have no choice in the selection of our parents, just so, according to Roth, we have no choice other than to receive the guiltiness they inculcate in us. Portnoy has no responsibility for himself. Simply, inevitably, he has incorporated the inhibiting lessons taught him in early childhood. How, as the product of such a death-dealing education, Roth's protagonist has achieved sexual success at least with his Gentile girls—and it is considerable: there are Gentile readers who would envy him—Roth doesn't say. He also doesn't explain where, except from his training in guilt, Portnoy learned his contempt for his own sexual fate although it is this which of course makes the basis for his condemnation of his parents.

Portnoy has brought his complaint to the psychoanalyst's couch, which would seem to imply that he and his author acknowledge the Freudian unconscious, hidden and beyond conscious control. But no: it turns out that nothing, really, is hidden from Portnoy. His unconscious is more than visible to him, it is peculiarly spongelike, rejecting nothing in the parental teaching; Portnoy has himself apparently made no contribution to his unconscious life in terms of interpretation or distortion of parental doctrine. Not merely his parents' victim, he is their entire creation on every level of his psychic being except that on which he assesses and protests the victimization. We apparently have at least this one immunity to the process of personal determinism: the free choice to be angry at what has been done to us.

In Roth's view, guilt is only and always an alien substance in the human composition, introduced for the destruction of joy and the perpetuation of old sorrows. Because guilt intervenes so grossly between us and our fullest humanity, it incapacitates us in our relations with others, especially the relation of the sexes. And this, I conclude, is why the Jewish condition, supremely guilt-laden, is now thought to offer literature its best means for describing the modern condition: the alienated Jew becomes representative of alienated modern man. From a view such as this, it is logical that Roth should not permit Portnoy's doctor to speak during the course of Portnoy's analytical sessions, or not at least until the last sentence of the book when he says, "Now vee may perhaps to begin." While this can be read as a comic gag, compliments of Mike Nichols and Elaine May or, more generously, as preparation for the doctor's assault on Portnoy's self-deceptions, it is at this point that the book ends. No version of Portnoy's grievance other than his own has been put on the record. It is therefore fair to understand the last words of Roth's novel as the Q.E.D. to the book's hypothesis: if guilt is what makes us inhuman and there are no guilts hidden from Portnoy's consciousness and if, too, Jews are so guilty a people, what else is there for Portnoy's physician to say except that for Jews their beginnings lie in their end? By extension we may understand Roth to be telling us that for all of us, Jew and Gentile alike, social creatures all and victims of the grotesque idealisms and ambitions handed on from one generation to the next, our beginnings lie in the end of society as it has established itself and its proscriptions, perhaps in particular those that masquerade as benevolences.

In other words, Roth's funny book is yet another offensive in our escalating literary-political war upon society, and intuitively it has been welcomed as such by most of its reviewers: the popular success of a work often depends as much on its latent as on its overt content. Indeed, it is not too difficult to trace the connection between *Portnoy's Complaint* and Norman O. Brown's *Life Against Death* of a few years back, the investigation into Freudian theory which made our present culture's most scholarly attack upon civilization as we know it in the Western tradition and as Freud gave it his tragic acceptance. It is a nice irony, however, that while Brown's book ensues in a call to the Eden of the polymorphous perversity of infancy, Roth follows his graphic tour of the perversities with what in actuality is a call to Mental Health: "mature" genital heterosexuality-cum-love. No one, in fact, could present us with a more traditionally sanctified system of sexual values than Portnoy. He knows just what kind of sex is wholesome and life-enhancing and what is debasing—there is the moment in his story when he wonders how, with his upbringing, he sank only to the low status of a compulsive masturbator and of someone able to perform only, alas, with Gentile girls and never took what he manifestly regards as the next step downward, that of becoming a homosexual. But Brown is not Jewish and Roth is. Perhaps the Jewish unconscious is more pertinaciously puritan and hidden from us than the author of *Portnoy's Complaint* is ready to recognize.

This is all a far cry from Ackerley, the farthest possible. Ackerley's book has no such fashionable antisocietal doctrine to impart; in fact, no doctrinal intention whatever. Yet it, too, is about sexual deviation, of the sort which for Portnoy represents the lowest rung in the scale of our dehumanization. It is the underlying assumption of *My Father and Myself*, though never argued, that homosexuality is simply a form of sexual choice, like any other; and it is only if we ask why Ackerley was impelled to tell us his story that we raise the possibility that he was driven to counteract some buried torment of personal or social disapprobation. When, as a boy, Ackerley masturbates, no doubt to the accompaniment of homosexual fantasies, or when, as a man, he devotes all his nonworking hours to the pursuit of male sexual partners, he never wonders how he was spared that final degradation of becoming a heterosexual; he is a witty man but not funny. There are men who want women, and men who want men: the variation between the two is no more remarkable than the variations among the many ways in which a person exercises this primary sexual choice. Ackerley himself happened to be the kind of homosexual who wanted young, clean, healthy boys as nearly normal—heterosexual, that is—as could be consistent with their responding to his desires; this requirement, difficult to meet except transitorily, made his life lonely, barren of affection. But what he describes is a personal disposition; it doesn't refer to a system of moral and social values. It does not defer to a social norm in the way that, say, homosexual writers do when they translate their homosexual emotions into fictions of heterosexual love. Ackerley sought a lasting relationship because he thought it would make him happier and not because it would bring him into closer conformity with the heterosexual ideal. The social norm appears not to be worth mention: it was never an option for him and therefore doesn't operate as a standard.

Although in his own fashion Ackerley is no less accomplished a craftsman than Roth, his manner is as self-effacing as Roth's is flamboyant. Ackerley was already an established figure in England when the author of *Portnoy's Complaint* first opened his eyes on our cosmic disorder: this age difference may account for Ackerley's more "classical" style. But surely more significant in the formation of Ackerley's modest literary manner is the fact that his father was able to secure for him a social position sufficiently privileged to send him straight from his public school to an officership in the First World War: social advantage is as implicit in Ackerley's literary as in his homosexual style. Where Roth, child of an indiscriminate mass society, undertakes to command attention by the use of the broadest possible strokes, the author of *My Father and Myself* can afford the well-heeled presumption of understatement. No matter how redundant and unchaste the activities on which he reports, Ackerley writes the economical prose of the advantaged classes of a class-structured nation.

But between 1932, when *Hindoo Holiday* was first published, and the completion of *My Father and Myself*, the English middle-middle class had begun to lose its old moorings in inherited privilege. The authority once vested in Ackerley by his superior schooling was no longer to be taken for granted. Ackerley's memoir shows little awareness of these altered social circumstances. A comparison of the first edition of *Hindoo Holiday* with the reissue of 1952 discloses several additions to the text after the passage of twenty years; these new sections are all of them explicitly homosexual—in 1932 the kiss between men could not be published, the request that a boy take off his clothes for the pleasure of another man must be deleted. And obviously it was the cultural change dramatized in the new permission given to homosexuality that finally made possible the memoir on which Ackerley would seem to have been brooding for some time. But the permission to publish explicit sexual statements seems to be the only cultural change that bears in upon Ackerley. If there was no boldness of action which was not allowed someone of his class when Ackerley was young, in his older years there is no literary fashion which can seduce him into betraying the standards of taste in which he was trained. The laws of good taste always demanded that a gentleman speak directly and straightfor-

wardly, without ostentation, without squeamishness or gentility. For Ackerley, the sexual outspokenness of contemporary
democratic England would seem simply to have caught up
with his own class rearing.

But more than an aesthetic was prepared by Ackerley's social situation. His social place had also taught him that he
must take responsibility for what he was and did. When *My
Father and Myself* refuses, as it does, the idea of personal
victimization at the hands of the family or society—and this is
where it most significantly differs from Roth's sexual investigation—it is in line with England's continuing resistance to the
principle of personal determinism of any kind and, in particular, the Freudian determinism. It has been and remains the
belief of the dominant English literary culture that as individuals we create ourselves. While Ackerley has the old-fashioned
distaste of his class for raging at the world and especially at
one's parents because one's life has been unsatisfactory, he
also shares the distaste of even his present-day countrymen for
searching out personal causalities. He is thus as representative
of present-day England's pre-Freudian literary culture as Roth
is of present-day America's post-Freudian literary culture.

In America we still take what we want from Freud though
our psychology increasingly moves in other directions. For
reasons which perhaps have to do with the more structured
character of British society and even with the persisting desire
of the English to regard the organization of their society as the
natural given of life, in England Freud is neither a point of
rest nor of departure. The human malaises which we in this
country so easily ascribe to the family, or to society working
upon the individual through the institution of the family, the
English are prone to ascribe to personal idiosyncrasy and the
mysterious workings of free will; and they have a large tolerance of the idiosyncratic. Certainly Ackerley has the largest
possible tolerance of his father's refusal to marry Ackerley's
mother until the children of the household were grown, and of
the secret division of Ackerley Senior's paternal offices be-

tween two sets of offspring. Although both for good and for
bad the elder Ackerley was no common instance of British
fatherhood, in the view of his son he is accepted for the
quirky, decent mystifier he was. As to his mother, who gradually, quietly, moved toward madness all her life, Ackerley's
attitude is one of gentle remoteness. Her life is her own and if
she needs her privacy he gives it to her, makes no claim for
more love than she was able to give. That it is solely the father
and not the mother who piqued his biographical curiosity, that
he made his research only into the paternal past, no doubt has
a double explanation: it is a response to the greater drama of
his father's life but also to the fact that his father was once a
homosexual like himself.

The possibility that his father's homosexuality influenced his
own is not explored by Ackerley. Ackerley merely gives us the
story of his father's young manhood: his enlistment in the
Royal Horse Guards, his connection with various men of station and means, his introduction to the business which eventually made him rich. He draws no conclusions from the parallel
between his father's early sexual proclivities and his own or
from the divergence in their later sexual development. More
interesting: although his own sexual preference was absolute,
so that he was never tempted to even an experimental moment
with women, he registers no surprise that his father was bisexual even in his earlier days and later centered the whole of his
abundant erotic energies on women. The simplicity with
which Ackerley accepts this move from one sex to another, as
if it were routine and expectable, is likely to be bewildering to
American readers accustomed to the idea that, once a homosexual, always a homosexual. But for an English audience it
can have no such startling impact: as recently as four years
ago an American boy in an English public school could engage
his schoolmates in a discussion which would be inconceivable
in a school in his own country; to his question, itself impermissible among American schoolboys, "Are all of you queer?", the
answer was that some accepted this mild impeachment while

others were being homosexual *pro tem*, until they moved out into the world and met girls. Legally, homosexuality in England may be considered inimical to the public interest; but socially, or culturally, at least among the educated classes, it is regarded as a not unnatural phase in growth and no deterrent to heterosexual adulthood. Even where it is a ruling sexual persuasion it is considered entirely consonant with manliness and with the proper discharge of the manly duties of citizenship; among the "so few" to whom England owed "so much" in the Battle of Britain it is a fair guess that there was more than a small component of men whose homosexuality would have excluded them from military service in the United States. And indeed the American in England is bound to be struck by the nonprevalence of such manifest signs of homosexual effeminacy—high-pitched voice, giggling, camping—as we are familiar with here.

Whether this social and psychological tolerance of male homosexuality plays a part in England's unreceptivity to Freudian theory, it is difficult to say. Yet it seems reasonable to suppose that a culture which believes that a man is exercising a free choice when he engages in homosexuality, and even that he is free to change his sexual direction at will, is likely to be resistant to Freud's deterministic doctrine: in our country, too, there is unquestionably a connection between our present increase in tolerance of homosexuality and the decrease in our acceptance of the Freudian psychology. There are of course Freudian psychoanalysts in England—Anna Freud, her father's powerful successor, lives in London—but the Freudian authority has always been weaker there than here and the teachings of Freud have never penetrated British culture as they have ours. While it may be that the English Freudians still hold to the orthodox analytical assumption that any male (not female) who has actively engaged in homosexuality is effectually debarred from making a successful transfer to the opposite sex, the opinion has not made itself strongly felt. Without formulating a principle that it is feasible for an individual to move from homosexuality to heterosexuality, the English simply act on the belief that it *is* feasible, with the result that it becomes so; at least, England seems to produce enough examples of an apparently successful changeover to challenge the Freudian belief that the transfer cannot be made. We have no way of knowing how satisfactory the senior Ackerley's "adjustment" to women was. But of course neither do we have any way of knowing whether he did any worse than men who have never indulged their homosexuality. What we do know from his son's biography is that, not alone among Englishmen, he moved from his own to the opposite sex without, so far as we can see, any of the guilt which in our own country would inevitably have trailed him.

The guiltlessness with which Ackerley reports his own homosexuality is thus a gift to him from a society whose cruel laws governing homosexual practices—and they were even crueler before the famous Wolfenden Report made its impress on the courts—constitute not only a peculiarly acute division between culture and law but also a peculiarly ugly hypocrisy. But it is we who make this judgment, not Ackerley; the author of *My Father and Myself* no more calls his society to account than he does himself. Where the whole pedagogic point of Roth's book lies in its insistence that our personal disorders are a consequence of our disordered civilization, the pedagogic point, which is also the human point, of Ackerley's book lies in its reminder that imperfect man makes for an imperfect world. In his actual conduct, Ackerley, like Portnoy, is of course singularly free, however conditioned we may regard his sexual preferences. Both men go after what they want with some address and degree of license. But unlike Portnoy, Ackerley doesn't deny that he has this freedom, nor does he call for a state of unconditioned bliss for all of mankind. What his book is saying is that socially unconditioned man, if such a phenomenon were imaginable, would still be man conditioned by his human disposition and therefore prone to suffering.

Life for Ackerley was in fact hell, such was the nature of his sexual need. As far back as his school days, he was aware that boys, not girls, excited him, but for some reason he was unable to avail himself of the sexual opportunities offered him. Probably this was an early announcement of the inhibition which in later life reappeared in the form of various disturbances to full sexual pleasure. As an officer in the First World War he was sexually inactive; his induction into sex would seem to have waited until his Cambridge years and even then, instead of finding his partners in his own class, it was necessary that he have recourse to a London house of male prostitution. The selection of his lovers from outside his own social world was to continue: in India it was the maharajah's young servant–attendants who attracted him; back in England again, it was among soldiers, sailors, the working class that he sought his partners. All his life Ackerley was in search of the Ideal Friend, the beautiful clean young boy on whom he could lavish his devotion. He never found him. The search was a nightly compulsion, driving him into the London streets and bars. But he never satisfied his longing to give love requited in loyalty, in affection, most of all in dependency—until at the age of fifty he got his dog Tulip and the quest ended. The indignities and dangers to which he so regularly submitted were undoubtedly as much a requirement of his life as the sating of his sexual desire but this hardly alters the reality of his frustration and suffering.

It was more than helpful that he had money: Ackerley paid for the services rendered him. He records, as I recall, no instance in which his lover was as well fixed as himself; indeed, this too was apparently a requirement, that his partner be someone in want of money. He played the paternal benefactor to his young men much as his own father played the benefactor to him. Often his partners were bisexual, even married. Once he was told that the money he paid for a boy's services was to be used to underwrite the boy's wedding. But the closer he got to "normal" sexuality, the better he liked the partnership, which is why he particularly favored the Guardsmen, members of his father's old regiment. Young, hand-somely uniformed, manly, always short of cash, *and* the company in which his father had deployed *his* homosexual resources, the Royal Horse Guard offered an attractive prospect.

The fact that Ackerley Senior had by his own wits and charm been able to make the social leap from being used to having a son who did the using makes its own success story of a specifically English variety: the author of *My Father and Myself* had reason for gratitude to his self-made father who had put him in the class of those who do the buying. Still, the social class from which the father had sprung would seem to have colored the homosexual style of the son. Although litera-ture and other social records provide us with some general notion of the sexual habits of the British working classes, it is only now, with books like Ackerley's, that we begin to discover the character of their private sexual behavior: the restrictive-ness that went along with, perhaps still goes along with, their apparent laxity. Ackerley gives us a forthright report of his sexual practices with the lower-class men he went to so much trouble and expense to bring to his bed. In the main the activ-ity was limited to mutual masturbation, and this was not only because of his own disinclination for anal or oral intercourse but because of the almost universal reluctance of his partners to vary their exercise from this, the most permitted one, the one that least outrages a conventional sense of the sexual de-cencies. On the single occasion when Ackerley thought he had at last found someone with whom he might establish a perma-nent relationship, the young sailor with whom he had set up house in Portsmouth disappeared forever after Ackerley had persuaded him to fellatio and we have the feeling that the sailor's disgust was met with a considerable sympathy on the part of his mentor, himself released to such "perversity" only by his love for the boy. We have not yet the evidence on which to conclude that Ackerley's own restraint or those of his part-ners have their root in working-class morality, but it is clear enough that not only his own sexual freedom but that of his companions was streaked with prohibition. And it throws a new light on the relation between economic actuality and sexual custom to discover, as we do from Ackerley's book, that a class which can accommodate itself to male prostitution as a means of earning a bit of extra money will draw the line this firmly on what should or should not be done in bed.

Yet even when Ackerley speaks of his rare excursions into activities usually forbidden him, it is not guilt that he points to as a deterring factor but personal preference. Indeed guilt is not mentioned in this autobiography until its Appendix where Ackerley at last deserts objective narration to comment, briefly, on the psychophysical difficulties that attended his lovemaking: we learn that he was always liable to premature ejaculation and in middle life became entirely impotent. This was when he got his dog Tulip. Tulip was an Alsatian bitch, and without, so far as we can tell, indulging in bestiality, Ackerley loved her with the deep and lasting passion he had never achieved with any man; after he got Tulip he never sought another lover. We leave it to the psychoanalysts to tell us why it was a female rather than a male animal that Ackerley so much loved, and why, other than because of her entire dependence on her master, Tulip was able to elicit and sustain this tenderness. Ackerley was himself not psychoanalyzed, and in his Appendix he expresses regret that his knowledge of the psychoanalytical therapy for guilt came to him too late for him to avail himself of it. But the guilt he is speaking of is not the guilt of being a homosexual; he had no wish to be cured of that. What he is talking about is his perception that it must have been guilt that caused his insufficient self-control in love-making and his eventual impotence; of this he would have wished to be cured. The distinction strikes one as being clinically sound: it may very well be that psychoanalysis, accepting his homosexuality, would have rid Ackerley of the hindrances to his sexual enjoyment. It is also a useful distinction to apply in the case of Portnoy: had Portnoy accepted himself for the less than totally "normal" person of his imagination and not demanded that society be so perfect that all its children be perfect too, probably his psychoanalyst would have spoken sooner and to plainer purpose.

The question is, then, which of these sexual "confessions," so radically different from each other, is closer to the truth of our human condition: Roth's, which blames society for the fate we suffer as individuals and, legitimately or not, invokes Freud on the side of his own grimly deterministic view of life, or Ackerley's, which, in returning us to the working hypothesis of free will, suggests that society is no more than the context of personal anguish? No doubt the answer is, neither. Each aspires to truth; both are undertakings in honesty; neither finally attains to more than frankness. But on behalf of Ackerley's old-fashioned nondeterministic view of life, it can at least be said that it proposes, as Roth's more modern view does not, the not inconsiderable virtues of courage, kindliness, responsibility. Curiously, Ackerley's homosexual memoir is the more manly— if that word still has meaning—of the two books.

[1969]

Easy Rider and Its Critics

BERNARD SHAW'S *Quintessence of Ibsenism* was first presented in 1892 as a lecture to the Fabian Society in London. Shaw's justification for bringing the theatre into discussion with people chiefly engaged in government, politics, economics, and the law was his belief that the drama has a significant influence upon the individual life and the life of society. "Art," Shaw said, but he was speaking primarily of the theatre, "should refine our sense of character and conduct, of justice and sympathy, greatly heightening our self-knowledge, self-control, precision of action, and considerateness, and making us intolerant of baseness, cruelty, injustice, and intellectual superficiality and vulgarity." Although today a formulation like this verges on quaintness, we recognize that Shaw is voicing a conviction which in much-transmuted form is still alive for us. Certainly it is some such appreciation of the moral function of the theatre that warrants our appeals for government support of the stage and makes the basis of our condescension to the commercial theatre.

And his statement of the high purpose of the dramatic art makes plain why Shaw found it appropriate to talk about Ibsen to a group of people whose first commitment was to political and social improvement. For if it is the purpose of the theatre to instruct us in character and conscience, then all men of character and conscience, all persons devoted to the public good, should be informed of the way in which the theatre discharges this important duty.

There can be no question that were Shaw addressing himself to present-day affairs he would put the film under as strict scrutiny as the stage, or even stricter, and not only because the movies reach so much wider an audience than stage plays but also because he would be bound to respond to the special force of the visual as compared to the predominantly verbal medium. Indeed, I have only the most formal hesitation in borrowing his authority for the belief that no art now exerts more moral influence than the film, and that for the present generation, particularly the best-educated young people, more than personal character is being formed by our filmmakers: a culture, a society, even a polity.

It is as an exemplification of this power of moral and social instruction that I wish to discuss *Easy Rider*. But perhaps I should first say what I mean by instruction in this context. I do not mean overt pedagogy, nor do I mean what the famous director Jean-Luc Godard presumably had in mind when he said recently of his film *See You at Mao*, "The movie is like a blackboard. A revolutionary movie can show how the arms struggle may be done [*sic*]." *Easy Rider* is not a film of this order. Although it is highly tendentious it wears the mask of disengagement. Its atmosphere, in fact, is that of a pastoral, its method that of implication rather than assertion. Its notable achievement lies in its ability to communicate states of feeling: it does its work of persuasion through the creation of mood.

The plot of the movie can be briefly summarized. Two long-haired young men, Wyatt (Peter Fonda) and Billy (Dennis Hopper), purchase some cocaine or heroin in Mexico, sell it at a handsome profit to a sleazy character who emerges from a chauffeured Rolls-Royce, and, with their money, buy a flamboyant pair of motorcycles and set off on a journey from California to New Orleans. It is a handsome travelogue, their West-to-East voyage. The landscape has known no desecration other than the building of the highways on which Wyatt and Billy

ride. There are no buses, no billboards, no cars, and the very
few people they meet have entered the scene for only symbolic
reasons.

The riders stop at a ranch to repair one of their motorcycles.
The rancher is shoeing a horse. The land is his to the horizon.
As part of his open-handed, trusting hospitality, he and his
Mexican peasant wife, joined by their large brood of happy
children, give the riders dinner—the farmer's table has been
set up outdoors, idyllically. A little later, they pick up a hitch-
hiker who takes them to his rural commune. Here we are
shown another pastoral, less self-consciously nostalgic than
that of life as a rancher, but presumably of an idealistic piece
with it in its (drug-induced) innocence.

But as they near New Orleans, the two riders meet an
ACLU lawyer, gentle, tolerant, the defeated son of a town boss.
He is going to New Orleans to visit a brothel. The three men
stop at a modest restaurant and attract the attention of the
sheriff and some cronies of his who mobilize a quick brutal
hatred of the hippie outsiders. That night, as the riders sleep
at the roadside, the sheriff and his people sneak up on them—
they manage to kill only the lawyer. The pop music which
functions as a kind of Greek chorus to the mounting doom of
Easy Rider carries much of the emotion with which Wyatt and
Billy receive the death of this new friend. Determined to complete his journey for him, they go to the brothel in New Orleans where they join up with two young prostitutes—but not
sexually, only in comradeship, and they all go to the Mardi
Gras, then continue the day in a cemetery where they get high
on pot and liquor. By the time Wyatt distributes the LSD he
has in his pocket, the girls are too intoxicated to care what
they are taking. The inhabitable world vanishes from the
screen: as in one of Dr. Leary's psychedelic celebrations, the
film is now given over to describing the psychic states induced
in Wyatt, Billy, and the two girls by the acid. When one of the
girls takes off her clothes, no one has use for her naked body:
with the help of drugs Wyatt and Billy have transcended more

than society, more even than their minds: their bodies. *Easy Rider* celebrates not only a pretechnological but also a presexual, or certainly pregenital, world.

But they have not transcended death. The acid trip over, their other journey across an America which once was, and presumably might still be, resumes. The two men get only a short distance beyond New Orleans, however, when they are overtaken on the deserted road and shot down, in coldest blood. Whether it is the same sheriff of their previous encounter who commits the murder or some ready counterpart, is not clear. But it cannot matter; we have been shown vigilante America at work, out to destroy whatever loves freedom and is different from itself. The film ends in a bloody dawn, with Wyatt's and Billy's smashed bodies lying in the road. We understand that their murderers will go unapprehended.

Although while I was in the theatre I was aware of weighty reservations on the score of *Easy Rider*'s moral content—they were first provoked by the dope sale at the start of the film—I was also considerably seduced by it. But ironically, my seducer was America. I say ironically because, in addition to the fact that the point of the film is its indictment of America for failure to fulfill its promise to us, the America of *Easy Rider* is in chief part a pictorial illusion. The landscape it draws for us is mythic in its lack of industrialization, of technology, even of population. I daresay there are still sections of the Southwest where one can travel long distances without seeing a billboard or a hamburger stand and where farms exist in isolation but I doubt that one can travel from California virtually all the way to New Orleans on main highways which are this bare of people and vehicles. And yet no other film which I can recall has so poignantly reminded me of the lovely heritage of this country. It was the American land which seduced me in *Easy Rider*, and this would seem to suggest that I too, like the makers of the film, am caught in the dream of a country unscarred by modernity.

But the longing for an unravished land is not a new emotion

for Americans. It appears in our literature well before the existence of a technological society, in the work of Cooper, Thoreau, Whitman, and of course Mark Twain—when Huck Finn lit out for the territory he too, even in his time, was trying to escape the restrictions of civilized modern life. And in our more recent literature it has played a decisive part in the imagination of Hemingway. For all of these writers the unspoiled forests, prairies, mountains, and rivers of America make not merely the setting of their quest for freedom but also a condition of life which makes it possible for them to discover their wholeness and worth as individuals. *Easy Rider* leans heavily upon the charm and authority of this literary tradition but the unravished countryside which makes the landscape of its dream of the free life has, in fact, no integral relation to the film's representation of freedom—it is nothing *but* landscape. Its beauty is used to validate the only freedom of which Fonda and Hopper would appear to have any genuine conception, that of the drug experience. A first and basic dishonesty of *Easy Rider*, that is, is its proposal that more than a kinship, an equivalence, or at the least an interdependence, exists between the fulfillment which we seek in moving beyond the frontiers of civilization and the gratifications to be sought in extending the frontiers of consciousness by drugs.

But a dishonesty of this dimension requires other deceptions to sustain it. The search for a new frontier beyond which life will have retained its innocence may be recurrent in American literature but it is not the only American dream, nor ever has been: our nostalgia for the fair and innocent land has always had for companion another dream, that of F. Scott Fitzgerald's Gatsby, of happiness through power and wealth. This was the conqueror's dream, and today we direct our sternest disapproval to those who celebrate it. Wyatt and Billy are so plainly offered as the very negation of predatory America that when at the end of *Easy Rider* they are murdered by the forces of darkness, we are intended to feel that more than individual lives have been lost. Virtue itself has been destroyed.

Gatsby, we recall, tried to buy his transcendence over limiting social circumstance by bootlegging: Fitzgerald conceals
from us no part of Gatsby's moral implication in his way of
getting rich. Wyatt and Billy try to buy their transcendence by
trafficking in drugs but they are made to bear no moral responsibility for *their* way of getting rich—unless we were perhaps to argue that their death at the end of the film is a
punishment for wrongdoing, in which case *Easy Rider* would
have to be accused of having vested its moral authority in cold-
blooded murderers. The transaction in dope is indeed em-
bedded in moral obfuscation. We see the expensive white
powder being given to the man in the Rolls-Royce, we never
see to whom he gives it other than himself: we are never
shown, say, the children who will become our newest statistics
in addiction and death. Certainly nothing in the film suggests
that the money with which Wyatt and Billy undertake to
escape this tainted world of ours is itself tainted—the sale of
the dope behind them, Wyatt and Billy continue throughout
the film as spokesmen for its appeal on behalf of America's lost
purity.

And just as the filthy business in which the heroes of *Easy
Rider* make their wad is somehow disinfected by the manifest
worthiness of their intentions in life, just so their recourse to
LSD or other drugs is somehow obscured by the innocent
pleasure they have from marijuana. In general, the enlightened public now makes a distinction between marijuana and
the other drugs which increasingly come into use. In fact, the
argument, not that all drugs should be legalized in order to
take them out of the sphere of criminality, but that marijuana
should be legal because it is harmless, rests almost entirely on
the proposition that the use of marijuana is an activity of a
quite different order than the use of "real" drugs. The evidence of *Easy Rider*, however, is against such a distinction.
For Wyatt and Billy pot is merely the basic daily fare which
makes life supportable for them between their adventures
with more potent medicines. We see the two men sniff their

nameless white powder only once, at the start of the film, but their practiced performance is fair evidence that this is not an initial experience. Similarly, their composure after their acid trip is proof enough that this is not their first use of LSD. It is difficult to see how the young filmgoers who chiefly make up the audiences of *Easy Rider* can fail to conclude from the example of Wyatt and Billy that the taking of LSD or other drugs is simply an alternative to smoking pot, or at least that dreary medical warning to the contrary notwithstanding, the taking of these more drastic drugs can be slipped in and out of at will, between joints.

Nor can we place more confidence in the social-economic import of *Easy Rider* than in its medical instruction. The film implies that spiritual freedom depends upon an escape from technology and it gives us the happy rancher in example. In his barn a horse is being shod and we are shown the wheel of a wagon—there is no farm machinery, there are no farmhands, and the rancher's sons are too young to help him. Apparently we are to believe that it requires only one man plus a horse and wagon to put a huge tract of land under cultivation. We could perhaps accept a simplification of this sort as aesthetic concentration were it not for the extreme social and political disingenuousness of the film as a whole, including its core assumption that one has only, like Wyatt or Billy, to be the target of evil social forces to be oneself wiped clean of evil. This curious belief of course established itself in American liberal thought in the McCarthy period, when one had only to be the object of McCarthy's malignity to be certified as forever blameless.

As in a traditional Western, *Easy Rider* divides the world into good and bad guys. But what gives it its chic is its definition of good and bad: good guys want to be left in peace to live out their lives of natural freedom, bad guys want to impose their way of being upon others. Obviously in the revolution of the seventies, the contending social forces are no longer capital and labor, nor even the movements of progress versus the movements of reaction. They are the passively virtuous and the actively wicked. The proletariat of an earlier revolutionary day, with its auspicious place in history and its decisive role in determining the fate of mankind, is transformed into a pair of mindless copouts (not to say criminals) for whom there is neither past nor future, imagination, curiosity, desire. Symbols of what we are to suppose is our present social idealism and aspiration, Wyatt and Billy lack the energy to create anything, comment on anything, feel anything except the mute, often pot-induced pleasure of each other's company.

But the muteness of *Easy Rider* not only accurately represents the anti-intellectualism of the contemporary revolution, it is also essential to the myth-making impulse of the film. By this I mean, simply, that were *Easy Rider* more verbal, it would be more accessible to the intelligence. For example, the pivotal moment of the film, or at any rate what many viewers have taken to be its moral climax, depends upon our interpretation of a sudden statement by Wyatt. It consists of three words: Wyatt and Billy are again about to hit the road after their acid trip, and Billy murmurs something about their having made it, to which Wyatt replies, "We blew it." To some viewers of the film this utterance indicates that Wyatt believes that their journey has fallen short of its moral goal or, which is not too different, that he has come to recognize his moral responsibility for the drug transaction. But nothing in the film supports these interpretations, and I myself incline to the opinion that the ambiguousness of the statement is a conscious deviousness, designed to let the viewer draw from the film whatever conclusions make him most comfortable. By failing to clarify Wyatt's summary assessment of his and Billy's quest, the authors of the film at one and the same time permit us an adverse judgment of their central characters and yet protect them as examples of innocent victimization. But of course it is as examples of innocent victimization that Wyatt and Billy have entered the pantheon of contemporary heroic dissent.

Here, then, are some of the actual ingredients of this popular film, and an enticing brew of the fashionable, the false, and the pernicious it is. How are we to respond to such an offering? Surely not by legal censorship, which in America doesn't even raise questions of the control of moral and social ideas, only of what may be thought pornographic or obscene, and which in countries where it does treat questions of social suitability necessarily operates to suppress anything which challenges the official culture. But the rejection of censorship implies that we put our faith in moral and social intelligence either as exercised by the artists themselves or by those who receive their work.

It is a piety of our art-loving culture that between moral and social intelligence and artistic intelligence there is an inevitable congruence. *Easy Rider* is demonstrable proof that this is not so. As an instance of the art of filmmaking it is sufficiently to be praised: it is well played, imaginative, adroit, visually pleasing, and it undoubtedly fulfills the intentions of its authors. But these positive qualities not only coexist with grave deficiencies of thought: they give authority to the film's false view of the moral and social life. If *Easy Rider* were less attractive as a piece of movie making, we would not need to be concerned about its influence. It therefore rests with us who receive the film to exercise the moral discrimination which the authors fail to exercise. In particular, this responsibility devolves, I think, upon those whose work it is to tell us how well the theatre is fulfilling its high mission of instructing us in character and conscience: the critics.

I have the sense that, more than any other group within the critical profession, film critics have the public's attention—less than a week after the warm critical reception of the film Z, it was impossible to get a seat in the theatre at eleven o'clock in the morning. I was out of the country when *Easy Rider* opened but from the reviews I have since retrieved I have the impression, certainly not of general unqualified approval—only Penelope Gilliatt of *The New Yorker* would seem to have given it that—but of a response in which any critical unease it engendered was always eventually buried in the reviewer's need to concur in its message: it was as if Fonda and Hopper's observation of Middle America's hatred of anything different from itself and of the American capacity for mindless violence constituted an insight of such freshness and magnitude as to render paltry or carping any adverse judgment the critic might make on the film's validity as a document of American life. Except for Paul Schrader in the *Los Angeles Free Press,* who boldly ridiculed *Easy Rider* for its indulgence in stale left-wing ritualisms—and it is worth noting that with the publication of this review Mr. Schrader's connection with the paper was terminated—even critics who, like Richard Schickel in *Life,* spoke of the air of self-congratulation in which Wyatt and Billy have their being, or, like Joseph Morgenstern in *Newsweek,* mocked the sententiousness of the film, raised these objections in a context of appreciation.

And Mr. Schrader himself went but half the course. Although he denounced the nondimensional politics of *Easy Rider,* he never mentioned the means by which Wyatt and Billy financed their journey. The oversight little distinguishes his reception of the film from that of the other reviewers. To be sure, Vincent Canby of the *New York Times* wrote: "After all, Wyatt and Billy, the heroin pushers, may be the same kind of casual murderers as the southern red necks." Stanley Kauffmann of *The New Republic* wrote: "In cold factual terms, Fonda and Hopper are pretty low types—experienced drug-peddlers, criminal vagabonds. . . ." And Joseph Morgenstern, again in *Newsweek,* wrote: "Neither of these two riders . . . is conspicuously innocent. They've gotten the money for their odyssey by pushing dope." But these comments, which at least express disapprobation of drug trading, are curiously brief, unreverberant—they scarcely constitute a rousing opposition to the film's own acceptance of drug dealing—while the other reviews I have read fail to rise even this inadequately to the moral occasion. For Dan Wakefield, writing in the *Atlantic,* the drug in which Wyatt and Billy traffic is cocaine—he is positive in the identification—and extensively outraged as Mr. Wakefield is by the bad treatment hippies receive at the hands of their fellow citizens, he finds it possible to concentrate his judgment of Wyatt and Billy's drug transaction into a single sentence: "The two hippies . . . make a highly profitable sale of some cocaine they score in Mexico to a sinister-looking connection in Los Angeles, and with the money stashed in the red-white-and-blue Stars-and-Stripes painted fuel tank of Wyatt's motorcycle, they take off east for New Orleans. . . ." In fact, later in his piece Mr. Wakefield makes explicit his faith in the two central characters of *Easy Rider* as figures of virtue: "Why," he inquires, "the needless death and destruction of these fairly innocuous, generally pleasant, and harmless young men?" But it is left to Miss Gilliatt of *The New Yorker* to bring the moral and social-political concerns of the film into most reassuring accord with each other. Of Wyatt and Billy she writes: "By smuggling dope across the frontier and selling it to a gum-chewing young capitalist disguised as a fellow-hippie, they make enough money to live life their own way." With a stroke of the pen Miss Gilliatt certifies the central characters of *Easy Rider* as proper symbols of the lost decency of American life: they are genuine hippies, not capitalists disguised as hippies, and—oh, important point!—they do not chew gum.

We are accustomed, of course, to the reluctance of our critics to submit to rigorous examination any political or social idea which is presented to them under the aspect of enlightened dissidence. It is indeed by its accessibility to whatever is opposed to established values or whatever may be regarded as innovative thought that criticism defends itself against the imputation of academicism and brings itself into the full current of strenuous contemporaneity. Are we to conclude, then, from Mr. Wakefield's or Miss Gilliatt's unperturbed acceptance of drug dealing, and from the diffidence on this score even of the critics who oppose it, that drug use has made good its claim to radical-ideological status?

I do not think so. I think, rather, that what we see in the response of the critics to *Easy Rider* is their acquiescence in the modern injunction against moralizing about art. Quoting from Shaw, I said that the language in which Shaw described the function of the theatre was bound to sound quaint to contemporary ears. I meant that outright moralizing puts us in mind of cultures of the past, when there could be firm working formulations of right and wrong and when there were wise men, teachers, whose job it was to guide us through areas of doubt. Our sense of our own times is the opposite of this. So extreme, in fact, is our awareness of the absence of such rules and persons and of the consequent need for each of us to improvise his own morality that we have all but lost sight of the continuing dynamics of culture, which is to say that we have forgotten that codes for the guidance of our moral lives *are* constantly being proposed for us by the culture even where the social standards which are being invoked seem most precisely to prohibit recourse to moral criteria of the sort which concerned Shaw.

In the fashioning of these codes artists, especially in the popular media, have a primary role. But the role of the critic, though neglected, is far from negligible. It is the critic who is supposed to warn us not to be seduced by art and who is delegated to ask questions about the worth of the codes which are being offered us. It is always a first task of the critic to make the implicit explicit. His is always—or so, at any rate, I believe it to be—a moralizing function, whatever additional critical purpose he may also be pursuing. And it is today, when he gives sign of being most eager to forget this responsibility, that we have most need to recall him to it.

[1970]

Women's Liberation

1. Female Biology in a Male Culture

As a subject of conversation, women's liberation is unmatched for putting everyone, women as well as men, in the happy state of mind which results from establishing one's superiority to whatever is benighted and ridiculous in human activity. I think of only one other topic which equals it in provoking ignorant mirth among the well-educated and that is psychoanalysis; not psychiatry, which people are willing to recognize as a serious subject, but Freudian analysis. The parallel cannot surprise us. In both instances the derisive response represents a defense against confrontation with an uncomfortable truth. The amusement with which, even at this late date, the mention of psychoanalysis is so often met is evidence that we do indeed have a life of the unconscious which we are afraid to bring to consciousness. And the ready ridicule of women's liberation is confirmation that women are indeed regarded in our society as of a second order of being and that we are reluctant to have this truth revealed to us. By "us" I of course mean women no less than men.

It is both appropriate and ironic that in undertaking to speak of the present movement for women's rights I bring it into such immediate connection with Freudian thought. The appropriateness lies in the fact that for many years my own view of the relation of the sexes was substantially shaped by Freud's perception of the differing biological natures of the sexes and of the consequent differences in their psychological lives and social roles. Recently, this influence has been modified: I now tend to give considerably more weight than I once did to the cultural, as opposed to the biological, determination of our sexual attitudes. For example, I am no longer persuaded, as I may once have been, that a woman's willingness to cede power to men necessarily represents her wholesome acceptance of a biologically determined passivity; rather, I tend to see it as a cultural conformity or even an expediency or laziness. The irony of bringing Freud into immediate conjunction with the subject of women's liberation lies in his having had such an invidious view of the female sex. I am afraid that the man who sought to liberate the human psyche from the hindrances put upon it in infancy was interested not at all in liberating women from the special restraints imposed upon them in our society. Nowhere in his writings does Freud express sympathy for the problems which pertain to women alone. On the contrary, his misogyny is now taken for granted even by his most admiring students.

Freud's condescension toward women is rooted in his castration theory, which plays a vital part in his theory of neurosis. According to Freud, it is the male sexual organ which constitutes what might be called the natural, or ideal, endowment from which stems the envy particular to women because they lack this genital equipment and the anxiety of men lest they lose this essential male distinction. And no doubt it is as an extension of his view of woman's basic biological inferiority that Freud makes his forthright statement in *Civilization and Its Discontents* that it is men who are the makers and carriers of culture; he adjures women not to interfere with man's adventures in this sphere.

The adjuration could scarcely be more irritating, especially as we contemplate some of the activities that men have come to regard as a sound life in culture, like inventing hydrogen bombs or planting the flag of their nation on the moon. On the other hand, there is nothing in Freud's formulation of the castration fear that I'd be prepared to fault or which people far more competent than I am have yet succeeded in refuting. While it would be pleasant to accept, say, the idea proposed by Dr. Karen Horney, the mother of Freudian revisionism, and widely propagated by Margaret Mead, that womb envy, man's envy of women because they can have babies and men cannot, plays as much part in the life of men as penis envy plays in the life of women, this appealing reassignment of biological advantage is supported by neither men's literary metaphors, their dreams, nor their free associations during psychoanalytical treatment. As to Freud's statement of the different relation of men and women to culture, it would seem to be historically indisputable that for better or worse men have forged the ideas and provided the chief energies by which cultures develop while women have devoted themselves to the conservation of what they have found valuable in the efforts of men. We may protest that there is no work in culture more valuable than childbearing and child nurturing and that women's ability to create and conserve the human race over-shadows any other accomplishment of which we can conceive. But this of course begs the question of why women have not made even a small fraction of the intellectual, scientific, or artistic contributions to culture made by men.

Or we may protest that women's small contribution to culture doesn't indicate a lack of capacity but merely reflects the way men have contrived things to be: we can blame women's small place in culture *on* culture. But this leaves unanswered the question of why it is that over so many hundreds of years women have consented to follow the male dictate and allowed men to fashion the culture according to male design. It also leaves unanswered the even more fundamental question of why it is that in every society which has ever been studied—so Margaret Mead tells us—whatever is the occupation of men has the greater prestige: if men do the hunting and fighting, hunting and fighting are the status-giving occupations of the society but if men do the weaving and baby tending, then weaving and baby tending are thought the superior activities. If we are moved to conclude that this value system is something that men impose upon women, we are still left to explain why it is that even where it is the women who bear arms they have not enforced a different system of values.

The reference back to biology would seem to be unavoidable, and we are returned to Freud's use of the words "passivity" and "activity"—female passivity, male activity. Almost inevitably the words themselves imply a pejorative judgment, especially in a culture like ours where passivity connotes such unattractive attributes as inertness, laxness, the uncritical acceptance of whatever is handed one. Even as a concept in the purely sexual relation of men and women it suggests that man is the seeker and that woman yields to man's importunities, a description of the sexual life which is not notably congruent with our modern sense of reality. But actually this distinction between the active and the passive sexual roles is an irrefutable fact in nature: the most active seduction or sexual participation on the part of a woman cannot relieve the male partner of his primary physical responsibility in their union. To put the matter at its crudest, the male has the biological capacity to rape; the female has not. We may, if we wish, accuse Freud of drawing too many, or mistaken, inferences from this primary biological difference. But to try to ignore the difference, as some of the women's liberation groups do, is to narrow rather than widen the prospects opened up to us in dealing with biology.

It is reported of Freud that he was not without bitterness at being thought dirty-minded because he wrote about infant sexuality—he would point out that he had not created the condition, he had merely recognized it. And he of course didn't create the different sexual endowments of men and women nor the emotional consequences of the difference, he only recognized them and attached the words "active" and "passive" to the differing roles they decreed. But after centuries of female subjugation we should not be surprised that the essential lack of sympathy for women in orthodox psycho-analysis, and in particular its emphasis on women's envy of men, with its implication of hostility, is one of the aspects of Freud's thought which has been most easily received by our society. There is small doubt that Freudian doctrine, often scarcely understood, has greatly powered the development in recent decades of what amounts to virtually an anti-female movement in American culture.

It has been the informing sentiment of this movement that women, whether as wives or mothers, are bent on the destruction of men. As statistics have been gathering on the appalling number of men who die from heart disease in this country, increasingly the blame has been put on the American wife for the killing material demands she makes of her husband: houses, cars, washing machines, clothes, costly gadgets. She has been pictured as ruthless in the economic exploitation of her male partner, a sort of domestic statement of what is taken to be our national imperialism. And as Freud's views on the childhood source of mental disorder have permeated our culture, there has been mounted a wide campaign of mother-suspicion and mother-discreditation. From Sidney Howard's play *The Silver Cord,* in the mid-twenties, to Philip Roth's more recent *Portnoy's Complaint,* our literature has disseminated the idea that American women alternate a diet of husbands with a diet of sons.

Nor is it solely on the ground of her inordinate appetites that the American mother has been chivied and mocked: if she cannot be blamed for devouring her young, she is blamed for rejecting them. For some fifty years now, it has been impossible for a woman, especially a mother, to be anything but wrong in our enlightened culture; the more "advanced" the community, the more varied and virulent the attacks upon her, to the point where one often has the impression that the prestige of our best, or certainly our most consciously progressive, nursery and grade schools is built on the humiliation of young mothers. Moreover, this pernicious assault on women's minds

and spirits comes not alone from men. Much of the time, especially in the schools and playgrounds, it comes from other
women moving on the lines of thought and feeling which a
male-dominated culture has cleared for them.

Any adequate statement of woman's inhumanity to woman
would perhaps make it appear that what eventually is wrong
with women is that there are other women in the world, and
that women are to be condemned out of hand for their be-
trayals, overt and covert, of their own sex. But an assessment
as harsh as this ignores the range and subtlety of the difficulties by which women are beset, the accusers along with the
accused. It may not be edifying to contemplate the spectacle
of women acceding in the disparagement of their own sex in
order to provide the reassurance that men deserve the status
conferred upon them by their superior biological endowment;
but if a woman's sexual and maternal satisfactions depend
upon male self-confidence and if, too, the male in our society
is willing to pay for his bio-psychological advantage by assuming the financial support of his wife and family, it is more than
understandable, it is plainest reason, that a woman should
place the male will, whether real or only fancied, above that of
other women.

In particular it is understandable that women should come
to feel that they are not defeated but fulfilled in the
acceptance of man's primacy. For to live by deference to the
needs of those one loves among the pleasanter modes of
existence; also, I might add, among the most taxing. It is a
grave fault of modern culture that it trains us in the belief that
whatever defers to others is an *in*action and therefore of
secondary social value.

And yet even while we record the appeal on behalf of female passivity, the question is pressed in upon us whether our
female-ists, who stress their satisfaction in devoting their lives
to being good wives and mothers, would settle for this domes-
tication, and be happy in it, if they lived in a society in which
different requirements were made of them than are made in

our culture. We are told that the women in the Israeli kib-butzim who serve side by side with their men in the fields and even in the army and who give up the larger part of the rearing of their children to communal nurseries show no sign of being unfulfilled as women. Nor, apparently, do their men feel castrated by this female activity. It also seems clear from Solzhenitsyn's remarkable novel *Cancer Ward* that although a woman surgeon in the Soviet Union may return from a grueling day at the hospital and, like working wives everywhere in our servantless world, still accept it as her job to do the marketing, cooking, cleaning, and laundry, it is not in her home and family but in her "real" work—her man's work, if you will—that she finds her chief pride, including her peculiarly feminine pride. It is undoubtedly one of the significant revelations of Solzhenitsyn's novel that in a situation where the women doctors have equal responsibilities with men it is still the men who hold the top hospital posts, but equally fascinating is its account of the numerous unself-conscious ways in which the women physicians manage to irradiate even their grimmest hospital routines with a sexually distinguishing gentleness and delicacy. From evidences such as these it is fair, I think, to conclude that women are considerably more flexible in the matter of how they are able to achieve fulfillment than we seem to recognize, and that it is perhaps only because our American culture requires women to find their best satisfaction in the activities of home and family that women obediently discover it there.

In other words, we are all of us, men and women both, the creatures of culture: we do and feel what our societies ask us to, and the demands put upon us are not always consistent or precisely correlated with biology. In wartime, when men are away and women not only take jobs in factories and on farms but make all the financial and practical decisions usually made by the male head of the family, no one thinks of accusing them of conduct unbecoming a woman. Or if a woman is forced through widowhood to earn her own living, no one is moved to put a brake on her competitiveness with men; she is regarded as a castrating woman only if she switches the dependence she once had on her husband to her children.

And in a similar reversal of values, I can imagine a perhaps not distant moment when the conserving instinct of women will become the most active force—I emphasize the word "active"—in the continuing life of society. Among the active roles that women may soon be called upon to play is that of rescuing the modern world from pollution; called upon, that is to say, not by men but by their own assessment of the exigency of the situation. Since thus far it has appeared to be impossible for men to mobilize the energies they use for the conquest of other planets for the preservation of life on Earth, women may well have to take over the job. And this is but one activity in culture, one form of competitiveness outside the boundaries of home and family, in which the female sex should excel, the competition to perpetuate life, though I fear it is not the kind of program to which women's liberation has turned its imagination.*

But when I say that women are the creatures of culture, while I obviously mean the prevailing culture, I do not necessarily mean only the dominant culture of the society. It may be that among those who now dissent from our dominant culture, particularly among the young, attitudes will be forged which will importantly alter the relation of the sexes in the dominant culture of the future.

I suppose it is natural enough that in the matter of renovating the relations of men and women it is on the score of women's professional and legal rights that the voice of contemporary protest is making itself most clearly heard. This is perhaps the area in which men actually feel themselves least challenged and it is of course the area that was first opened up for us by earlier efforts on behalf of sexual equality. It is

---

* As this book goes to press, we learn of a powerful movement, initiated by women but also opposed by women of different political preference, to bring peace to Northern Ireland.

nevertheless possible—and I say this with no intention of provocation or reductiveness—that the cause of women's professional rights, their demand for equal pay for equal work and similar advancement for similar merit, may be becoming, in the sexual sphere, our newest liberal ritualism, embraced as a way to avoid the need to look more closely at less overt, more insidious manifestations of the lack of parity between the sexes. I myself happen to think, for instance, that although it will indeed be a significant day for women when they are appointed to full professorships at our leading universities on the same basis as men, that is, on the basis of their merit, it will be an even better day when, in their own living rooms, they are naturally paid the same heed, given the same credence, as men can now count on for their opinions and speculations.

But finally it is not the organized agitations on behalf of women that I especially have in mind when I ponder the possible effect our present-day dissent may eventually have upon the dominant culture. I am not yet closely enough acquainted with the dissident young to know exactly what decorousnesses, rules, and formalities pertain to their sexual relations or what constitute their criteria of sexual worth and loyalty. What is nevertheless apparent even at my present distance is the devaluation of those appurtenances of masculinity and femininity which our culture—and here I chiefly speak of our competitive economy—sanctified for an earlier generation. I was myself of a generation in which any deviation from the specifications for female charm set down by Madison Avenue or Hollywood was thought the gravest hindrance to a woman's sexual bargaining power. While we couldn't fail to understand that the models by which we were supposed to measure ourselves were the exceptions in any race of mortals, we suffered much secret anguish in living under the sexual dictates not of nature but of commerce. One recalls the father in Dostoevski's *Brothers Karamazov* who believed that there was no such thing as an ugly woman: the possibility that an opinion like this would one day infiltrate substantial sections of our society was beyond our power to imagine, strained as we were by the demand put upon us by advertising and the movies to meet their ideals of beauty. This strain would now seem to be disappearing in the radical effort to disavow the ruling capitalist culture, and as a woman, though not a revolutionary, I hope it is gone forever.

And gone, or going, with it, through the same effort, is the social-sexual differentiation between men and women in terms of dress and hair style. While I have no love for the shared slovenliness of many young men and women with whose mode of physical life I have acquaintance, and indeed believe that it derives from a deficiency of self-respect, I welcome the unisexual appearance of the sexes if only as a criticism of a culture in which sexually differentiated styles of hair and dress, designed not by God but by man, have been treated as if they were biologically given. As I perceive it, or at least as I hope it, anything which rids us of false sexual assumptions and puts its stress upon biological actuality is bound to reduce men's and women's suspicions of each other and thus permit them a fuller expression of their human potentiality. Free of the cultural shards of our sexual differences, perhaps we can now come to a more satisfactory knowledge of our distinctive maleness and femaleness, and from this knowledge bring biology and culture into sounder relation with each other.

[1970]

2. The Prisoner of Sex

[Ten months after the delivery of the previous paper in Cambridge, Massachusetts, I participated in a meeting in New York at which Norman Mailer proposed to defend his recently published book, *The Prisoner of Sex*, against the criticisms of a panel of four women. Although less than a year, and a mere two hundred and fifty miles, separated the two meetings, the second occasion bore no recognizable relation to the first, which had been all propriety and grave reasonableness. In a subsequent speech on feminism and women's liberation, not reprinted in this volume, I described the second evening as follows:

"In the spring of 1971 a curious, highly publicized and much-attended event—tickets twenty-five dollars in the orchestra, ten dollars in the balcony—took place in Town Hall in New York: Norman Mailer, the celebrated author of a recent book called *The Prisoner of Sex*, his statement on the theme of women's liberation, undertook to defend his views against a panel of women variously critical of the beliefs he developed in that volume. It was no less than a confrontation, though it also turned out to be something of a happening; and it was appropriate that it took place in Town Hall because by imaginative extension the evening might, I suppose, be regarded as a present-day version of an American town meeting: it offered opportunity for the fullest possible exercise of our democratic right to free opinion and expression. I was a member of the panel that evening, the last of the four women speakers on the platform, but there were times in the course of the meeting when it seemed as if everyone in the audience was, if not a speaker, a highly vocal, often inexplicably angry participant in the goings-on.

It would be difficult to exaggerate the disorder of the evening: the raucousness, the extreme of polemic, invective, obscenity. Although it was 1971, the spirit was far more that of the sixties than the seventies; and it may be, in fact, that it required an event like this to put a seal on the previous decade of violent demonstration and disruption. The Theater for Ideas, sponsor of the meeting, had, I was told, invited several women to be members of the panel who had either refused outright or backed away at a late moment on the ground that it was an indignity to be chaired by a male, worst of all by the black-souled author of *The Prisoner of Sex*. It seemed to me that objections such as these overlooked the fact that Mailer offered a fair *quid pro quo:* he would chair the evening and in return his female panelists could attack him, his book, and his ideas as freely as they wished. Actually it is the single instance I know of in which the moderator of an evening has wittingly doubled as its victim.

"But as it turned out, Mailer was little moderate; it would have been impossible that he should be inasmuch as, from the moment the curtain rose, he was under most intemperate assault from the women in the audience. He of course gave as good as he got in the way of insult and dirty talk, and I found myself glad of this—when I had consented to join the panel I had not contracted to be present at a symbolical slaughter. Still, his working posture, half boss-man and half Old World gallant, was not well contrived to please or subdue: the ambiguousness of being the unwanted chairman of a gathering at which he would manifestly have preferred to play the generous host to his female adversaries made something of a mockery of his customary charm.

"And one must surmise that he was thrown off base by Germaine Greer. Miss Greer was the star attraction of the evening, sufficiently confident of herself to accept with generosity her place as second speaker. This put her at Mailer's right at the table. She had made public announcement of the reason why she, unlike others of the sisterhood, had consented to be on the panel: she wished to meet Mailer and go to bed with him. This was probably heady stuff even for him. When I arrived in the Green Room of Town Hall the two of them were already there, together with Miss Greer's team of BBC television reporters who, much like Mailer's TV retinue on his Pentagon march, had been pertinaciously attendant on Miss Greer's tour of America. Mailer and Miss Greer were being photographed together by a score of cameramen with Mailer holding up, not his own book, but Miss Greer's recent volume, *The Female Eunuch,* for the cameras. If an old-line feminist like myself expected an audience of militant women to take it amiss that one of their foremost agitators publicly grasped the educational occasion as an opportunity to forward her personal ambitions, both sexual and commercial, I obviously failed to appreciate the distinguishing contemporary fact that by being so overt about her desires Miss Greer had scored a victory for our sex: transcending reticence, she had transcended traditional femininity and moved all of us up a notch in the scale of male-female equality. Throughout my speech, friends in the audience later informed me, Miss Greer behind me passed little notes to Mailer, an upstaging technique for which she had already become known from various public appearances: if it was perhaps not an entire success in diverting the audience from what I was saying, it must have been distracting enough for the chairman. At any rate, it is so that I account for his sharply calling time on me in the middle of what I am afraid was the only admiration he was to receive that evening for the poetic force of some of his writing on the relation of the sexes.

"But the fact that I was permitted to give my speech at all was remarkable: a plan to disrupt the meeting just before I spoke failed. Jill Johnston, columnist for the *Village Voice* and a leader of the Radical Lesbian group which had recently announced its imperial role in women's liberation, was the third speaker of the evening. At the conclusion of her talented remarks two of her young women friends, like herself dressed in well-patched jeans and boy's shirts, rushed to the stage and the three of them, locked in embrace, having lost their balance, rolled on the floor, hugging and kissing. It was a miscalculation to have thought that a Lesbian exhibition could break up a meeting like ours—in New York City, 1971, no curtains were rung down, no one was outraged unless it was Mailer; it was he who demanded, in what must surely be the nicest malappropriateness of the era, "For heavens sake, Jill, act like a lady!" To make ostentatious perverse love in the sight of an audience which, with the best will in the world, finds itself unable to be shocked is bound to be deflating, and soon, in some embarrassment, Miss Johnston and her friends slunk away.

"But apparently it was not alone in addressing Jill Johnston that Mailer had used the word "lady." At some point in the discussion he seems to have referred to me, in all apparent neutrality of intention, as a "lady writer," or it may have been a "lady critic," and now, when it came to the question period, a member of the audience inquired of me whether I didn't object to this designation. The question was so mild that I took it to be a mere formality of friendly participation from the floor. I replied that perhaps I ought to object but actually I didn't. My answer was careless, in the mood of the moment. At a meeting in which all sexual differences were being wiped out not merely on behalf of equality for women under law and in the world of work but for all purposes of life itself; in the context of an evening in which one half of the human race, man, was being treated as expendable, I felt the need to separate my position from that of the other women panelists and their audience and, at any cost, to put myself on the side of sexual duality. It was only when the dust of the evening had settled and I was no longer moved to counter the extremity of opinion and behavior which had characterized the discussion that I let myself see that the question was of course not an expression of concern about the genteel connotations of the word "lady"; it had seriously to do with professional condescension to women. It was addressed to the pejorativeness in the mechanical sexual differentiation Mailer had indulged in, and its point was not negligible: to be a lady writer, a woman writer, a female writer is not the same as being a writer. It is a professional value judgment; implicitly, a *de*value judgment, analogous to the implied condescension with which one speaks, say, of a male nurse: no nurse is a lady nurse, she is *a* nurse. No man is a man writer, he is *a* writer. The unqualified professional category, the literary profession itself, is apparently the property of the ruling sex, and women who enter it require identification tags, like visitors at an army installation. . . ."

It was in this context that I delivered the speech which I reprint here.]

When, some weeks ago, I was first asked to join the discussion this evening, I of course already knew that women's liberation represented no single movement, no single point of view about the condition of women, but that it probably had as many definitions as there were women attracted to the idea of changing their lives or men aware of the mounting tides of female unrest in our society. I knew that there were those for whom it provided a new strategy of personal assertion, those for whom it offered a new occasion for cultural and institutional assault, those for whom it meant a long-delayed revivification of the women's rights movement which once went under the name of feminism, those for whom it was a prophetic vision of an erotic utopia, and those for whom it was Thurber's war between men and women as it might be formulated, twenty-five years after he had created *his* fancy, in the darkest imagination of the Pentagon. What I did not know, and learned only as I heard that one woman speaker after another was refusing to participate in the occasion, as if under penalty of some special ingenuity of female torture should she submit to the presence of a male chairman, in particular this male chairman, was that women's liberation was an authoritarianism already notably advanced in purpose and efficiency. Here we have accomplished virtually nothing on behalf of women other than perhaps to open a first outer door on grievances which we have either suppressed or lived with in loneliness: are we already so sure we can name the enemy and get him into our gunsights? To me, such certainty—certainty as virulent as this—would seem to suggest that among women no less than among men the energies we have most ready to us are the energies of rage and imposition, we who are supposed to be so contemptuous of governments, or sexes, that rage and impose.

Well, I am not at all sure that I am able this easily to identify the enemy of my sex. But much as I dissent from some of the attitudes which inform Norman Mailer's recent book about women, I am fairly certain it is not Mailer. Knowing him, I know he will forgive me for saying that, big as he looms on the modern literary scene—and I long ago put myself on record as considering him the most important writer of our time—he is not *that* big. He is not as big as biology, for instance, or culture. Certainly he is not as big as the combined forces of biology *and* culture.

Although, as I recall, Mailer makes little or no explicit mention of biology in *The Prisoner of Sex*, the concept of biology permeates it. Indeed it is biology which provides the chief determinant of Mailer's view of the relation of men and women. This cannot come as an entire shock to anyone acquainted with his work: one could have deduced much of his present position from his old and continuing rejection of birth control. Still, I doubt that we could have been entirely prepared for this degree of biological emphasis in a writer who, in so many areas other than that of the relation of the sexes, has been so pre-eminent a spokesman for the unconditioned life: an unconditioned culture and an unconditioned politics. After all, was it not Mailer who, for our time and far more immediately than D. H. Lawrence, made the conjunction—it is no minor one—between social-political revolution and a revolution in personal consciousness? Nothing, surely, puts a more terrible shackle upon unconditioned selfhood, nor more effectively weakens the metaphors by which we undertake to make a revolution in personal consciousness, than to introduce into our imagination of life, as Mailer does in *The Prisoner of Sex*, the stern determinisms of nature.

And in fact one has only to turn from Mailer's piece to another current statement on the situation of the sexes, Germaine Greer's *The Female Eunuch*, to recognize how great is the breach which an emphasis, like Mailer's, on the biological determination of life makes between, on the one hand, a willingness to confront this fundamental condition of our sexual being and, on the other hand, the dominant mood of our radical times. As whoever has read Miss Greer's book must recall, biology is finally the vanquished villain of *The Female Eunuch*. (Psychology is also defeated but in 1971 this takes fewer pages—seven and a half, to be exact.) Miss Greer's vision of female transcendence starts nowhere if not in the need to rid ourselves of biology other than in a single manifestation, that of female sexual desire. It would appear that in the service of sexual impulse anything is well lost for Miss Greer: love, motherhood, the nurturing instincts, even the pleasures of a developing relation with the same lover. For Miss Greer sex is not sex unless it is *only* sex, a triumphant refusal of any other of the forms in which libido may present itself. *The Female Eunuch* is said to be a book about feminism. I find this misleading, as if we were to say of Norman O. Brown's *Life Against Death,* with its celebration of the polymorphous perversity of infancy, that it is a book about what we have always wanted to know about children but were afraid to ask. Actually Miss Greer's book is its own call to a new order of consciousness in which the fullest possible unhindered release of female sexual impulse will alter our way of personal feeling and, in consequence, alter the way in which we conceive society.

In fact, it is perhaps not to Mailer but to Miss Greer and the Radical Lesbians, to all the strange contradictory voices which make the present-day chorus of radical female protest that we should attend if we are to hear our latest message of a society altered by a revolution in consciousness. But this is not to say that Mailer cedes his rule of the kingdom of metaphor without a last flourish of trumpets—for in a world as crowded and desperate as ours, what is it except a figure of speech, a discordant one, to ask for the constant apotheosis of sex in parenthood? Even as he professes the stern actualities of biology, Mailer reveals his attraction to what I would call the *poetry* of biology, and in so doing takes his place in line with those major male writers of our century who, like him, are so vulnerable in terms of social reality and with whom he is linked in the attack upon him by militant women—D. H. Lawrence and Henry Miller were similarly concerned with the body as the gateway to heaven.

And yet, much as my own taste runs to prose in matters

which have to do with the proliferating—and starving—populations of the world, and vigorously as I oppose myself to the dangerous poetic excess of Mailer's stand against contraception, I as vigorously disincline to join his current female opposition. For the plain fact is that I prefer even an irresponsibly poeticized biology to the no-biology-at-all of my spirited sisters. I think the former proposes, at least where life is supportable, not only more but better life.

But even as I reject the antibiological views of the extreme female liberationists, I also disincline to join any attack upon them which has at its source the wish to protect the sexual culture in which we now live. Mailer accepts little of our general culture, but he does accept much of our sexual culture as given, in particular that part of it which has to do with the relative status of the sexes. Where I separate from most of the radical liberationists who are winning the facile assent of women understandably troubled by their present sexual situation is that women's liberation seeks a culture which will invalidate the biological differences between men and women. Where I separate from Mailer is that, while honoring biology, he implicitly acquiesces, as I do not, in the intolerable uses which culture has made of the physical differences between the sexes.

In this, Mailer, who I know thinks of himself as in remorseless disagreement with Freud, in actuality gives support to Freudian doctrine precisely where I believe it to be most absolutist and questionable. Freud's use of the words "activity" and "passivity," male activity, female passivity, have recently come under hostile examination by women concerned with women's role in society; and justifiably so. Almost unavoidably the words themselves, in our culture, imply a value judgment, favorable to "activity" as being energetic, positive, productive; unfavorable to "passivity" as being lax, inert, uncritically receptive to whatever may be socially given. Even as a description of male and female roles in mating the words suggest what is unacceptable, that man is the seeker and woman the yielder or object. For an active woman to be told that hers is the other, the passive role, activity being the prerogative of men—surely this must seem the very negation of spirit. And applied to the conduct of the sexes in coupling it suggests the denial to women of their full freedom of initiation and participation.

But in anatomical fact the distinction between the active and passive sexual roles is an ineluctable condition in nature. Granted that there can be sexual pleasure for both men and women which is attained without activity on the part of the male; sexual union cannot be achieved without it, nor the propagation of the species. It is nevertheless one thing to accept this irreversible condition in nature and yet another to carry it beyond its biological confines as Freud did when he said that men were the makers of culture and that women mustn't interfere with man's life in culture. In a paper she wrote a few years ago, Dr. Phyllis Greenacre, an eminent woman psychoanalyst—it was she, by the way, who discovered that babies are often born sucking their thumbs, thus releasing mothers from yet one more blame for the terrors of the race—conjectured that perhaps the reason why men have made the major artistic and intellectual contributions to civilization lies in their possession of a thrusting assertive inquisitive external genital; and in something of the same speculative spirit Dr. Erik Erikson speaks of the existence in women of something he calls "inner space" by which they define their sense of themselves and their gifts. It is not my impression that either of these talented clinicians is undertaking to put limits on the capacity of women to employ and enjoy their fullest possible range of activity outside the home. But Freud unhappily is undertaking exactly this and so I think is Mailer though he doesn't put it as bluntly as the middle-class Viennese physician. It is required, then, that we remind Mailer that just as there are men who make no thrust toward the new and untried, there are women who refuse to be imprisoned in inner space even though their sense of themselves may in some important degree be conditioned by it. I defer to none in my regard for Freud. But I take from him only that which affirms and adds to life, discarding from his work, as from the work of anyone, including that of Mailer, including that of the female liberationists, whatever is impoverishing or absolute.

And among those efforts of the women's liberationists which I find most impoverishing, most absolutist, is the doctrine now being promulgated on the female orgasm. I find it remarkable that the same people who properly criticize our society for its hard treatment of homosexuals have no hesitation in dictating to women—and it *is* dictation, make no mistake about that, especially when it is directed to the young—where they are to find their presumably single path to sexual pleasure. I am talking, of course, about the campaign now being mounted to persuade women that there is no such thing as a vaginal orgasm, and that they therefore might just as well dispense with men even in bed. This is one-dimensional neurological mapmaking falsely representing itself as psychophysiology in depth, and it takes meanest advantage of the endemic ignorance about our bodies, perhaps especially in their sexual uses, which still persists into our present day of supposed enlightenment. So swift and strong, indeed, is the effect of anything which offers itself as scientific sexual information that we may have already reached the stage where whoever would wish to increase rather than thus narrow the range of women's sexual responsiveness will be thought to be boasting an unnatural advantage. Nothing in the sexual culture of recent decades has been more justifiably attacked than the idea that there is a single definition of what is or is not normal in sexual desire and response. As an added benefit of our deliverance from a presumptuous and even tyrannical authority in our choice of sexual partners or in our methods of pursuing sexual enjoyment, it would be good if we could also be free to have such orgasms as, in our individual complexity, we happen to be capable of, without having to consider whether they are of a kind and source which further the politics of sex.

If, however, I find it sad and dangerous that the nature of the female orgasm has now been brought into the realm of sexual politics, I find it appropriate that a political attitude be brought to bear on many matters in which the personal impulses naturally take a public form. Mailer makes the assumption—and here I am moved to charge him with disingenuousness since his experience must necessarily have demonstrated the opposite—that not just a few but most, perhaps even all, women are wholly fulfilled in love and motherhood and that, unlike men, they have no unused libido which presses for sublimation in art or in work. He fails to confront even the fiercely practical fact that women often have to support themselves and the babies he recommends to them in such abundance and that in consequence they require not only equal opportunities with men and equal rewards but also special protections demanded by the special biology which he celebrates. These are indeed political concerns and proper issues for public agitation. I have just come from Harvard in Cambridge, Massachusetts. At Harvard at this moment there are twelve women assistant professors together with a few dozen female tutors and teaching assistants. Harvard is Mailer's university; does he know these figures? These women carry a man-sized share of the teaching duties of Harvard but they will achieve faculty rank and tenure only when there will be enough political agitation to shake the men who rule the university out of their complacent superiority. Otherwise, as things stand, there is no rank or tenure for women at Harvard.

Biology is all very well, Norman. All these women have biology and they might be happy to celebrate it with you. But they have, as well, a repressive, life-diminishing culture to contend with. Your book *The Prisoner of Sex* has your always-beautiful intention of life enhancement and also, in its own particular way which is your particular way, a splendid imagination of women: I suppose we could describe it as the imagination of women in love. It nonetheless fails in its imagination of the full humanity of women, and this is a charge which no one would be impelled to level against your imagination of men.

[1971]

We Must March
My Darlings

[In the spring of 1971 I spent close to nine weeks in Cambridge, Massachusetts, living in one of the residence halls of Radcliffe, my old college. What follows are three portions of a projected book concerning this experience. My title is taken from Walt Whitman's "Pioneers! O Pioneers!" of which I quote the opening stanzas.

Come my tan-faced children,
Follow well in order, get your weapons ready,
Have you your pistols? have you your sharp-edged axes?
                Pioneers! O pioneers!

                For we cannot tarry here,
We must march my darlings, we must bear the brunt of danger,
We the youthful sinewy races, all the rest on us depend,
                Pioneers! O pioneers!

                *   *   *

                Have the elder races halted?
Do they droop and end their lesson, wearied over there beyond
                the seas?
We take up the task eternal, and the burden and the lesson,
                Pioneers! O pioneers!]

official of my Radcliffe era, the House Mistress, this information
never attained to even a first level of probability. It wasn't that
I found the location inappropriate: nothing was more logical
than to house whoever wished to keep the activities of the
hall under her eye exactly where I was myself now housed.
And certainly I didn't think that the post, either then or as it
was now developing under the House system, an English importation by way of Harvard, demanded a grander setting; on
only the most cursory inspection I had already come to the
opinion, from which there began to sprout various tentacles of
speculation, that like everything else in Currier House, the
master's apartment was unsuited to the manifest genuineness
and simplicity of the present incumbent and his wife, and lacking in congruence with the urgent democracy of present-day
institutional principle: a thirty- or thirty-five-foot living room,
all splashing color and deep-cushioned comfort, as measured
against the eight-foot cranny in which my poor Miss Purvis
had once pursued her official duties—in view of the new egali-
tarian consciousness of my old college, wasn't there something
paradoxical in all this ostentation? But my sense of dislocation
entailed nothing this portentous. I suffered a disorientation
due only to a fault of memory: try as I would, I couldn't
remember where Miss Purvis had lived in the dormitory and
certainly I couldn't place her in this suite assigned to my husband and me. The Mistress herself, that most tormented of
spinsters even in a period when spinsterhood was a solid profession or at least a guild for which the maidenhood of most of
my dormitory sisters must have been a sort of unchartered ap-
prenticeship, I remembered with no difficulty. It had been the
mid-twenties when Miss Purvis presided over Briggs. Of the
sixty or seventy of us who lived in the hall, there must have
been eight, or at most ten, whose nubility wasn't to be disguised or forever frustrated. But it was terrible to contemplate, the House Mistress's fear of us unregenerate few, the
unceasing nervous misery she undertook to hide behind the
perpetual simpering "sweetness" with which she met whatever

it was we so dreadfully proposed to her imagination—this was a period, it must be kept in mind, when nonmarriage still presented itself to certain sections of American society, notably in New England, as an aspect of gentility, a sublimated assertion of good breeding; when she took the job, breeding and what it implied of nonsexuality must have been something Miss Purvis took for granted in the students she would supervise. Where, though, had this unhappy lady lived and discharged the duties of her post such as giving or refusing us a release from this or that dormitory law, issuing the passport for a weekend visit, permitting us to be out when, by a stricter interpretation of our rules of self-government, we'd have had to be in? And where had she reposed in that bone-thin body of hers when at long last her day's ordeal was over and she had an interval of rest from the tortures that the disturbing existence of this tiny minority of us inflicted upon her? My visit passed with these questions unanswered. At night as I lay in my narrow cubicle, my husband in his little cell next door, and awaited surrender to the bad dreams which plagued me throughout the early weeks of my return to the past, I struggled to put Miss Purvis in either of our cots or, for that matter, upright in any space anywhere in this dormitory in which she had once maintained the brave front of her tremulous authority. But the mystery of the lost lady of Briggs was never solved.

Now it was couples the college employed as administrative representatives in the residence halls which, although incorporated into Houses, were not directly supervised by House Masters: these, or at least the wives, were apparently meant to provide the young women of Radcliffe not with surrogate mothers or maiden aunts but with "role models," that stylish contemporary evocation: see what it is possible for a properly enlightened female maturity, even one that includes marriage, to look like; it needn't look like a *parent,* it can look like your marvelous young self, slim, blue-jeaned, even sexually viable. And the present resident tutor, as I think he was called, with his pencil-slim, blue-jeaned, for-all-purposes-viable child-wife occupied a little housekeeping apartment at the farthest end of the first-floor corridor where supervision of the students' comings and goings was manifestly not a factor in their location. I am not suggesting that this nice pair now *in loco non-parentis* in Briggs was not regularly on hand for the students. In actual fact, if one or the other of them was out of sight for even a few hours, there was every likelihood that he, or more usually she, was entertaining the more exigent residents of the hall in their little kitchen where the oven was in constant use to meet that ever-more-pressing present-day moral, social, and even political need of the young, the baking of bread. One day when nothing of moment was going on in the dormitory, no party or dance, nothing festive, I caught a glimpse of the tutor's wife stealing into the living room to deposit a big chocolate cake and some tins of fruit punch, just so, no thanks asked for or given. There was no doubt she had herself baked the cake—in that small body there was a large-hearted girl. And this had of course also been at once apparent in the warm welcome she had extended to my husband and myself, in rather marked contrast to the tense restraint of the Radcliffe authority at its summit. To be sure, I had not asked permission of the president for my stay: if I was to be free to write as I wished, I wanted to avoid official obligation, and I could understand this might make the administration uneasy. But I had been unprepared for the president to be sufficiently annoyed so that she couldn't conceal her displeasure. As opposed to her quick reprimand not alone of me but even of those who had assisted me in my invasion of a student universe as open as it could conceivably be short of advertising for tourists, the behavior of the young couple in charge at Briggs was all kindliness and modest hospitality. In fact, the wife of the pair eventually went so far in support of my investigations—or perhaps it was only in identification with the students in the hall—as to give me an interview too; in both tone and substance it was hardly to be distinguished from the accounts given me of their lives by the undergraduates for whom she and her husband were the resident examples of college-certified maturity. By the time of her interview, however, I was well past the stage of worrying whether the students would talk to me. Was there anyone of this student generation who could resist the chance to talk about him- or herself, and not merely to someone willing to listen but into a tape recorder, perhaps even for publication?

Probably it was fortunate that it was a fairly dry spring, this spring of my return to Radcliffe, so that it wasn't until June and the day of my return to New York that grime, sweat, and even oozing mud were added to the picture of my old college this many years after my own undergraduate days. Suppose what would be normal enough at the beginning of April, there had been heavy rain the morning of my arrival and that it had then turned wet-warm in the mid-afternoon, so that I had emerged from the taxi which brought us to Briggs to confront a quadrangle running with delicious rich brown mud and to be greeted by the sight which in fact bade me farewell two months later: a dozen boys and girls—actually there was only one girl in the line, the rest were boys—dressed in normal college attire, hands clasped, tearing again and again down the length of what had once been a hockey field, racing in a long slithering curve, slapping down the viscous grass, until at last they dove, one on top of the other, into the glorious mud-hole they were contriving for themselves; with enough perseverance it would soon be of a size to accommodate a whole company of camera-mad buffalo. Irresistibly I thought, "Fifteen apparitions have I seen, the worst a mud-coated herd of undergraduates." But no, the reference had really little to do with my emotions as I stood watching this mud-play and was far from a reliable clue to the feelings which I'd been juggling, day after day all these weeks, only to reach a state of near confoundment about the present-day college student, at least at my own college. Who were these boys and this girl, who were these young men and this young woman who, after this many weeks of acquaintance, were still so mysterious to me that I could no more foretell their cavortings than their seriousness, or trust myself to know the difference between their frolicsomeness and their outrage? And it wasn't they who put this unmanageable distance between themselves and me; on the contrary, if anyone was doing the distancing, it was I, exhausted by the wild ups and downs of response they provoked in me, as acute as the fever course of a sick child. Indeed some of my chief instructors in the way they combined innocence and guile, insolence and delicacy, resulting in such wearing alternations of irritation and affection, of distaste and sympathy were out there today engineering this all–too–appropriate leave-taking. During my visit, whenever I had time between interviews, I took notes and I find in my notebook the following:

I must catch in anything I write about these students the fierce alternations I feel between an aching tenderness for them, on the one hand, and, on the other, my annoyance and especially my boredom. How they do bore me much of the time! These young people are so full of themselves, sometimes I think it's all they *are* full of, but then I wonder if it is fair to say this as if it described only this generation. Isn't it always true of the young, and why one seldom wants to return to one's own youth, that they are so unduly and dully full only of themselves? Yet fair or unfair, boredom is one of my pervasive emotions, chiefly provoked by the presumably most highly developed of them, the girls who knew they had it made even before the great hand had been laid upon them and they had been accepted at Radcliffe. I try to tell them that in my day you picked Radcliffe out of a telephone book, Radcliffe didn't pick you, but they think I'm being funny; they can't imagine a world in which they didn't have their superior destiny. What destiny? Where are they heading, these brilliant and self-conscious ones who are all hard-edged confidence and condescension? Then suddenly, just as I am about to join the shooting squad, the scene changes abruptly, though often retaining the same cast, and there is an encounter such as my conversation in the Briggs living room last night just as a house dance was being started, and I am undone by a pain of love for anything this vulnerable. There must have been ten of us of both sexes sitting around in a circle, and we began to talk about

Anaïs Nin's lecture in Cambridge the other evening which most of us, myself included, had attended—I hadn't realized how much of a cult figure she was for the rock generation. She had come on like an evangelist, demure dress, demure flowers, eyes of unusual width and brightness, or so it seemed to me from my distance, the full hypnotic equipment. Her following was so large that the Harvard building where she'd been originally scheduled to speak wasn't big enough to take the crowd and the occasion had been switched to a church on Mass. Ave. where she got a standing ovation. In her lecture Miss Nin had urged the young women in the audience to a more bounteous life by telling them they must create out of their "feminine secrecy." Back in Briggs last evening I remark of such talk that I deplore it, consider it suffocating in its narcissism. I give it as my opinion that women, like other human creatures, should direct their sensibility outward, to the world of social and human fact. For some reason that defies me, this launches us on a world tour of happy speculation; what, among men students, used to be called a bull session. Could I possibly have released them to the external universe? If any subject offers even a semblance of interest it becomes ours: natural law and the nature of fantasy; sex and imagination; genetics; the sources and meaning of leadership; penis envy; womb envy—does the latter really exist, as Margaret Mead has maintained and as I do not? The young men in the group turned out to be dedicated spirits, committed to giving women a fair show and to helping in the solution of their special "problem." But their sympathy constantly verges on self-eradication; they want assertion on *behalf* of women but are they themselves prepared to assert, to *do* an asserting, or only to sacrifice, surrender? I long to talk with them about this but I feel it might be tactless; it might sound like a sexual challenge. In the meanwhile the noise from the dance in the dining room is becoming horrendous: I frown and one of the boys smiles at me divinely and says, "Gee, you're going to be sorry to leave here." He intends no irony, and I am melted out of my mind.

My mind-melter is not among the mud herd now, on the eve of my departure, but I can be sure he is both represented and contradicted, or something between the two, by my student buffaloes. I stand on the terrace of Briggs watching the antics and I see that the lone girl in the line has all at once caught sight of me; I see her quick defensiveness as she nudges the boy next to her, calling me to his attention. Although I have interviewed neither of these two, I have been as aware of them as they of me, particularly of the boy who I surmise is hurt because I haven't invited him to participate in my blessed "research"; I have no formulated reason for having deliberately avoided an interview with him but instinct warns me to cooperate in his sardonic reserve and not disturb whatever it is he is trying to hide with his mechanical ironies. Now, alerted to the alien in their midst, he looks toward me for a charged second; then too elaborately, almost rudely, he shrugs his shoulders in indication that I am to be eliminated from their calculations; I don't figure. Yet when their play is over and he and half his dripping herd come clomping onto the terrace of Briggs within inches of me, against his own resolution he is impelled to address me.

"Are you going to put this in your book too?" he asks, his tone a poor mix of indifference and defiance. He has no flesh on him. He shivers in his caking of mud like an exhausted Channel swimmer in his coating of oil, and it takes considerable effort for me to put on a show of indifference equal to his and not hustle him off to a hot tub.

"Why not?" It is now my turn to shrug my shoulders. Without further comment he moves into the dormitory, leaving me wretched.

But to return to how my visit had really begun and how the dormitory quadrangle looked when I arrived in sweetest April sunshine, the sunshine of late afternoon in a place which is not one's own but to which one has ties of remembrance. A first glance around me as I stepped from the taxi startled me not only because of the presence of males on this once unsullied ground—for this I was prepared—nor even because the students of both sexes were so remarkably unkempt, males and females alike seeming to compete to destroy the body as an object of visual pleasure, the men with folded handkerchiefs or neckties bound around their foreheads, their beards uncombed and their torsos naked, their shoeless feet and legs, none too clean, jutting out of freshly torn trousers or shorts, and the young women, with covered torsos, doing their utmost to be indistinguishable from the men. For me the most dramatically new note was the quality of the intersexual companionship in itself, the ease and casualness with which the men and the girls seemed to have come together as the wish took them rather than in the ordered sexual confrontations of my own day, here a few girls enjoying the sun alone or together, without benefit of male partners, there a spattering of men alone or in pairs or groups, and yet somewhere else a couple locked in embrace; there was even a coeducational volleyball game in progress, obviously organized with an entire freedom from sexual coercion or constraint. This was of course a first quick impression. In the next weeks my sense of this new blissful relaxation would be often enough overturned, and I would have reason to recall D. H. Lawrence's remark upon all programmatic freedom: "Men [and women too, he might have added] are freest when they are most unconscious of freedom. The shout is a rattling of chains, always was." Certainly "ease" was scarcely the word which would spring to my lips to describe the relation of the sexes at Harvard and Radcliffe as I came to know something of the endemic isolateness of Cambridge undergraduate life, the extreme paucity even of warm association let alone of friendship, the endless dismal straining for self-definition by young men and women who on the surface, especially the women, seemed so enormously assured. In interview after interview the Harvard students who, last year when the possibility had been offered them, had elected to transfer to Radcliffe dormitories instead of remaining in their old all-male strongholds at Harvard gave me the same explanation for the move: loneliness. Girls were friendlier, in their opinion, and they had moved to Radcliffe halls for friendship. And had they got what they came for? Ah, here was the rub: not one I spoke to had got what he came for even when he had got more than he had before. Whether it was a Harvard

or a Radcliffe student to whom I put my questions about
friendship, always I was given the same terrifying report of an
empty world. Radcliffe students with roommates found no
cure of their own affliction which was also the affliction of
those with whom they lived so closely. Radcliffe girls and
Harvard men who went to bed together seemed to be solaced
not at all in their painful sense of nonconnection—theirs was
indeed a generation for which coupling worked no union. In
the matter of course offerings, Harvard is noted for being a
great smorgasbord table, spreading countless delights for its
students, often an undigestible banquet, but emotionally its
students were starving. It could be that this is so everywhere
today, at every college including Columbia and Barnard on
whose borders I live, but I was taking testimony at Radcliffe,
at Harvard, and among the students of Radcliffe and Harvard
there was famine in the midst of an overwhelming plenty. The
scene I had encountered upon arrival was thus wholly an illusion. Where once, in my own day, there had been an empty
quadrangle, naked space rather than naked bodies, there
might now be the look of an abundant male-female companionship triumphant over our old cruel laws of sexual separation, and the illusion was at first convincing enough for me to
wonder if it mattered that the once soft green lawn around
which the dormitories were ranged was no longer green, no
longer even a lawn but only a stretch of roughly mown field
punctuated with bare swatches of earth where the grass had
given up its claim to survival. After all, what price the prim
aesthetic achievement of a fine lawn as against the richly ex-
foliating joys of human connection? For a few brief moments I
was seduced, I had the comforting assurance of progress:
where there was this much free companionship between the
sexes, there too one would find other improvements over the
life I had known as a student, other good portents of the
future. I had not yet learned to put everything to question.

But the day had not passed before I had my first lesson in
the pitfalls of hasty conclusion. Scarcely unpacked, I had come

out to sit in the communal living room of the hall and fallen
into conversation with a student of whom I inquired about
something that had caught my eye near the entrance to the
dormitory, some rubbish piled on the field awaiting collection.
Why, I asked, had this unseemly mess been left open instead
of being stowed in bags, boxes, refuse cans, whatever it is in
which the detritus of housekeeping is usually hidden? And
why had it not been collected: was Cambridge having a sani-
tation strike? The giggling answer was that what I had seen
wasn't rubbish. There was no strike. This spread of old
scarves, discolored T-shirts, filthy torn sneakers, stained bu-
reau runners, unusable curtains, frayed brassieres and under-
pants, and broken-down boots—I had now of course gone out
to look at it for a second time—was a dormitory giveaway.
The residents of the halls had put out on the field the things
they no longer wanted but which other students might have
use for; what I had observed was a considered act of virtue on
the part of the (dominantly middle-class) student population.
I couldn't have been more shaken—how could anyone in direst
poverty use anything this disreputable? Was it from discards
such as these that the contributors meant their fellow-students
to take their pick and, if so, what did this imply of disrespect
even for themselves, not to mention those to whom their ill-
conditioned generosity was directed? I think back to a year my
husband and I had spent in Oxford when one evening during
the first week of our stay, preparing dinner, I had suddenly
understood that the elderly live-in caretaker of the house we
had been given, a retired college servant who stood watching
me trim and discard the great slabs of fat which the butcher
had left on a leg of lamb, wasn't interested in my strange
foreign ways in a kitchen but longed for the grease I had cut
away. She was badly paid, I would soon find out, but it was
not lack of funds, it was class-bred ignorance of how to use the
money she did have for food that made her want the lamb fat
I threw away; throughout the week the only meat or meat
product she and her husband ate was their Sunday steak-and-

kidney pie; but every afternoon, at tea, they had pastries from the local Lyons bakeshop. Was there, I wondered, validity in the parallel I was inclined to draw between this caretaker's distribution of her funds for food and what struck me as an equally class-derived manifestation of how the students at Radcliffe allocated their funds of fellow-feeling? Nothing could have made a less appealing, a more alienating reintroduction to my old college but I admonished myself that if I had it in mind to cultivate emotions which would so decisively separate me from the students among whom I would be living for the rest of the semester, I had had available to me a more direct means of accomplishing it: I could have stayed home. Once again, but this time on the score of adversary judgment, I cautioned myself against premature conclusions.

Yet the days went on and now I not only had as many interviews as I could handle, I also made notes and the making of notes quickly goes beyond its first purpose, to remind one of what might otherwise be forgotten; it takes on a life of its own; as one writes, observation plus speculation yield to certainty. It was at the start of my stay, for instance, that I made explicit, and permanent, my ambivalence about the students, the conviction that there could be no escape from the tension between the favorable and unfavorable responses they aroused in me. It was from the start too that I allowed myself the opinion—and both these early perceptions were to stay, finally, at the core of my Radcliffe "findings"—that as compared with my wearying but eventually not unpleasant conflicts of feeling about the students, my response to the "authority" of the college, that force, at once so concrete and abstract, which governs the life of institutions, was hard, unitary, and only unhappy. For, put baldly, I had no idea of what this college thought it was up to. I didn't understand what this particularly celebrated institution of higher education proposed to accomplish or what it *had* accomplished on which it congratulated itself so ardently, encouraging its students in a quite unparalleled self-admiration. And without knowing what

the institution wanted, other of course than to stand for whatever is certified as most forward-looking in contemporary culture, how could I know what it was that the students were
coping with without help or how they would react were they
to have the institutional direction I felt they should be given
and—so I thought—sought? A story related to me by a Radcliffe
student I interviewed was no doubt told me far too early in
my visit; it had an ineradicable effect on me, becoming a kind
of magnetic pole of adverse assessment. The girl who told it to
me was very young. The previous year, for the better part of a
semester, she had spent many nighttime hours curled up on a
library chair or sitting on the steps of her dormitory corridor in
order not to have to hear her black roommate and the roommate's boyfriend making love in the bunk above her own. And
when at last her parents had got to know what was troubling
her and asked the college to change her room, the administration replied that the situation would be remedied at the end of
the term: room changes weren't made in mid-semester. The
year was a year of extreme black separatism in the university.
Even an outsider like myself was able to persuade only one
black member of the college community, a woman tutor of no
intellectual gift but of some personal courage, to cross the
fiercely guarded color line to speak to me. In the Currier
dining hall where I took most of my meals I never saw a
racially mixed table; once or twice, when I ventured to take
my tray to a table held by blacks but only half-occupied, I was
unable to enter their conversation. All of this is to say that I
was aware of the difficulties which confronted the administration in handling the racial problem. But what is a college
saying to its students about equality, justice, the courage of
one's decencies if it quietly folds before threat, permitting a
student to suffer the aggression directed against this girl? And
what is it saying about sex?

Slowly, after not one dozen but several dozen interviews
with young men and women of widely differing social and
family background, I learned how false was my initial assump-

tion that the Radcliffe-Harvard coeducational life was a newly invigorating nourishment of the young human spirit and that it was not only in the mind of someone like myself, whose ideas about sex must obviously be a Victorian relic, that it was possible for doubt to arise about the ultimate usefulness of side-by-side bathing and toileting, and the abolition of all hindrances to student coupling. In possession of even minimal first-hand knowledge of the sexual sterility into which the students were being inducted, I had to ask myself how, except in answer to their wishful thought, the authorities of the college who had these young people in daily view could suppose their sexual experience was a happy one? Or to be more immediate: how, except by refusing to question the dreary instrumentalism in which she had been schooled, could Radcliffe's sex counselor have failed to discover and disseminate the difficult truth that sexual fulfillment involves something more than institutional permission for the sexes to cohabit? Still young, I should guess in her early thirties, Radcliffe's sex counselor was not a college employee. The students themselves had engaged her out of their own scant funds to aid and comfort them in dilemmas as old as the college itself, and always new, new as the creation of her office. It couldn't surprise me, it was only a sorrow when it wasn't an anger, that this young woman's expertness lay in her dedication to Masters and Johnson whose opinions on female biology in relation to the female sexual emotions she was determined to establish as indisputable doctrine for her young clients. Of all the interviews I recorded on my Radcliffe visit, hers alone so assaulted me with its arrogant confidence that I precipitously broke it off for fear of losing my temper.

The 1969 uprising on the Harvard campus only two years in back of us—this had been the disruption which Harvard's Archibald Cox, called to New York the previous year to head a so-called fact-finding team on the Columbia insurrection, had said would not be possible at Harvard where the life style was so much superior to that of Columbia—it was striking that apart from the racial issue, which announced itself only in attitude, not in disruptive acts, the college was as politically serene as I found it. I am not suggesting that it was untouched by politics past but there was no discernible organization for political action and only the most formalized political talk: Harvard too had been overtaken by the new quietism of the Left which had all at once descended on the American campus; the college was unruffled by the April antiwar march to Washington in which many Harvard and Radcliffe students joined. But it seemed to me that a corollary of this new peaceableness on the part of the students was their new passivity, what psychoanalysis might perceive as a marked diminution of ego drive. This will-lessness appeared to be much more a male than a female phenomenon. It was nevertheless only among the blacks—or so I was told—that it was met with female resistance. The young white women at Radcliffe gave every sign of acceding in the loss of will of their male companions even while they retained much of their own energy of assertion although for the present they applied it chiefly to their special female concerns as citizens and as members of the academic community; of the girls if not of the men one felt that should an occasion arise in which political activity were invited, they still had the potential for politicalization. It was not that the two sexes were divided in political outlook as much as that for the Harvard students of left-wing persuasion their personalities seemed to be more of a piece with their principles. They rejected the society in which they lived, refused to compete for its advantages or subscribe to its middle-class values of ambition and success, and in making this choice they had a political, or perhaps it was only a cultural, rationalization for the retraction of personal effort, a justification for indolence. The young women of left-wing sympathies might give assent to a similar cultural-political line, but it apparently didn't preclude their desire for achievement; they mobilized a considerable degree of discipline in their schoolwork despite their principled aversion from a society which rewards the good grades they strove for. They were thus less consistent, less whole-minded, than their male opposite numbers; or perhaps they constituted a case of female activity moving into the vacuum created by a sudden pervasive male inactivity. Ever since, many years before, separate Radcliffe instruction had been abandoned and Radcliffe undergraduates had begun to attend classes jointly with Harvard undergraduates, there had been complaint at Harvard that the girls made things hard for the men; they worked more and were better in their work. Nothing I saw on my visit suggested that this state of affairs had altered. But according to information given me by faculty friends, among the blacks actual strain was developing between the sexes because the women felt that their men had insufficient ambition and aggressivity, so that it even occurred to me to speculate whether it was a dressing-down from his girlfriend that had inspired a black Harvard student to protest, as he did one night, the condition of the Currier dining room floor—indecent slop, he accurately and furiously called it. As a matter of fact, I had myself been aware that at every meal, within an hour after the doors opened, a river of unheeded spillings splashed around the counters where milk, tea, and coffee, also a remarkable daily variety of fruit drinks, were served. This, however, was the single reproach of the students' carelessness of their environment—and how distinctive a feature of present-day college life it is!—that I would hear throughout my visit.

But to speak of anything that pertains to Currier House is to be more forcefully reminded of the mad luxury of this newest of Radcliffe dormitories than of its students' lack of thought for its upkeep; or perhaps the two aren't to be separated. When I speak of luxury I'm not even thinking of the beautiful May morning when I was present at so different a giveaway than the one which had greeted me on my arrival at Briggs: the philanthropy at Currier was a free offering of all the champagne one could drink as accompaniment to strawberry breakfast. Somewhere in this house there were of course children of poverty, some of them blacks, and children of the financially constrained middle class, and I wondered what these young people who came from homes where money didn't grow on fathers made of such lavishness; but I tried to give the college the benefit of the doubt of its wisdom by deciding that it had simply, unthinkingly, borrowed the traditional strawberry ritual of Oxford and trimmed it up with champagne. No, I had a worse charge than this against Currier which stemmed from the way in which it had translated what, in an earlier Radcliffe time, had been the quiet warmth and charm of the common rooms of Barnard Hall or Briggs Hall, with their soft-colored walls and pretty pictures, their nicely upholstered sofas and chairs, their chintz curtains and pleasant rugs, into the glaring panoply of color and metal of the interior decoration of this newest residence hall, and then added to this primary ostentation of taste the ostentation of personal indulgence, the wild elaboration of "conveniences" which the hall seemed to regard as necessary to the well-being of its inhabitants. There were three girls, intimate friends, in Currier—I call them Carrie, Betty, and Annie in order of age, Carrie being the youngest and a freshman—who asked to be interviewed together, and what follows is taken from one of my extended sessions with this trio:

D.T. But you were talking about the conveniences of Currier. Tell me about the kitchens.

BETTY. Why don't we start first with our suite?

ANNIE. Well, Betty and I have this suite. There are two on the floor, but one of them has a tutor in it, and we've got the other one: two bedrooms and a hallway, and then across from the bedrooms our own bathroom.

D.T. How did you rate this?

BETTY. Sheer luck.

D.T. They're not more expensive?

ANNIE. No, it's crazy. Partially it's because Currier House was brand-new this year and a lot of people came in over the summer. Well, in the hall there's a large common kitchen and then we have a smaller kitchen in our suite, with a small refrigerator and a three-burner stove, and an oven and a sink and quite a bit of shelf space.

D.T. Now you're talking about the great big—

ANNIE. No, our own private kitchen.

D.T. Your private kitchen has that?

ANNIE. Oh, sure. And then in the corridor there's a large kitchen with a full-size refrigerator and tables and chairs and sofas and things. Six big cabinets. And there are other private kitchens, distinct from the corridor kitchens: three of them, and they have rooms that are fifteen or maybe twenty-five feet square. They're kept locked but you can get the key any time you want. They've got service for about twenty-five or thirty people. They've got large living rooms with three or four sofas, a large table, several little tea table type of things, and lots of armchair type of things. And beautiful rugs and tables that are pullout leaf tables. They can pull out to about twenty-four, otherwise they seat about eight.

BETTY. And a locked bar. (*Laughter*)

ANNIE. I haven't figured it out because if you open the drawer to the locked bar you find there's a key in it and you find out that the bar is empty. And the kitchen has all the glassware you need, probably two dozen wine glasses and two dozen water glasses; they have large eight-ounce tumblers and four-ounce tumblers. Salad plates. You know, very well equipped.

D.T. Um.

ANNIE. Just incredible amounts, lots of pans, complete silverware, steak knives. An electric coffee pot. A huge decanter for coffee and round pitchers that are huge, and trays, dish towels—

BETTY.   All probably from Design Research.

ANNIE.   Oh yes, everything you need in a kitchen and in good taste. Mats, and you can get other things, linens, if you ask for them.

CARRIE.   Oh, you can? How lovely!

D.T.   I gather that you've had a party there and I'll come back to that in a minute. But now tell me, you say you have kitchens upstairs that are available to all of you, as well as the kind the two of you have in your own suite. What's done in these kitchens? Do you skip meals in the dining halls and make your own? Or are they just for snacks?

ANNIE.   Some people do. There's a lot of dessert-type things: brownies, cookies, cakes. And there's a lot of birthday cakes made.

D.T.   Someone said something to me about there being a man on one of the corridors who's always baking bread.

CARRIE.   Two girls on my floor bake bread.

BETTY.   It happens.

D.T.   And suppose somebody bakes a loaf of bread. When does it get eaten?

ANNIE.   Between meals. I've skipped meals and eaten later there. And I'll every once in a while miss breakfast and I can't operate without feeding my stomach, so I have to cook something if I'm going to get up before noon.

D.T.   Are you allowed to take things from the dining rooms to use up there? For instance, could you take a couple of raw eggs and bread?

ANNIE.   You're not supposed to but if you don't go to extremes nobody says no. If you take two eggs, nobody will say anything. If you take two quarts of milk they'll probably nab you and say don't.

D.T.   Do you ever have tea parties? Is tea something you drink around here?

ANNIE.   There's a good deal of snob value about tea, about different kinds of tea. I like this kind of tea versus that kind of tea. In fact, most of my friends know a fair amount about tea. I mean it's something that they drink all the time, much more than coffee.

BETTY.   Yeah, but the thing is that coffee you can't quite do that with. I mean, discussing whether you like Yuban or Chock Full O'Nuts or percolated or what.

ANNIE.   Yes, you can. You could talk about Turkish and all that kind of thing.

BETTY.   I suppose so. It depends. But tea is usually—if people stop by during the afternoon or in the evening, I'll make a pot of tea and I usually ask what kind of tea they want.

D.T.   And your kitchen has a tea set supplied by the house?

BETTY.   No. I bought it. Our kitchen came with nothing in it, actually.

ANNIE.   Two ice trays. Actually most people will serve coffee or tea or something even if they have only a little bit of room. I mean, some kind of hospitality is offered.

D.T.   What about drinks?

BETTY.   Liquor? Oh, yes.

ANNIE.   I took a bottle of port upstairs. And I have a small bottle of wine in case something happens—

D.T.   That was going to be my next question. Do you ever have wine parties?

ANNIE.   Oh, it's the type of thing where a friend of mine got an honor and he just showed up and said, hey, guess what! Well, two of us were there and so we had a bottle of wine. And then I have a friend, a boyfriend, I don't know how to describe him, who lives in New York. When he comes up we usually have something.

D.T.   Now tell me about that package I keep eyeing so curiously. You bought something special for some special purpose,

I gather. Obviously it fills some terrible crying need in Currier House. (*Laughter*)

ANNIE. Well, I like cooking with this friend from New York and when he comes up I usually take over one of those big kitchens for the weekend.

D.T. What do you mean, you take it over? You take it all over?

ANNIE. Well, no, I just use it Friday and Saturday and Sunday.

D.T. You mean one of the downstairs party kitchens?

ANNIE. Right. And that way, if you buy food you can leave it in the refrigerator and nobody eats it.

D.T. So just for the two of you, you have this twenty-four-person service available?

ANNIE. Right. That is a little presumptuous, I suppose. But gee whiz, when I'm cooking two or three meals a day—I mean, if you sign up for dinner you sign up from three o'clock in the afternoon till midnight.

D.T. What is your impression, that these rooms are always in use?

ANNIE. No, I'd say that, of the three kitchens, there are probably fifteen days a week that they're in use. In other words, there's six that go unused.

CARRIE. Fifteen kitchen-days per week.

ANNIE. An incredible number of people just use them for an afternoon, or they just use them for dinner, for something or other.

D.T. What about cocktail or sherry parties?

ANNIE. Sherry or wine parties, or cheese parties.

CARRIE. And dances.

D.T. There's enough room to dance in the living room?

BETTY. Oh, yeah. A room like thirty feet long and fifteen feet wide—

D.T.   And you all know how to cook?

ANNIE.   There must be some Radcliffe girls who don't. You have to make a kind of distinction about cooking because there's following the cookbook recipe which is basically your high school chemistry approach to cooking, which is pretty much what I use, and then there's Betty's type of cooking: well, I guess I'll look at the recipe, but I'll change this, this, and this. And it's a real difference. I think probably most Radcliffe girls know how to use chemistry-cookbooks like *The Joy of Cooking*. That's a favorite cookbook here.

D.T.   Did you know that the first female rock group was called "The Joy of Cooking"? They were the first ones to be successful in getting a cross-country tour. It isn't all women either; three of them are men but the two girls got it started. That's an important breakthrough because there's never been any successful female group in rock music, it's an absolutely male-dominated activity in this country. But now let's get back to your package. Is it some kind of coffeepot? (*Laughter*)

ANNIE.   Right, it's a coffeepot. The thing is, if you have a dinner party and you have a coffeepot that serves twenty-five, you feel pretty stupid putting the coffee into it. You know, four cups of coffee. And so I wanted a small coffeepot that was silver or something—

D.T.   Why did it have to be silver?

ANNIE.   Well, I wanted it to be nice so that it could be on the table. And I didn't think I was going to be able to manage anything financially much more than Pyrex or something like that.

D.R.   But why not Pyrex or something of that sort? Is this your own standard or one that other people share with you?

ANNIE.   It's probably my standard.

D.T.   But then aren't you being idiosyncratic to your culture? Aren't you doing something symbolical here (*all the girls chuckle*), something that you intend to be subversive of the general radical preference of the student body?

ANNIE. I think it probably has nothing to do with that. It's just that my family likes collecting dishes, coffeepots, glassware of various sorts. We figured it up once that with all the dishes in our family we could probably serve a hundred and fifty people at one time. Appetizers, dinner, dessert, and, you know, water and wine and liqueur of some sort. This was with silverware and so forth to match. Oh, it's just, you know, a collecting habit, and I'm used to crystal and Spode and so forth and I don't like Pyrex, unless it's a casserole.

D.T. Okay, so it's your standard. But surely you must have some awareness that this doesn't exactly go with the life of torn jeans and unbuttoned shirts.

ANNIE. I wear jeans because they have pockets in them.

The interview had continued with my asking what, in the opinion of this Spode collector and her friends, made the dominant political culture of the college and with my being a bit testily answered that there was no dominant political culture at Radcliffe—"it's just a very diverse kind of thing," said Annie, not entirely honestly as she would herself indicate a few days later when I was talking to her at lunch and she bitterly denounced the "by rote" anti-Nixon, anti-Kissinger sentiment of most of her schoolmates. If her earlier crassness rang true, this hint of her political direction rang true no less.

But it was not the politics of any individual student which interested me or even her personal predilection for silver coffeepots; it was the space the college offered her for the exercise of this latter preference that troubled me. For were the elaborations of Currier House not a curious encouragement to—what should I call it?—consumerism and the bourgeois life for a reputedly liberal college to give its students? After all, Radcliffe was one among many of our educational institutions which only a year before had suspended classes for a week so that its students could protest the Cambodian invasion and work for their favored political candidates. Yet here, in its newest residence hall, there was this plethora of kitchens, dining equipment, private eating rooms! What did this represent if not the indulgence of impulses deeply at variance with the general movement of present-day student idealism and the official sanction which was given this idealism? Did it not have about it much to remind us of the "penthouse radicalism" of the thirties and the "radical chic" of our present moment? Granted that it was agreeable for students to have dormitory kitchens in which they could prepare food for themselves, and reasonable of the college to provide some sort of cooking facility on each floor of a new hall: was it reasonable for the students in this hall—and this hall alone, by the way—to have no fewer than three entire apartments at their private disposal, each with a handsome living room and a kitchen equipped to the last middle-class detail of glassware, cooking and serving utensils, linens, all for the entertainment of a student's friends to the number of twenty-four? There were modest student houses close to the dormitory quadrangle where girls lived cooperatively, preparing their meals instead of using the college cafeterias. Several times I had been invited to a meal in one of them and found the arrangement not only attractive but consistent with liberal administrative policy inasmuch as it permitted students the means to live more cheaply. But for a liberal administration to countenance the privilege of Currier House struck me as a failure of both social understanding and pedagogic reliability.

Yet how was I to raise these or any of my doubts about contemporary Radcliffe with its president when at long last we managed, certainly not an interview, but a brief encounter? Of President Bunting as a private person I knew and know nothing. Of her public academic performance I had surmised, even before my visit, that she was a woman with a marked readiness to meet the future: she was cheerfully presiding over the disappearance of Radcliffe into the great male university which was once only its sibling institution. I also knew what is not unallied to the sentiment of progress, the informality of her relation with her undergraduates. From the limited experience of my return to Radcliffe it could be nothing but impertinence for me to confront her with the social and political anomalies, as I saw them, of the present-day college. And as for my voicing my opinion that the sole future which awaited her students was one which, notably independent of their specific schooling, would be shaped by an unpredictable combination of genetic, familial, economic, and political-cultural accidents, obviously this was no more than I would have had to say of myself and *my* contemporaries, thereby bringing into dispute the very concept of progress, perhaps even the very concept of institutional education and its much-honored formative powers.

It was already June when this meeting took place. Carrying sandwiches for our lunch, as it had been suggested we do, we had both of us, President Bunting and I, attended the showing of a film about life at Harvard and Radcliffe produced by a pair of Harvard undergraduates in the Visual Studies Department. Then, searching my mind for comfortable ground on which to establish a long-delayed amenity, I accompanied the president to her office. Naturally enough, I wanted to discuss the impressions of my stay. I was conscious, however, that propriety dictated the avoidance even of subjects which, though essentially abstract, bore upon decisions in which the president had had a share.

For instance, I should have wanted to say that if it had indeed been her particular historical function to preside over the disappearance of Radcliffe and if this fate was an economic inevitability, I should have preferred that the grim practical fact be acknowledged gravely and unequivocally rather than that the death of Radcliffe be chalked up as yet another of its landmark achievements. Why encourage women in the self-deception that, in merging a once-proud female college into the male institution with which it had for so long coexisted while at the same time retaining its own identity, something awesome and beautiful had been accomplished for our sex?

Or I should have wished to say that although Radcliffe no doubt had more ground than I recognized for thinking of itself as the best women's college in the world, I was not only far from certain it had ever been the best women's college in the world; I was also far from sure that any educational institution could be even indisputably good, let alone best—was it not Freud who had pronounced three things impossible of successful accomplishment: to legislate, to educate, and to rear children?

Well, talk like this was patently impossible. But there was also little promise of agreement on less theoretical aspects of college life. For example, in the course of my visit my attention had been drawn to the wide disparity among the various kinds of instruction by which a student earned credits toward a degree. It was expectable enough that there should be inequality among the teachers in a department, one professor being more scholarly or stimulating than another. But there had newly proliferated on the campus shockingly lax peripheral teaching within what had once been a rigorous system of "tutorials"; "house courses" were now available which, though they gave credit equal to the regular departmental offerings, were outside direct serious control by the departments to which they were presumed to belong. Too, there had been a marked shift, since my own college time, from a historical to a nonhistorical emphasis in instruction, to the point where the students I interviewed were, with few exceptions, unable to come, say, within twenty-five years of naming the dates of the French Revolution. I had no reason to suppose that the student of classical or medieval history was ignorant of basic historical facts such as these in his special field of study; it was the nonhistorians, many of them staunchly left-wing in their politics, who gave sign of almost total ignorance of the historical background and source of their beliefs. In evidence I could present the series of questions pertaining to recent or not-so-recent history which I had taken to asking everyone I interviewed: one such question had pertained to the Spanish Civil War; no student I interviewed seemed even to have heard of it. I had recounted this to a reporter on the *Independent,* a Harvard newspaper, and an article about my experience had appeared which provoked such anger among the students that I came to feel like Malcolm Muggeridge criticizing the British queen. Among those loud in their rage, one Radcliffe undergraduate had at least the fortitude to accept my suggestion that instead of railing at me on the telephone she come to see me in Briggs and convince me that my criticism was unfounded. The poor girl appeared at my room swollen with sullen fury.

"Perhaps my report was unfair to you," I apologized. "I was generalizing from a random sample of students and I could have been mistaken in your instance." I prodded, in fact all but pleaded with her to put me in the wrong. "You do know about the Spanish Civil War?"

"I don't know much," her words were concessive but her voice was not, "but I do know enough to know it was our fault!"

This was no different in kind, however, from the historical morass in which the students had floundered in a house seminar in which I joined one evening in the first week of my return. The seminar, held in a dormitory living room and conferring full credit, dealt with writing by and about American women and, the evening I attended, the book being discussed was Mary McCarthy's *The Company She Keeps.* In view of the fact that Miss McCarthy's book had first appeared in 1942 and I had not read it in the intervening years, I had warned the instructor who invited me to the class, one of the two teachers in charge, that I would only listen, not talk. But I had not then imagined a literature class in which there would be so little note given the historical context of the work under examination, indeed no note at all. The evening began with a student's prepared discussion of Miss McCarthy's stories—everyone referred to the book, erroneously, as a novel—as an investigation of the "identity crisis" of its heroine. The two

teachers expanding upon this report soon made it torturingly
plain that neither of them was equipped to supply the students
with even the roughest summary of a political-cultural background for the book: what Miss McCarthy's country and world
had been like in the thirties. The Great Depression of that
decade, the radicalization of the American intellectual classes,
Roosevelt's New Deal, the NRA and the WPA, the struggle for
power in Germany and the refusal of the Communists to make
a united front with the Social Democrats, which had given
Hitler his victory, the civil war in Spain, the Moscow trials
and purges, the unwillingness of so many liberal intellectuals
throughout the free world to admit the tyranny of Stalin's
rule—all of this which made the factual substructure of *The
Company She Keeps* was left unmentioned to a class which,
when I could no longer refrain from intervening, showed itself
to be hungry for the knowledge of which it was being deprived. Was I now to speak of experiences like these to the
president of the college? Was it for me to tell her that this
crème de la crème of American young womanhood had no idea
of how the world it inhabited had come to be as it was, only
the idea of its own superior place in that world? It was impermissible—and not only on grounds of courtesy but on grounds
of justice, since the Harvard students I had encountered both
in and outside this seminar had as little background as the students at Radcliffe for their criticism of contemporary society;
and it was a fair guess that if one made a survey of colleges
across the country it would yield the same conclusion.

I decided that my simplest recourse was to chat, speak
of things "merely" human such as the isolateness of students
today as compared to my college time. And so it was that I
came to report a conversation I had had with a young Radcliffe
woman about the possibility of awkwardness in the students'
use of the new coeducational bathrooms, an exchange which
had eventually led me to inquire, "But suppose you were sick,
suppose you were vomiting in one of these thin-partitioned

coeducational bathrooms of yours. Would whoever was in the next cubicle call in, do you think, and ask what was the matter? Have you ever had this happen?"

The girl nodded. "Nobody would pay any attention. I've had it happen." This was a serious girl, among the most trustworthy I had interviewed.

I had gone on. "Then is it sexual unself-consciousness *with* each other or nonsexual unconsciousness *of* each other that we are dealing with here? Does any of you care what happens to the other people in your dormitory, not as friends but simply as other human beings?"

The president's reassurance as I told her of this conversation came faster and more firmly than any I had had from my interviewees. The report I had been given was exaggerated and prejudiced, the president explained quickly. The Radcliffe student of 1971 couldn't be more thoughtful of her fellow students: only this very semester she had heard of a group undertaking in one of the residence halls to assist a dilatory senior in the completion of her honors thesis; of course there were always a few people in any residence hall who were unable to make friends but theirs was not a problem which one found multiplied in the Harvard-Radcliffe community. Her reply couldn't surprise me, nor was it necessary for her to add what I had known about before I returned to Cambridge, that everywhere the counterculture flattered itself precisely on its "humanity": college students, that is, sat up with each other during bad LSD trips. I had virtually by heart an exchange at my own dinner table in New York a few months earlier with a student at Columbia, my husband's college. This young man, son of acquaintances of ours, occasionally came to have a meal with us and this evening I'd inquired about his plans when he graduated.

"I don't think that way."

Believing that I had been misunderstood, I explained, "I mean, are you going on to graduate school?"

Not without impatience, my visitor repeated, "I don't think that way."

"I'm asking you how you intend to earn your living, or do you expect your father to go on supporting you?"

"I don't need much money. I earned my own living last summer in Europe."

"But you knew that if you didn't find work, you had your father to turn to."

"For a whole month I didn't even know where my father was."

"Oh, what matter?" Suddenly I was very angry. "You knew where we were, you knew where a dozen friends of your family were who'd always help you if you were in a jam for money." I had an important social message to transmit to this self-important young man. "That's the difference between you subversive middle-class kids and the poor. There are a dozen people to bail you out if you're in trouble but a working-class kid has no one!"

"I don't make my appeal to the middle class," was the cool rejoinder. Our young man wore his silky black hair uncommonly long, almost to his waist, and it was held at the base of his head with a barrette. "Wearing my hair this long is my entrance to my own class. It brings me friends wherever I go: the other people with long hair. We recognize each other."

Well, no doubt the counterculture did have this solidarity which the rest of us lacked. Why then didn't it offer *its* members relief from loneliness? Sitting up with your friends during a bad LSD trip didn't look to me like the total and lasting beneficence which warranted the risks involved in the use of the drug. My young friend whistled in the dark, indeed in blackest emotional midnight, like all the adherents of the counterculture I had ever talked with. He shared with the squarest of the Harvard and Radcliffe undergraduates whom I had interviewed this terrible loneliness of his generation. I thought back to my own college years: adolescence is inevitably a lonely time, it always was and it always would be. It is a time when one yearns for what seems to be unreachable: one has given up those powerful figures of the family romance and not yet found a substitute in a family life of one's own creation. Still, no one I had known at Radcliffe when I was a student had ever spoken of loneliness the way the students did today: there was always the girl next door, there were always the girls at your dinner table with whom you made conversation which paved the way for the development of intimacy if you wished it. What, I asked myself, had happened to us that our young were atomized to this degree?—the question had become obsessive. Why should young men and women who were voluble about "community" as we in my college day would never have thought to be, and who inhabited a society in which people talked about love, love, love as if they were advertising an anodyne for the sick soul, have to be instructed in the commonest notions of human awareness? In that great neglected book, *Hope Against Hope*, Nadezhda Mandelstam writes: "To some degree . . . we all had the temptation to rush after everyone else, to join the crowd that knew where it was going. The power of the 'general will' is enormous—to resist it is much harder than people think—and so we are all marked by the times we live in." She is speaking, of course, of politics but as in the life of politics, so in the life of feeling: the students of today rush after one another into emptiness. I talk with a freshman who has never had a date, yet she submits to the general will of her historical moment by assuring me that the sexual activity around her bothers her not at all. Were she to say, "It makes me miserable," or "I disapprove," which I am certain she does, she would be separating herself from the crowd: that would be a wrong kind of loneliness. Yet to be ordinarily outgoing would also be eccentric to the general will and it would isolate one from the isolates. I ruminate on my encounter the other night with a young man in Briggs who invited me to dinner at Moors Hall with a group of other

students. Issuing the invitation he described the difficulty he
had had to overcome before he spoke to me. Later I made
notes:

We gathered in the living room of Briggs among the day's quota of
empty beer and Coke cans, scattered newspapers and magazines and
used paper cups, cigarette butts, and the multitudinous remnants of
attempted schoolwork—on Saturday and Sunday mornings, when
there is no maid, I steal into this room which is next to my own
and manage a modicum of tidying up from the previous day but
this evening I am afraid of being caught *in flagrante*. There are five
of us and we walk together to the nearby hall; the cafeteria is only
half-filled and we easily find a table. My host is a junior at Harvard.
He reports that he is much happier living at Radcliffe than he was
in an all-male residence hall. Apparently he had been studying in
the Briggs living room at a time when I was reading in the same
room and suddenly he had said to himself, "I want to ask Mrs.
Trilling to dinner." But he had felt too shy so he had gone upstairs
to the library to study, except that he couldn't stay there either
because he kept thinking he wanted to ask me to dinner. So then
he had gone to the basement to work but again I had intruded on
his attempt until finally he had got angry at himself and decided that
if all he was going to think about was whether it was all right to
ask me to dinner, he'd better ask me and be done with it—at which
point I was no longer in the living room and he had had to knock
at my door. I accept gladly, a bit awed by his self-mastery and
enormously, curiously, relieved by his reference to an emotion, that
of shyness, with which I had had acquaintance at his age. "I was
shy too when I was young. I still am," I tell him, "but I never had
the courage to overcome it the way you did. I couldn't do it today!"
The young man is properly pleased at his accomplishment and
happy to have it recognized. He explains that he had had no friends
at Harvard and that it wasn't until he had been initiated into the
routine of washing and brushing his teeth at the next washstand
to a girl's that he had broken the loneliness barrier: he now has a
girlfriend who will be joining us. Yet this same person who learned
so competently to bridge the age difference between himself and
me has no "deportment" with which to handle his little dinner
party. He walks through the door of Moors Hall before me, all but

slamming it in my face and in the faces of his other guests, including his girlfriend who brings up the rear of the party. Neither he nor anyone else in the group hands me a tray or gives precedence to me at the food counters. When we finish dinner the two girls rush off to jobs: his girlfriend doesn't say what her job is but the other girl is scheduled to babysit—I have already gathered that these are not the indulged offspring of the well-fixed middle class; all of them come from homes of limited income and perhaps this is why they have gravitated toward each other. But strangely it is with these students that I find it possible to talk most freely about manners and even about the part that servants had played in the more sustaining social life of my own undergraduate time when meals had been served us at tables at set hours by maids in uniform. Yes, there had been a substantial patrician population at "my" Radcliffe. The upper-class students nevertheless had no more claim to good manners than the daughter of immigrants; we learned together and from each other how to be ladies, and a useful goal it had been, always within limits. Now I speak to my dinner companions of manners as a protection against being overwhelmed by our crowded and difficult world: I am not sure they understand me but they try. And when I say, "After all, if you ask me whether you can take my tray or bring me a glass of water, we have made a human contact, haven't we? It's at least a first step," one of the boys gets up and laughingly asks if he can get me a glass of water. I answer yes, please, and he asks the two girls at the table and they answer yes, please, too. At the end of the meal, one of the girls takes away my tray. I recall the nursery school edict of the early fifties when these students had been at the start of their educations: "It is not formal manners we are interested in, but internal feelings." How wrong could they be? By what road straighter and faster than that of external forms does internal feeling travel to another person? Even our chitchat this evening at the table: has it not helped us dispel our anonymities? Are we not far less alone than had we fed in edgy silence as usually happened in the dining halls? Despite my protest, my young friend pays for my dinner, insisting I am there on his invitation. It has been a beautiful evening.

But all of this is too complex to open up in these few moments which remain in my visit with the president. We speak instead about inconsequentialities, skirt my distress that soon there will be no Radcliffe other than in the fading memory of a few oldsters, avoid even that nicest of the impressions I have gathered in my return to Cambridge, that if there was indeed a generation gap anywhere except in the myth-making mind of feature writers it was of a different order than was being institutionalized by our improving journalism: in my firm view, what separated the young from us who were older had almost nothing to do with the number of years they and we had been alive, though this had certainly made for the age division in my undergraduate era, but depended solely upon divergence in outlook, differences in values. To be sure, in the campus uprisings at Columbia in 1968 and maybe elsewhere too, there had been sudden ugly division on lines of age alone: insurrectionary students had exhorted old people on the street who were strangers to them to go home and die. But these cruel passions had now themselves died, and at Radcliffe, so far as I could determine, there had been buried with them all remnants of mechanical fear and suspicion of older people simply because they had been longer in the world. For instance, I find in my notebook one of its pleasantest reminders of the cordiality shown me by students who were usually incapable of similar warmth with their own contemporaries, except perhaps in the case of a single chosen partner of the opposite sex. The page is labeled May 8, 1971, and after the date I have written: "I came back from New York the night before." This refers to my absence from Radcliffe for a few days while I went to New York to take part in a panel discussion on Norman Mailer's *Prisoner of Sex*.

Several posters—they are decorated with carelessly painted daisies—announce a "Spring Party" in Briggs this evening at eight: food, wine, live music. It is Saturday morning, no maid at the hall and even at 9 a.m. when I go out to look at the *Times* in the living room, the room is so disordered that I stop and pick up—I move chairs into place, gather and dispose of used paper cups and napkins, straighten the magazines on the tables. For the first time I notice that the hall apparently subscribes only to *Newsweek* and the *Saturday Review:* who is responsible, I wonder, for this principle of pious literateness? Expectably, by afternoon the disorder has reestablished itself; even the huge refuse cans in the corridor overflow. Tonight my husband and I are wistful at having to miss the fun; we have engaged ourselves for dinner with friends in Boston and must leave at seven. My husband goes into the rain to look for a cab while I canvass the preparations for the evening's festivities. They are not elaborate: around the grand piano in the living room there looks to be a storeload of drums, also an upright microphone with a man's blue shirt draped on it—the shirt is filthy, covered with graffiti. In welcoming me back from New York, the tutor's wife warned me of the noise on either side of our rooms tonight; with the sweetest of smiles she explains that it will be more than noisy, it will be very, *very* noisy and the din will be coming not only from the direction of the living room but that of the dining hall as well. Yet even as she apologizes she can't resist boasting the quality of the jazz which is being provided: "They're friends of someone in the house and they're coming all the way from New York to play for nothing." I comfort her that the noise will bother us not at all; we just hope to be back in time to see the party.

Now there enters out of the wet night a boy and his girlfriend; he is shaking his umbrella strenuously. I know him slightly through his always bothering to greet me. "Hi! Where are you going?" he asks me. "To Boston." "That's nice." He smiles. "To a show?" "No. Visiting some friends." He eyes me warily, as though there's a hidden content to be penetrated. "But you'll be given dinner?" I assure him it's a dinner date and he visibly relaxes. But he is still studying me while his girlfriend waits patiently. I'm studying him too, believe he can't be more than twenty, at the most twenty-one. "Your hair looks nice," he decides. "Oh, thank you." I'm pleased though embarrassed: when I had been twenty, you didn't give older people compliments; they looked awful to you. "Are you going to the dance?" "No, to the Library," he laughs. "Unless there's a dance in the Library." "Have you so much work that you can't spare an evening?" "No, that's not it. I have work all right but that's not it. I'm just not going to the dance." He is talking solely to me, and I have the impression that for some reason he is putting his girl at a distance. But suddenly he turns to her and says, "Shall we go up?"

and she nods; they both smile at me and say goodnight. Then on the steps the girl stops and announces: "I'd love to go to the party tonight." The remark is not addressed to me but clearly I am its target. His response is a grinning gesture of despair; he *wants* to capitulate and I say to his girl, "Twist his arm." At this he puts it around her and calls down to me, "I guess I'm going to a dance tonight."

But if he did show up, he had left by midnight when we returned from Boston because I especially look for him, prepared with my excuse—"I've hurt my knee"—should he insist that I dance. At first I had thought to say it was my ankle I had injured but such is my sense of the young with whom I live that I daren't limit my injury to an ankle lest he offer to rub it for me; a knee is a more reliable generation-divider. The party is in progress and I decide it can't be judged a failure though the attendance is so sparse, not more than thirty-five or forty people; in fact, it's a splendid success for those who have come. But among this number only a handful opt for the jazz session in the living room; the rest dance to the rock in the dining hall, a dozen, two dozen yards away. The resident tutor has met us coming in and apologizes for the noise, urges us to join the fun. He holds a large red-and-white paper cup in his hand, so I look around for the source of his drink: no doubt it is one of the jugs of wine, all of which now appear to be empty—with no replenishment in sight I wonder how the party will sustain itself for another two hours. But no one is drunk unless it's the jazz musicians, and probably they're high on pot rather than wine. I lack the skill to assess their abilities; they are accomplished players and accustomed to each other but apart from a strong beat and shatteringly magnified sound, their distinction is not mine to appreciate nor do they seem to have great appeal for their contemporaries, most of whom are in the dining room where the jazz is not. Of those who are dancing to the rock, on records from the early sixties, the wife of the tutor has already murmured to me: "These people were only little kids then."

In the living room the mess spreads. Everywhere there's a litter of paper drinking cups; the morning's newspaper has miraculously reappeared and spawned. Cushions have been lifted from one of the sofas and made into a floor seat in a corner of the room where a long-haired youth and two long-haired girls decorously visit together.

The single other occupant of the room sits in a chair near the door, alone, stoned. I watch her for an hour in which she never opens her eyes though she is awake, her foot tapping and her body rocking with a strange tense insistence on capturing the beat of the music— she looks like someone practicing for a performance on doomsday. Coming in on the party from our Boston evening, met by the fierce blast of sound, I had fretted that the two of us, my husband and I, what with our "straightness" and our outsidedness and burden of years would be made to feel that we were blighting the festivity, that we would be unable to reach the sanctuary of our rooms without spreading the gloom of our experience of a time unknown by this student generation. But where had I learned this anxiety except in my own past which had had no acquaintance with the generosity with which we are accepted by the present-day young? It starts with the resident tutor and his wife who spread protective wings about us as if to shield us against our own unkindness to ourselves— can they know that when I and my ladylike dormitory contemporaries were nineteen and twenty we were agonized if graduates ten years older than ourselves appeared in the halls? We treated them like ancient artifacts. Between the attitude of a present student generation toward their elders and ours in my own generation, there is surely no bridge.

So then what bridge to the past did I seek in this party? Were the girls to have put rosebuds in their hair and worn flowing chiffon to countermand the rain? Should the boys have perhaps left off their white gloves but put carnations in their buttonholes? Should President Bunting have presided over this occasion as our own Dean Brown, then all of twenty-nine, had presided over a well-remembered dormitory dance of the twenties? Poor Miss Brown, what would she then have made of girls who came to a dance in blue jeans and bare feet and of boys in sweated-out shirts hanging from their pants or precipitously discarded, thrown into a corner, partner wholly disconnected from partner, privacy the tune they danced to? Still, the privacy they danced to had *some* kind of inclusiveness unknown to my college generation, and if only for these weeks of my visit I am its beneficiary. No one thought to put us from sight or mind because we were outsiders and of an older human species. On the contrary, and this made the great contemporary conundrum, it was the very particularity of our place in their uni-

2. An Interview

D.T. Tell me about the house you live in. It's a Harvard house but it has women in it?

X. That's right, it began having women last year.

D.T. About how many women are there? Are you equally distributed?

X. No, not at all. Perhaps a third. Of course we're still at the point of self-consciousness and we notice the girls more than the other boys do at Harvard, so it seems there are more of them.

D.T. And I take it that they are all on the same floor?

X. No, not at all. When I first came here I'd come from a year of sexual segregation in Harvard Yard so I was quite astounded, not shocked but simply surprised, by finding that the girls would be distributed throughout the dorm. I'd assumed they would all be on one entry or perhaps one floor.

D.T. Suppose you'd known in advance that they were going to be distributed as indeed they are distributed? Would that in any way have diminished your anticipation?

X. On the contrary. I was disappointed when I anticipated that they wouldn't be accessible.

D.T. They are very accessible, then. On your floor there are girls and they live in suites of four or five girls with their own bath? Is that the idea?

x. Yes.

D.T. But you haven't any communal bathrooms, have you?

x. I don't think so. But it's not so shocking a possibility that we would necessarily have heard about it if there were any. I'd be willing to bet that within three years we'll have coeducational suites. It won't change things very much.

D.T. Now, that's what I wanted to talk about. You say it won't change things if there are coeducational suites. There are already communal bathrooms in Briggs and in Barnard Hall because they're old Radcliffe dormitories; they weren't built with suites the way Harvard houses are. In Briggs—I haven't yet been upstairs because I don't think they'd like me wandering around too much but I know from having lived there myself when I was at Radcliffe—there are two bathrooms, I think, at either end of the corridors and then in Barnard Hall, as I remember, there's one in the center of each corridor. But I'm told by everybody, male and female, that this makes no problem. In fact the boys, even more than the girls, speak of it as a coziness because they feel it is nice to get acquainted by using adjacent washbasins and if you're brushing your teeth you don't have really to get into much conversation but then the next day you're brushing your teeth again and pretty soon you're friends just because of this easy contact. Is that what you have in mind when you say that coeducational suites wouldn't bother you?

x. Yes. That, of course, too. But what I suppose I'm really saying is that many of the barriers in people's minds against treating other people as human beings, rather than as different categories of human beings, are artificial, they've simply been built up by habit and as soon as the reality is presented, they just fall in the wind. As in my own case: in two weeks it never occurred to me that people could live any other way than the way I'm living.

D.T. There are already a few suites—I've not interviewed anyone in them but I've been told about it—in which there are girls and boys, and the girl was reported to have said that she found this perfectly okay, it didn't bother her in the least. Inevitably she was asked by someone of my generation, "Isn't it odd, with you in bed in one room and then some boy in bed right in the next room," but she said, "Not at all," and went on to explain that she had her own boyfriend as he had his own girlfriend and so they were nothing but suite mates, maybe adjacent cliffdwellers. Tell me, can you explain how the transition to this new style of living was accomplished? Are you all like doctors who have developed the ability to associate in a certain degree of physical intimacy with members of the opposite sex and yet abstract from the relationship anything that has to do with sexual excitement but without castrating yourselves? Obviously doctors aren't eunuchs; they reassert the sexual connection when the situation is appropriate to it.

x.   I'm sure you've heard from a lot of indignant people of my generation how they feel when it's explained to them that it used to be assumed that human beings are absolutely governed by physical urges beyond their control, that they're animals or robots. Like other people of my age, I react with horror to a statement like that.

D.T.   But I don't think anyone's ever said that except perhaps in hyperbole. They may be pointing to something they mean seriously but they're certainly not saying that there's nothing in any man's mind except how he's going to get in bed with some woman or other. Not literally.

x.   But isn't it common for your generation to think that people are not in complete control of their passions when in close proximity with people of the opposite sex, even those they don't know; some magnetic force is at work which has to be battled and countered at every turn?

D.T.   Well, there's been a change in movies since the early days: that's true enough. From the idea that men are some kind of tearing maniacs of lust to the idea of more sexual control. But that was quite a long time ago, you know.

x.   In the act of love itself conscious control and restraint are good things. Similarly in the most social aspects of sexual attraction restraint and control might lead to more pleasure.

D.T.   Well, perhaps so. But tell me, if this is how your age group feels, there must be a contradiction we're dealing with here. I mean, it's commonly said of your generation that you are particularly uncontrolled and undisciplined.

x.   I do think we're more uncontrolled and more undisciplined. But I don't necessarily think that's a bad thing.

D.T.   But you've been saying that you are more controlled sexually than we are. Aren't you contradicting yourself?

x.   I'm not sure, I argue with equal ease on both sides. It's possible that we're just lazy—

D.T.   Yes, that's a possibility. But let's not mix up passivity with control or uncontrol. Maybe passivity is itself a form of control but then so is illness, or death. But tell me what you think about laziness.

x.   Well, when a barrier is to be torn down, among those who wish to tear it down would be two parties. When I was still in school in Europe we wanted to abolish all the rules. Some people want to tear down barriers so as to have more freedom to go forward. Other people want to have them torn down simply to have less resistance to stagnation. And the same is true in sexual relations: there are some people who have no need of boundaries, who have their own inner control, but there are some people who hate control altogether.

D.T.   I'm not inclined to think that there are necessary correlations between the different areas of life in which a person does or does not exercise control. I think, for instance, that my generation may have far more control than yours about such things as where we throw our used beer cans or what disposal we make of the paper napkins we have just used. We don't just drop them on the floor. And we're perhaps more controlled in our ability to stick with an assignment or put ourselves through a difficult task of comprehension. I think these are very important indeed in terms of the intellectual culture, and I'm much worried about their loss among the young: they seem simultaneously to have had reduced the demand put upon them in their educational institutions and reduced their own capacity to meet high requirements. But I'm not sure that in bed there is anything to be said generationally for the younger as opposed to the older male partners in terms of their actual self-control in lovemaking. I'd make an educated guess that it doesn't work that way at all, though eventually it may. All this sexual control and freedom you speak of may eventually work out to be a boon to men; they may be benefited. But I don't think we know enough about it now to tell whether it's a benefit or hindrance.

x.   But doesn't it have to be a benefit if only because the only thing that separates man from other animals is the fact that his sexual urges are under some sort of mental control, and therefore sexual control must stand for a development and heightening of humanity, a progress? I've heard older people say that sex depends on furtiveness.

D.T.   And you find that a terrible thought?

x.   I've heard few statements that irritated me more but I haven't been able to answer it.

D.T.   All right, let's get to that because some of the students were talking about it the other day—I think I had been talking about D. H. Lawrence, hadn't I?—and you remember I said that I thought furtiveness and sin might well be an enhancement of sexual pleasure: furtiveness *or* a sense of sin, I meant to say. You didn't seem to agree with that.

x.   No. But I can see that sin and sex is of course an important idea.

D.T.   Look, when sex is brought into the realm of mental and physical hygiene, there can be a terrible sterilization of the emotions. This awful hygienic attitude: it began to come into our society in the thirties. It hadn't been there before but the spread of psychoanalytical perceptions, some of them very misunderstood or misapplied, introduced it into the culture.

x.   That seems to me a different thing from what we are talking about today. The idea that sex is good for you is just as absurd as the idea that sex is bad for you. What we have now is a much more relaxed consciousness that sex just *is*.

D.T.   All right, but you know you've won that consummation over a couple of dead bodies, if I may put it that way; dead psyches, anyway, from my generation. But let me ask you this: would it be fair to say that for your generation sex is little more than a friendliness, perhaps an exceptional friendliness but only a friendliness?

x.   No, I don't think so. I don't think sex is merely an extension of friendliness. Before we talked about friendliness as a substitute for sex. I really didn't mean that one takes the place of the other. That implies they're different.

D.T.   Do you know anything about the Freudian concept of sublimation? Freud believed that we sublimated our excess erotic energy in art or in work. Would it be fair to say that for your generation sex is sublimated in friendship?

x.   I suppose a theoretical argument could be made for that. But I like to think there's a sort of compartmentalization and that one can separate a girl whom one sees as a girl from a girl whom one sees as a friend.

D.T.   Yes, but if you are having these de-eroticized friendships, what's new about that? The world has always believed in friendship, at least in male friendship though they've never had any great belief in female friendship. But now we're talking about men being friends with women and I'm not saying it's not possible or even desirable but it does give us the right, I think, to raise the question of whether you people aren't de-eroticizing women, or somehow subduing a great deal of your sexual drive.

x.   Yes, I see what you mean though I'm a little reluctant to admit it. Of course it's true that you can't banish the erotic element altogether—

D.T.   I'm sorry, I'm going to interrupt to ask you why you think that you *ought* to resist what I'm saying, that you ought to be reluctant. What do you think I'm attacking: friendship? womanhood? manhood? moral values?

x.   One would like to believe that friendship with a girl is a good for its own sake rather than merely an outlet, something which is a small function of something else. Let me turn to one other possible source of sublimation which you talked about last time, that of rebellion. Such as political rebellion. It seems to me there's a certain requirement in each human being for rebellion against fixed ideas and against the past, otherwise we wouldn't have progress. I think that each person has been given a certain amount of impatience with what is, a certain amount of desire to cast it down and set up something else in its place. Everybody feels a little bit rebellious unless he's been absolutely trampled on. What I am trying to suggest is that it's a natural quality of man, on a par with curiosity, and that it's universal. One tends to throw stones at whatever walls happen to be nearest. Some of the strongest rebellious emotions a hundred years ago were sexual because most restrictions were sexual. They were beset on every side with barricades and detours, labyrinths and mazes, all sorts of reverses and traps. But nowadays that's less true. Now the energy for casting down walls is expended in other areas than sex by the younger generation. If you've spent all day protesting and picketing against the restraints of society, you simply have no need to face any more barriers in bed that night.

D.T.   But if I may say so, your generation never had to face any in bed, that was done for you. You didn't do it. You've built this fine unbarricaded structure of yours on land that was cleared for you by us. It was we who had that fight. We battled against the restrictions and guilts, and we handed you the permission of your bodies. That's why we're interested in what you're doing with it. We'd hate to have it issue in de-eroticization: the territory was won for sex and we don't want it lost for sex. Not that I'm sure it is, but I'm going to go along on that assumption for a moment in order to get as much out of this conversation as we can. And I hope you understand that sometimes I'm just trying to draw you out and I'm not entirely voicing my actual beliefs. So let's go back to how you said you have no rebellions to fight in bed: you feel pretty good about your bodies and about sex and full of energy, and you don't think your sexual energies are being deflected by your need for friendship.

x.   I don't think they are. Of course, I never knew the *ancien régime*, I have no idea how it was. I have a suspicion, though, that the assertion of the older generation that sex and sin are intermingled is a sort of post hoc rationalization.

D.T.   Yet it annoyed you very much and I want to know why. Is it because, when we say this, you recognize that what we are countering is the notion of sex as hygienic living?

x.   That's absolutely loaded with pejorative connotations. The word "hygienic" conjures up images of sterility. That seems to me a basic contradiction.

D.T.   Not sterile, then. Just morally antiseptic.

x.   In other words, inhuman. But I think our idea of sex is anything but inhuman. I think it's *more* human in that it involves more sensitivity, more of the human emotions, a greater play of the human mind over the somewhat baser impulses of the body—

D.T.   Oh, let's stop right there! Baser impulses of the body? Have we hit it now?

x.   I don't think they're baser—

D.T.   Okay, I don't want to catch you up on every word and ask you why you said it if you didn't mean it. But I do feel I should stop over that. You know, I remember a long time ago a girl I knew was telling me about her early sexual experience, and she said, "Well, you see, I had been taught that sex was ugly but love made it beautiful."

x.   Exactly, that's an opinion held by many of my generation. In fact, by most of my friends. Almost all.

D.T.   That sex is in itself low and only the feelings that you bring to it really make it all right?

x.   Yes, I think so. It's not that we think it's sinful. Just less than it could be.

D.T.   But why less? By what standards?

x.   I'm not sure.

D.T.   Is it a standard you get from romance, or what?

x.   Maybe just by observation. After all, even the most naive observer would say that something is added to the physical pleasure of sex when you like the partner. Perhaps more is added if the like is intensified into love: it's more fun. I'm sure that's measurable.

D.T.   It isn't measurable. A subjective report is all we have to go on. But you think that most of your contemporaries feel that there is something inadequate about sex unless it is imbued with love?

x.   Not so much inadequate as incomplete. But I'm not sure about my feelings. They seem to be on two levels. I'd like to believe that sex is a good thing in itself, that it's fun, it's pleasurable, it does no harm, and that it's made better by love. But what I think I *really* feel is that sex really isn't very good at all unless there's love. A bit of personal history: for the past year I've had a girlfriend. I said good-bye to her about two weeks ago.

D.T.   Oh, I'm sorry.

x.   It's of no consequence.

D.T.   Really not? I should think it would be.

x.   No, it was simply a necessary, almost an historical, development. Anyway, the point of this is—

D.T. Let me interrupt. You don't have to tell me if you don't want to but it would make things clearer if you did. You went to bed together?

X. We used to do exactly what you were talking about with so much surprise last week. We used to sleep together without any feeling of the necessity of making love, to use the standard phrase. Because we didn't think you could *make* love when you're not *in* love. I think there's a revealing linguistic insight there. We said that if we ever fell in love then we could make another decision, but until then we would keep some correspondence between the level of our emotions and physical passion.

D.T. So you just slept in the same bed with each other without any sexual activity of any kind, no caressing, no intercourse? And no excitement on either side?

X. That's right.

D.T. And situations like this are typical of your generation. I gather that you and she aren't special instances.

X. First of all, Harvard is not my generation, and neither is Radcliffe. I think they're different in many ways although I wouldn't say that in public for fear of being stoned. Nor are we typical of all of Harvard. But let's say that there's a very large proportion of people of my generation who think and act this way.

D.T. And the girl accepted this perfectly happily? Just as you did?

X. Of course. Perhaps I was even somewhat conditioned by her feelings. If she'd been all for casting aside these restraints, if she'd argued that it was artificial, I probably would have agreed.

D.T. Do you think you would have fallen in love with her?

X. I don't think so.

D.T. But suppose—now please don't shy away from this question—suppose you had actually had a sexual relationship: isn't it possible that that's what was missing?

x.   I think the opposite is true. I think we'd have broken with each other faster than we did.

D.T.   Faster? Because you were in a sexual relation? Did you move apart at the same rate?

x.   No. I guess I wanted to break off the relationship first.

D.T.   Did she really get tired of you too or was she just taking it like a lady?

x.   It was an unusual sort of relationship. It was based on many misconceptions. But I guess I get tired of everything faster than most people; maybe it's because I think I've seen more things, lived in such a lot of different countries, met so many kinds of minds—the interest of any one idea pales for me after a while when I compare it with other ideas. She's just discovered the world of ideas: it's a very charming time of her life.

D.T.   And your taking her by the hand and inducting her would be very attractive for a while. But I can see that that role could begin to get wearisome.

x.   It doesn't work, finally. Also, it isn't fair because she has just as much innate ability as I have.

D.T.   Do you think it's part of the assumption of the people you know around Harvard that intellectual communication, intellectual stimulation, is important in the relation of men and women?

x.   Terribly. That may be why ours foundered. In the last months all we did was eat and sleep together. That seemed to me fairly barren, the same way as sex without love would be though it's not exactly the same thing. I've been here now for two years and during that time I've lived with the idea that love is necessary to sex, so that I've postponed sex waiting for love. I've been looking for two years for a girl that I could fall in love with and haven't found her yet. If sex had been my only interest, I probably would have compromised that rather stiff ideal, but I don't think that I will. I think I'll just go on looking until I find somebody I can fall in love with and then everything else will follow naturally.

D.T.   Well then, let me ask you the most intimate of questions and you can tell me it's none of my business if you want to. Don't you feel sexually uncomfortable, physically driven by desire, or is your generation—does your generation not have this problem? Has sex been absorbed into your affectional lives so early that you don't just want a girl to lay, whether you love her or not?

X.   There are other ways of getting sexual release without actually making love with a girl.

D.T.   But surely they're not very satisfactory.

X.   It's a release.

D.T.   You know, somewhere in all this we must indeed be getting to the question of masturbation. This was the great permission we gave our children somewhere along in the thirties, forties, and fifties—it had been the chief thing that was forbidden my generation, surrounded with the most dreadful sense of fear and punishment. You people were re-leased from that fear and permitted your "outlets" for sexual pressures of a purely physical kind so now you assign your sexual feelings solely to your affectional relations, or maybe just subdue your sexual feelings to your affectional feelings. Perhaps that's what the whole thing is about, actually. Maybe you have to surround masturbation with prohibition if you are really to release sex in adulthood. What an idea!

X.   But there are pressures which aren't simply physical. Emotional pressures.

D.T.   You mean the need for someone of the other sex to love.

X.   Those are sublimated not only in affection but in a sort of return to courtly ritual.

D.T.   Tell me about that.

x.   Well, especially in the co-ed houses where the incest taboo is very much in effect—

D.T.   Tell me about that too.

x.   I'll come back to it. Obviously in our treatment of girls a whole new series of rituals is arising in response to new needs and new conditions. We have a return to gallantry after having rejected it for the past few years.

D.T.   Where does gallantry show itself? I haven't seen it.

x.   It's just beginning to show itself: first of all, in a return to the old small rituals such as opening doors, holding coats, offering chairs, that sort of thing. It also demands a kind of elevated gallant metaphorical language which you'd be amused to hear at a Harvard lunch table, two people treating each other as something special and putting their communication on a higher plane in such purely utilitarian statements as "Pass the salt." But interestingly, it is not sexually discriminatory as the old gallantry was. It's mutual and the girls enter into it in the same spirit and in almost the same role as the boys. My best friend is a girl in my house—I have no close male friends or close girl friends either, except this one person. We have carefully rigidified our relationship so that we meet once or twice a week at lunch but no other time, and we talk for about two or three hours. We never talk about ourselves. I found out yesterday from a third party that she's living in Radcliffe next year. Of course that will be the end of it. So apparently there's a need for barriers but it's more fun to create your own than accept the old ones, lock, stock, and barrel, because along with the old barriers comes a sense of guilt or a sense of shame, neither of which is very much fun, whereas with the erection of the new comes a sense of gallantry and restraint, a sense almost of artistic creation.

D.T.   When you say erect them for yourselves, do you think you're creating your culture in that sense? Or is your culture creating you and your new gallantry?

x. Well, I'm perhaps reassembling it out of elements given me by my culture. Also, I don't think this is entirely typical. I don't think you will find many people who've created an artificially stilted relationship and get any pleasure out of it. However, I have and I'll be very sorry when she goes to Radcliffe.

D.T. It ought to be possible for you to ritualize the few blocks that will separate you, don't you think? You could say, "I'll come to Radcliffe on Mondays, you come to Harvard on Thursdays."

x. I suppose we could do that. I knew a boy whose girlfriend went to school five hundred miles away and she was thinking of transferring to a college about sixty miles away so as to be near him. I asked him, "Why doesn't she transfer to a college in Boston?" and he said, "Oh, no! That's too close. Sixty miles is the perfect distance."

D.T. Just what you were talking about: the creation of an artificial barrier.

x. The perfect distance may vary from generation to generation.

D.T. Sixty miles for your generation.

x. The rules of the old generation may seem to us like a five-hundred-mile distance. Still, we wouldn't want to live together all the time. It's like the operation of the eye: you can't see anything that's pressed right up against your face but neither can you see anything a mile away. There's an optimum distance for the greatest appreciation of an object.

D.T. Now tell me about the incest taboo in the house. You live together like brothers and sisters so you mustn't have sexual relations with each other?

x. Well, maybe it isn't really a taboo because many people break it, as I wouldn't do. There are lots of love affairs raging out of control like forest fires in every house at this very moment. Let them be the exception.

D.T.   Love affairs, not just sexual affairs?

X.   Well, there are some of those too, I guess, but fewer. If you're going to have a sexual affair on a few weekends, you're more likely to have it with somebody outside of the house.

D.T.   Because they're difficult to end if you're seeing each other at breakfast every morning or if you live in rooms on the same corridor.

X.   Exactly. The sexual affairs seem to me to be based on a sort of benign mutual deception. The idea is that each of the partners is more attractive, more beautiful, more nearly ideal than he or she really is. Sex is that way, isn't it?

D.T.   No. Love is often that way. Love idealizes, or at least traditionally that has been one of the differential diagnoses: love idealizes, adds, but sex is just body meeting body, sometimes with love, sometimes with affection, sometimes with neither, just for the fun or satisfaction of it.

X.   I suppose that what I'm saying is that sex would like to, but love does. For example, to see your girlfriend at breakfast looking just terrible, completely bedraggled, or *bed*-raggled, would not hinder a relationship of love but it might shatter one of just sex.

D.T.   Perhaps it's not that simple either. But that brings me to something else: I see the girls in Currier House come to breakfast in their dressing gowns. To be sure, I've never seen a girl come to the table without having combed her hair, but in buildings where there are common bathrooms, she would be walking to the bathroom with her hair not combed. Does this upset you? In my generation, we never wanted a man to see us with our hair undone or when we weren't properly dressed.

X.   Those were role-conditioned, those fears of being seen out of character. But if one no longer has to feel that one is playing the role of a sex object, or a sex pursuer, then these appurtenances are useless.

D.T.   And are we all so humanly beautiful that we don't need the appurtenances of sexual attraction? What an act of faith this all is!

X.   Well, we might need them if we were playing that game but—this is going to be too complicated.

D.T.   Oh, go ahead. Let it come out too difficult, what difference does it make?

X.   What I was saying is this: that if I were expected to fall in love with the girls I see in the halls, I'd be terrified seeing them as they look in the morning. But if I'm not expected to fall in love with them, if there's no expectation that I'll have any reaction at all, why should I care how they look? Also, this generation has more distrust of how things look.

D.T.   In a speech last year on women's liberation, I said how wonderful it was for us to be living in a period in which Dostoevski's statement that there was no such thing as an ugly woman was at last coming true. Of course I don't mean that absolutely and literally but I said it seriously in that speech because I was talking about the terrible Madison Avenue–contrived notions of sexual attractiveness that were imposed upon the girls of my generation and how dreadful it was to be made to think, as I did, that you had to conform to some impossible standard of advertising beauty in order to be in the sexual running at all. How can anyone of my generation do anything except celebrate the fact that this is no longer how things are?

X.   I feel guilty about demanding a certain standard of physical attractiveness in girls I might fall in love with. I think that's wrong.

D.T.   Oh, my God!

X.   Well, if we're rejecting Madison Avenue we're supposed to seek the essence, not the appearance; the contents, not the packaging. And it's unjust to judge a girl by something that's not under her control. Her personality is under her control to a certain extent. Her interests and emotions are under her control and what she does with her appearance. But the way she was born isn't. That really isn't part of a person and shouldn't be.

D.T.   Even at your young age you've surely seen girls with few of the conventional features of beauty who are beautiful.

X.   But it would be much better if we could ignore appearance altogether and seek something more important. But I don't think anybody ever will.

D.T.   Would it be a better state of things if we dispensed with all aesthetics?

X.   Well, gosh—

D.T.   —or just the aesthetics of sex? Surely you can't want that. The very generation that is saying our cities are too ugly and we've got to make them beautiful can't be caught saying that it's only in the external world that we are going to maintain standards of aesthetics, that there need not be any in sex at all.

X.   If there were no aesthetics of sex there would of course be nothing to differentiate one person from another on the exterior. What I'm trying to say is that there's a certain dignity in saying, "I choose you." But with no aesthetics at all it would no longer be a question of choice. I'm putting this badly, but do you see what I mean? That in selecting one person from hundreds of others and saying, "You're special. I separate you from the others," you're somehow lifting the relationship between the two of you. Badly put, but I think you see what I mean.

D.T.   So many of the students I've been talking to are lonely. Are you lonely too?

X.   Terribly!

D.T.   Everybody around here is. I don't understand it. I wasn't lonely in college except the way all human beings are ultimately lonely all through their lives, and the way almost everyone has an occasional bad hour or day. But that's not the loneliness of having no human connections, no friends.

x. I'm lonely not because I lack friends; I have more friends than I know what to do with: I know perhaps two-thirds of the girls who walk past this window. But I don't have any *close* friends, that's the difference. I wonder whether in the last generation the same conditions didn't prevail. And whether they were simply disguised from you by the whirl of social activities in which you were caught up. My mother has endless tales of dances and parties and gala occasions. She says, "Oh, I was never lonely," but I wonder if in the midst of all that she ever had any time to stop and have a close, real communication with somebody else. Anyway, that's what I lack.

D.T. Of course when I talk about friendship, I'm never sure what I mean. In some odd way I guess I always thought that friendship should sustain you wherever you needed it. But what I have found in life—it makes me very sad—is that one friend sustains me in one direction, another in another direction. What's missing are the friends who sustain one altogether. But then I say to myself, "And do I sustain them altogether?" and I'm sure I don't. I don't mean to fail them but I'm sure I do. And they probably don't mean to fail me, but they do. But at least in my undergraduate experience, there was always companionship of an interesting and supportive kind which you people don't seem to find. Maybe it's because you grew up faster and therefore you suffer your disillusionments sooner.

x. It seems like a contradiction that with all this new permissiveness and easing of rules and barriers, people aren't meeting. They're not, though.

D.T. You're living so intimately: why don't you meet? Of course we had our rituals of manners and they helped us bridge some of the gaps. To say, "Do you want the butter?" "Do you want the salt?" is a way of making a connection for which you people have to dream up a whole philosophy of respect for each other's humanity. Respect is implicit in my noticing whether you need the salt. I'm aware of you and what could be more respecting than that?

x.   That's true. Yes, I agree with you in that. Many of the old barriers were really not barriers at all, but bridges.

d.t.   Right.

x.   But those are barriers.

d.t.   I'm not saying that at times they aren't. But smoking a cigarette can be a barrier too, and I think I'm capable of knowing when a certain kind of social small talk is meant to protect people from getting to know each other. You and I could chatter over a cocktail or a cup of tea in a way that was designed to keep us from getting to be friends or even of having any human contact whatsoever. But there's also a way of carrying on small talk which is a way of saying, "Be at ease with me. Let's be friends." And I'm all for the teaching of conversational good manners for that reason. You said the same thing, really, when you said that you are yourselves building up little gallantries.

x.   Manners change, though. The manners of this century aren't the manners of the last, and because our generation is rejecting the manners of the previous generation doesn't mean that we're rejecting manners.

d.t.   Your middle-class generation was taught in nursery school that manners were internal, not the learning of forms.

x.   I was never taught that. We were told to behave like gentlemen.

d.t.   Were you really? What a nice retrograde upbringing you had!

x.   Never to *be* gentlemen. Not once was that mentioned. But to behave *like* gentlemen, as if it were some sort of imposture.

d.t.   Do you think that we are all of us a generation of hypocrites? You always are implying that; that you know we behave like ladies and gentlemen but we only have the forms of courtesy, we don't have the real thing, the decent human feeling that would result in better treatment of each other. You really do have that kind of low opinion of older people, don't you?

x.   Not of the generation as a whole, but some of them.

D.T.   And do you think that the attitude which you and your generation are so painfully formulating—your new idealism—is going to prepare you to make the world better than it is now? Do you see the road clear?

x.   I've read too much Burke to believe in great quantum jumps of human civilization. But I do think there's a certain amount of progress.

D.T.   Do you feel that my generation or your parents' generation made any genuine contribution to the progress of mankind?

x.   Of course. To believe otherwise would be reactionary. Naive.

D.T.   The thing is that your generation is confronted by some of the dilemmas created by the large steps forward we made in ours: politically, socially, sexually, every way. You know, liberalism had great triumphs in this century but it's left us with all kinds of new problems. And so it will always be—the children will always have to face the problems created by the progressive ideas of their parents.

x.   I wouldn't stop with liberalism. The children of political liberalism in this generation are extremists of both camps, but mainly of the Left. Extremism is a giant step backwards from liberalism.

D.T.   But isn't that because they feel that liberalism has been exhausted as a tradition and nobody has yet been able to deal with this in an effective way? On the extreme Left they think a nihilistic revolution, an assault upon the institutions themselves, will do it. It seems to me that what we're all waiting for at this moment is the next large breakthrough in civilized thought or, at any rate, some new way to approach our old ideas. Maybe we'll find it, or don't you think so?

x.   No, I don't think so.

D.T.   What do you think will take care of things then?

x.   I guess I have a simple faith in the powers of rationality and the powers of men's minds. Radicals deny those.

D.T.   Well, I can see why they get discouraged with the rationalist tradition, can't you?

x.   It's slow, of course. But I still have more faith in the rationalist tradition than in any other. I think that if things get bad enough people will begin to see they're bad and then they'll slowly begin to get better.

D.T.   Would you say that you choose your friends on the basis of their sharing this rationalist view of the world? After all, it's not exactly a popular view at the present time.

x.   No. I'd rather say that both my choosing of them and their holding of that view are parallel consequences of some other characteristic.

D.T.   Your intuitions lead you to something in someone that then turns out to be supported by rationalism?

x.   I like people who take the same pleasure in the use of their minds as athletes take in the use of their bodies; a pleasure in discovering new abilities. After all, we have to create our own challenges. The idea is central for me that there are parallel impulses in everybody for freedom and for restrictions; the barriers that we talked about earlier. When things get easy, you erect your own barriers. When the old ones fall down you have to erect new ones. That will remain constant and those who mistake the replacement of the old by the new for the rejection of barriers altogether are misunderstanding the situation. That's where reason comes in: it means using your mind hard and to proper advantage, the way a good athlete uses his body.

3. Daughters
of the Middle Class

"Alice" was the name I had given my first interviewee, a delightful girl of nineteen from the Middle West, golden-haired, energetic. She had come to Radcliffe with an excellent high school record and sophomore standing, planning to major in history. But the choice of this field of concentration had been vague; soon she drifted away from it—as she explained, she always had liked to draw and take photographs so that it was not unnatural that she should be attracted to the Visual Studies Department. From my first meeting with her, shortly after I settled into Briggs Hall, I liked her enormously, found her not only alert and quick-witted—all Radcliffe girls are alert and quick-witted—but, as would not always be the case with the students I met, genuinely warm-hearted and lacking in the intellectual arrogance that in my own day I supposed was characteristic of girls who went to Vassar but that I now associated with my own college. What made the basis for my confidence in Alice's intelligence, I have no notion. The quality of her interview, the answers she gave to my questions, were scarcely reassuring on the score of her mental powers; in fact, she talked sheer nonsense. There fell to Alice the unhappy task of acquainting me with a new division of Harvard education, the Department of Visual and Environmental Studies, which had not existed in my undergraduate time, and it was from her description not only of her own courses—this semester she was doing free-hand drawing, three-dimensional application of color, and a course in the psychology of art—but also of the intellectual atmosphere in which she worked that I came to suspect that Alice was never assigned reading in any of her classes and that, indeed, if one chose her field of concentration it was possible to graduate from Radcliffe or Harvard, even with honors, without ever reading a book or taking an examination. My dismay at this revelation was not lost on my interviewee. Pleasant creature that she was, Alice would have wished to comfort me and she undertook to do this by telling me that there was a sophomore study group to which she belonged where they often read and discussed books. Yet under the pressure of further questions Alice had to admit that, more typically, they invited guest speakers such as they were expecting that evening who, as Alice put it, helped them "to interrelate the fields within the department." The person who tonight would take on this weighty function was the sky-writer who had created an artificial rainbow over the Charles River as part of the anniversary celebration of the Boston Museum of Fine Arts, called "Earth, Water, and Air."

It would be less than fair to direct against a single under-graduate the full force of my opinion of this remarkable report. Obviously in describing her department Alice spoke not in her voice alone but for a large section of present-day fashionable culture, including, of course, fashionable academic culture. I was unacquainted with how the hundredth anniversary of the Boston Museum of Fine Arts had been celebrated but if Alice was accurate in saying that as part of the festivities there had been a program called "Earth, Water, and Air," which sponsored skywriting and had created an ad hoc rainbow over the Charles River, on what scale was one to measure the intelligence of a nineteen-year-old who believed that such manifestations belonged to the serious business of education? In fact, when I would look back on my conversation with Alice in the light of subsequent interviews with other students, a sufficient number of whom were at some pains to complain about their courses though failing to reveal any ground for their dissatisfaction other than a rather chic—or so I took it—general disbelief in their soundness, I tended to think that Alice might even deserve good marks for her loyalty to her program; and I appreciated more than I condemned her failure to challenge me on our differing views for I felt that when she refrained from engaging me in argument it was not from lack of spirit but because there was honor involved for her in preserving, at least until she had time to think things over, her faith in what she had already subscribed to. Honor, I said to myself, is a planting that can produce many attractive blooms.

But it may of course be that I'm rewriting my original response to Alice in order to make it conform with information that came to me some months later, after I got home from Cambridge: we had a mutual friend in New York from whom I learned that by the end of term Alice had become considerably discontented with her field of study; there was even talk that she might leave picture-taking and switch to law or medicine. Wholly tentative though this news was, any hint of change in Alice's plans for her life delighted me. While so sudden and sharp a swing might on the surface suggest that she was of less than stable temperament, I found her readiness to confront error far more reassuring about her character than I'd have found the determination to stick to guns which, as I saw it, were bound to misfire. For here, apart from whatever I felt about a student at Radcliffe who could earn a degree without submitting herself to an intellectual discipline or even being required to read a book for three college years, was the nub of my disquiet about Alice's choice of her "major": I had no confidence that she was committed to filmmaking or photography as a career or that she meant to succeed at it.

Now, it is manifestly irresponsible to conclude on the basis of a half-hour of talk with a young person that she is engaged in a work to which she is insufficiently attached. This had nevertheless been my conviction almost from the moment Alice came into my room and certainly as she went on to describe her curriculum: undoubtedly she was nicely occupied for many hours each day by her activities at the Carpenter Center for the Visual Arts but she was not where she belonged, of this I was sure; and so far as her "field" would count for a direction or a content or a significant enhancement of her life, she was in no field at all. She was not serious about films and photography; she was not actually interested in design. She was wasting her college opportunity and her considerable mental capacities. And it could be that on some level Alice knew this herself, which was why she gave me so thoroughly unimpressive a report of her department—perhaps she wanted me to raise the questions which she had not yet permitted herself to bring to consciousness. And anyway, the chief source of these quick firm conclusions I had come to about her was not Alice herself but long familiarity with my own sex. The stylishness of the decision to major in visual studies made her of course a child of her time, not mine; but exactly because the choice was so stylish, it was more fruitfully examined as an aspect of the present-day culture of the colleges than as the vagary of one individual undergraduate. On the other hand, the haphazardness, even the fecklessness, as I would call it, with which she seemed to have fallen into her present area of study made her a timeless female example, as representative of my long-ago college day as of her own student generation.

As I say, in my college time there had been no visual studies program to entrap our Alices. English literature was the readiest academic shelter for the unpossessed, with romance languages the runner-up. Alice's counterpart in the twenties would undoubtedly have majored in English, to come out of college as little advanced toward a professional career as when she had entered; for to address the problem on the simplest level of practicality, unless she also took courses in education or went on to a graduate degree she was likely to be thought unqualified even for teaching in an elementary or high school. She might be lucky: she might learn shorthand and typing and if she got a secretarial job at a magazine or in a publishing house—but this was a big "if"—her job would represent an uncommon vocational continuity with her college studies. I do not mean to suggest that the professionally unpossessed female was a product solely of Radcliffe: at Vassar and Smith, Barnard, Mount Holyoke, Bryn Mawr, Pennsylvania, Michigan, Chicago, Pembroke, Berkeley, wherever middle-class female students were college educated, together with or as well as men, there one would have found the woman undergraduate, the multitude of women undergraduates, who labored over their Chaucer and Shakespeare, their Milton and Dryden and Pope, their Restoration dramatists, their nineteenth-century novelists, their Cavalier poets, their Romantic poets, their Victorian and Georgian poets, only to end up ten years later, if they were that fortunate, behind a reception desk at whatever was the current equivalent of *Glamour* magazine or *Mademoiselle,* waiting with immodest hope for the privilege of captioning a picture or reading an unsolicited manuscript.

My own experience was not dissimilar. I majored neither in English nor in romance languages but in fine arts; the specific subject of study is less relevant, however, than the degree of slackness it accommodates. By slackness I certainly do not mean laziness, or low standards of accomplishment. What I have in mind is the lack of pledge to continuing serious work in the field in which one is being trained. It is difficult to imagine someone majoring in mathematics or physics because she has to major in *something*. The special aptitude called for by the study of mathematics or science is itself at least the beginning of a test of professional earnestness; at any rate, in terms of recognizing and weeding out the uncommitted student, no college department can do much better than what mathematics or the sciences do automatically—a girl chemist at college may not go on to graduate school and to a scientific career but on the other hand she isn't liable to feel she is suitably applying her college-learned skills if she ends up at the cosmetic counter of a department store. But like the study of

English or French, or even of certain of the new, more competitive subjects such as social studies or history and literature, art history is a field which demands no native bent such
as might promise a continuing involvement with one's subject. I
worked very hard indeed in my fine arts courses, and were I to
have been asked about my future plans, I'd have said I was
going on to professional employment as an art historian, or
perhaps to a museum or gallery job. Yet at the end of my
senior year, when I was offered two splendid professional
opportunities, one in fact in a museum and the other in teaching, I refused both without any sense that I was making a
professional sacrifice of some size. I had what looked to be a
most cogent excuse for acting this vagrantly; one always
does. Both jobs were in New England and although I had won
a family battle by going to college away from New York, my
parents had now made it plain that, having graduated, I was
to come home and stay there until removed by a husband. But
even if my refusal of these jobs was due to family pressure, the
fact remains that it disturbed me not at all to let them slip
from me. While I must surely have worn a fine air of professional seriousness to have been made the offers, in actuality I
was not only adrift, I had never been professionally anchored,
any more than had any of the women in my department
though we vied so strenuously with each other for good grades
and honors. But the men in the department were not professionally adrift; they all went on to notable careers; they were
the outstanding art history teachers and museum people of
their generation. It was easy for me to imagine working and I
wanted employment in my field. What I couldn't imagine was
a lifelong reliance upon work such as men commonly have
from their earliest years. Back in New York I made a few
halfhearted attempts at putting my rigorous schooling to use,
for the training I'd been given was in no way less demanding
than that of the Harvard fine arts students. But the art world
happened at that time to be a particularly tight snobby little
universe in which I had no ready place; in refusing my two

original offers, I seemed to have lost everything open to me at the time. But to find myself now virtually excluded from my profession caused me only social-psychological, not professional, pain; in effect I was being provided the ground for final surrender on a pledge I had never taken. By great good fortune, some years later, when I could better appreciate the value of a serious commitment to work, I was able to make a different professional career for myself. But in the interim—until I married, that is—my equivalent of *Glamour* magazine or *Mademoiselle* was the National Broadcasting Company where, fortified by what many people even then considered the best education available to women in this country, I earned a modest weekly paycheck shepherding five child actors, a dog, a cat, a singing policeman, and an organ grinder, plus monkey, on publicity tours to promote the sale of a shoe leather that was being widely advertised on radio.

I remember that once, while I still talked of the possibility of a museum or gallery job, my father said gravely, "If I wanted to work in a gallery, I'd offer to sweep the floors if that was the only way to get started." Even that long ago the formulation struck me as embarrassingly Algeresque. It nevertheless points to another ambiguity in what was presumably no more than an act of daughterly submission on my part: as between encouraging or discouraging me about working, my parents were definitely encouraging, or surely meant to be. My mother often spoke of her envy of my female generation because we wouldn't be trapped in homemaking; and even as a child I was told that when I was grown I'd have to prepare myself for some form of gainful employment in case I ever had to earn my living. "In case I ever had to earn my living." The words are not to be lightly passed over: how ominous they were made to sound, what an extreme of personal and social crisis they implied! When the deepest assumptions of one's culture suggest that female independence is a condition of direst emergency, either a social holocaust or the death, bankruptcy, or incapacitating illness of one's father or husband, perhaps a daughter of the middle class is to be forgiven if she fails to bring to her education the bright purposive energies we generally associate with professional goals.

Well, I write now in 1972 and the question I put to myself is, how much dissimilarity is there, really, between the view which I and my Radcliffe contemporaries had of our professional futures, and of the part played in them by our college training, and the attitude of the present-day female student? And I am afraid I find myself moved to the reply that in spite of the dramatic changes which appear to have taken place in the way women view their relation to work, the passage of time has made an astonishingly small change in their actual attitudes toward future careers. It is still the exceptional middle-class girl, a tiny minority of those who go to college, for whom a college education represents more than a cultivation of the art of self-deluding temporization. Some of the young women I interviewed on my return to Radcliffe did indeed speak of specific professional plans; but of these only a handful sounded a note of conviction. When I inquired, as I did of all the girls I spoke with, whether there was any woman they had known in school or in their families or public life for whom they had special admiration, hoping this would give me a clue to the future they projected for themselves, almost no one could mention anyone she wished to emulate. With the invention of the pill and the removal of the inhibitions which attended women's fear of unwanted pregnancy, women are of course no longer dependent upon marriage as they once were. The sexual revolution of which they are said to be the beneficiaries is part of a wide-ranging social revolution which is bound to have its influence everywhere in their lives: for instance, at this moment in the history of female progress, women are suddenly being awarded, if an award it can be called, the head-turning status of an ethnic minority; together with blacks they constitute a test of the moral-political premise on which universities base their right to federal funds, with the result that positions are offered them or even thrust upon them which previously were out of their reach. Yet even so, and even at places like Harvard and Radcliffe which are particularly responsive to an altered consciousness in the culture, Alice remains as little possessed by her work as she would have been a half-century ago when Radcliffe had not yet forgotten its beginnings as the annex of a powerful male institution. Perhaps, in fact, she is the more afloat because she is denied what, fifty years ago, was at least the possibility of a solid mooring in marriage and motherhood. Granting what is indubitably true, that every college population, Radcliffe's no less than that of other private institutions, now includes many more students than it once did who aren't of the substantial middle class and that everywhere on our college campuses, as everywhere in our fiction and films, the projects and prospects of the middle class are being put under a new adversary assessment or even being dismissed as unworthy of inspection, it is still the values of the middle class, in all their contradiction, which create the values of the colleges. And perhaps in nothing is the middle class less certain of itself, and more available to merely transitory shifts in opinion, than in the two things which come together in the education of women: education and women.

One dreams of a Tocqueville to deal as it deserves with the subject of America's present-day ambivalence toward the very idea of the middle class, that bulwark of American society which provides the economic sustenance of our idealism at the same time as, all anomalously, it nourishes the most lethal assaults on our tranquility. Surely there was never a period when our feelings about middle-class privilege, middle-class advantage, were as double-edged as they are today. On the one hand, we despise the middle class as the source and repository of those assumptions and attitudes at which, in our modern liberal consciousness, we are most angry and which we most fear. On the other hand, what *except* the middle class is the promised land toward which we wish to move all who were not born its citizens—after which it will presumably have so different a character that it will no longer generate anger and fear! This divided judgment was of course already in preparation in the twenties when H. L. Mencken, from his own firm purchase in middle-class America, taught us our contempt for its philistinism. But no one in Mencken's time, which was also my Radcliffe time, unless it was the tiny "old family" minority in New England, which thought of itself as a class of its own from which movement in any direction was necessarily downward, would have regarded membership in the middle class as other than desirable, indeed basic. It was the culture or lack of culture, not the power of the middle class that the writers of the twenties put under attack—Sinclair Lewis's Babbitt was never accused of giving aid and comfort to the military establishment, only of being insensitive to his wife's yearnings—and the attack came wholly from the bastions of intellect and art which were then much more remote from the general life of the country than they are today. Quite without self-consciousness Radcliffe in the twenties could look upon itself as a school for young ladies of the middle class. The scholarships were few and distributed chiefly among students who, to be sure, lacked money, but who were otherwise no different—certainly no different socially—from their college sisters. Even for men a college degree wasn't the economic *sine qua non* in the twenties which it has since become; and for women—at any rate, for Radcliffe women—it was not so much a means of entrance *into* the middle class as proof that one was already suitably, if not always abundantly, there. It happened that I was the first person, male or female, on either side of my family to graduate from college. Less than ten years after my graduation, by the mid-thirties, it would no longer have been possible to measure with this cruel precision my father's economic advantage over the other members of his and my mother's families: with the economic depression of the thirties there came the demand for a new social dispensation based on merit and not simply on money. And only today, with our present desperate recourse to the university as an appropriate instrument with which to make restitution to the minorities for the deprivations and injustices they suffered in the evolution of the American middle class to its uncertain eminence, has meritocracy come—though, even now, perhaps only temporarily—to the end of its road.

Still, through all these permutations, one aspect of American middle-class life would seem to have stayed constant enough: the assumption that woman's primary place is in the home and therefore that her place outside the home is naturally of a secondary order, especially in work which gives status within the middle class as, say, bank managing gives status but bank telling does not, or university teaching gives status but grade school teaching does not. I am not suggesting that this view of woman's role in society has been unvarying even in the past. In periods of war, for example, there is always a significant shift in the definition of what is appropriate for women to do—it was only after 1945, when the G.I.'s had come back to an economy trying to adjust to peace, that culture mobilized itself, via the women's magazines and with the help of our psychologists and anthropologists, to get middle-class women out of the jobs which during the war they had been urged to take; the widespread propaganda designed to persuade women in the late forties and early fifties that their mental health lay in devoting themselves to motherhood and the art of gracious living, to female-ism, as it was called, would have been thought subversive a decade earlier, before America required a reaccommodation to male economic dominance. I am also not suggesting that middle-class America is monolithic or that the line of its development is always easy to trace without hindsight. To refer again to my own college experience: I entered Radcliffe only a relatively short time after women had been given the vote, when one would suppose that the militancy and purpose of the female suffrage movement would still be at the center of a young woman's sense of her life, yet I can recall no evidence that women had attained to a new political responsibility. Obviously, of present-day Radcliffe I

cannot make the parallel statement that I see no manifestations of the social and political sensibility of this historical
moment; on the contrary, the evidence is considerable that
Radcliffe students are now far more aware of a connection
between their personal circumstances and those of their society than I and my contemporaries were. Nevertheless I have
the firm impression—it is nothing I can prove but it is also
nothing that someone else can yet *dis*prove—that for the majority of present-day middle-class students at Radcliffe and
Harvard their current concern for the black and the poor, and
their impulse to social renovation, will all too soon yield to the
sterner imperatives of class, their own class: such, it seems to
me, is the inevitability of historical process. Whether this will
eventually also include a return of the girls to the sexual role
determined in their middle-class origins, that of woman's emotional submission to men, a deference most quickly made
viable in economic abdication, is a question not so easily answered. But if there should indeed be this defeat of our current efforts on behalf of women, this much at least must be
clear: it would necessarily be inseparable from the defeat of
a liberation movement which has made its original most arrest-
ing appeal to sexual hatred of a peculiarly destructive kind, a
movement, that is, which has failed to locate and claim the
place where sexual equality supports rather than violates
biology.

But what I would emphasize here is the continuing determi-
native power of class, and its ability to override the intermit-
tent power of cultural divergence except perhaps in that small
part of the population which as revolutionaries, artists, or
bohemians sometimes manages to make itself marginal to
class. It is, if you will, a Marxist-derived view of the supremacy of economic interest over the "free" efforts of culture. And
I would also stress the existence of mutually contradictory
impulses not only within a single cultural period but also
within individuals, particularly in youth. If we are to recognize
Alice as a representative of her college culture, we cannot

overlook those aspects of her character which also make her representative of the middle class on which, so far as women are concerned, influences of this or that cultural moment appear to have little lasting effect, sometimes no more than that of a new dance step or a new fashion in hair style. For all the "radical" conformity of her dress, which is careless, verging on the unclean, and of her manner, unput-downable, and of her choice of the camera as the instrument of her self-definition, I foresee of Alice that at last she will turn out to be much too closely held to her family origins to do more than nibble at the edges of revolt against the kind of womanhood that was predicated in her respectable middle-class childhood. This of course doesn't preclude her finding a work which will command her fullest dedication. But in this discovery, if she comes to it, she will not have been helped by a college which despite its old pride in female education compromises women's full equality with men by evading their need, their special need, for professional seriousness. That is, even if she finds a profession, it will do battle against her class indoctrination; she will feel she has no right, or no *full* right, to it. I recall a Radcliffe dean in the twenties who, addressing us at assembly, cautioned us that few of our number would ever put our college educations to professional use but that we were nevertheless not to consider them wasted: because of our Radcliffe training we would be more efficient in our housework—in dishwashing, instead of scalding the plates one at a time, we would wait until all of them were scrubbed and then pour a kettle of boiling water over the lot; and, able to quote Shelley and Keats over the kitchen sink, our minds would be raised above our sordid occupations. This lady—I now make penance—was for too long a figure of fun in my memory of college. I now recognize that she was unique for honesty, and that those of us who scorned her prognostications were notable only for our high-spiritedness, not for our prescience.

Yes, I remember thinking one night in the spring of my return to my old dormitory, after a day in which I had interviewed a half-dozen Radcliffe girls no one of whom struck me as being nourished by anything more professionally sustaining than the mysterious and somehow awful knowledge that she was among the intellectually elect of her female generation, some means has to be found to rescue the female intelligence which, into late adolescence, is all shine and promise but which, in the case of so many women, will—failing economic or social disaster—be all tarnish and empty tokenism within a decade after graduation. How, though, was this to be done? The year before I came back for my stay in Briggs Hall, on a Cambridge visit, I had been asked one evening to a meeting of a Radcliffe student committee on curriculum reform. This was in the spring of 1970, a short year after the revolutionary standard had been raised in Harvard's University Hall and when the students were still eager to be participants in the democracy of university administration. The important business on the evening's agenda was a recommendation that all fields of concentration be abolished.

"All of you are concerned with women's lib?" I asked at last when I saw that none of the young women around the table was going to object to the recommendation.

There was a chorus of assent.

"But surely you must see that sexual equality rests on economic independence, and that economic opportunity is largely a matter of professional competence. No college woman is going to be able to compete with men for jobs if all she has to offer is some kind of vague desire to be employed. . . ."

One of the two male members of the committee interrupted me: "We don't want majors at Harvard either."

Since from his manner I could guess that he was about to tell me that his student generation had thrown out professional expertness together with other imperialisms, I went on quickly: "But men in our society have a strong economic incentive to make successful careers. Women in the middle class do not. That's why, even more than men, they need to have special competence."

I am afraid I persuaded no one. In speaking of education as tooling for a future in some recognized professional sphere, I was setting myself apart from the current culture; worse, by invoking economic ambition, speaking in the tones of establishment. And to make my retrograde appeal in the name of women's freedom was, in their minds, to pervert the cause of my sex. It was clear to me that I could hardly expect these young people to discriminate as I would have liked among all the brilliant temptations being offered them by their moment in history, not least the promise of a future which would provide and sustain whatever it was they would come out of college asking for: peace, love, justice, opportunity without division or struggle, and as much of these good things for women as for men. Here indeed was seduction; and like seduction in the traditional sense, it spelled far more trouble for the young woman than the young man who yielded to it. Coming out of college into the brutal world of economic competition which looks as if it will be our universe for still some time to come, whatever change in the basic pattern of society may be made by changing our educational institutions, eliminating entrance requirements, eliminating examinations, eliminating grades, eliminating required courses, eliminating fields of concentration, the male college graduate will soon enough have to meet the economic challenge or else drop out of life entirely—these will remain his simple, or not so simple, alternatives. It is the girl graduate who, though she stay *in* life, faces being depleted in will, robbed of power and satisfaction; and all the employment statistics which will be adduced in proof that college women hold this or that percentage of all jobs held will tell us nothing about our unemployed women graduates or about the miseries suffered by those who *are* employed through lack of a decent correlation between the capacities they brought with them to college and the kinds of jobs they do. Yet as I talked with these Radcliffe students of the early seventies, these highly developed, self-confident young women, I had no heart to tell them what was more and more coming to seem to me to be their indicated alternative to education for a serious working life: no college at all—and what, I asked myself, was so world-shattering about that?—or else a frankly proposed, strictly supervised general education, an education for honest living, for honest female living, within the middle class. Again I looked back on my own college days and decided that of all the things which had been wrong with it, what had not been wrong had been the necessity which concentrating in fine arts had put upon me to know who had decorated the courts of the French kings or who had picked up what influences on the pilgrim routes to St. James of Compostela in Spain: the absorption of what might now be regarded as irrelevancies had been my means of learning about the past and though I had never put this learning to use in a professional way, I was deeply grateful for even the diluted instruction it had given me in the terrible and beautiful history of Western civilization. But what had been bad indeed was that I had been led to suppose that all a woman had to do was have the same education as a man in order to have, and make, the same choices in life; that if I had accepted, say, one of the positions offered me at graduation, my development as a member of our society, as a female in the middle class, would have been straightaway and clear. This had been a deception of some magnitude and, practiced as it was not merely on my own but on several generations of young college women, I held it responsible for much that was and is nervous, lost, disoriented, ungenerous, and, not least, histrionic in our best-educated female population. The histrionism of modern American women is a great unexamined scourge in our society, but how should a woman frustrated in the belief that she is special among her sex, at once more talented, more energetic, and destined for more accomplishment than the general run of women, *not* be impelled to act out in gesture and facial expression the fantasies of personal power which were engendered in her at school but find no sustenance in her actual experience of life?

If Alice studied law or went to medical school, there was at least the hope that she would be spared some of the less appealing indications of a life of unused capacities if not of the conflicts due to special pressures on her sex. If, on the other hand, she graduated into some never-never world where a taste for sketching was supposed to combine with a knack for taking pictures to forge a satisfying career, I foresaw for her only a future of tossing together some kind of make-do existence from the bits and pieces dealt out to her by fortune. To be sure, she could opt for no career at all: there were women for whom marriage and motherhood were sufficient gratification, all they wished of life. But were many of them likely to have found their way to Radcliffe? It would seem to me that, especially today, a process of natural selection was necessarily at work to put the mark of restlessness and unattained aspiration on most of the girls I had interviewed. Obviously there were dangling men at Harvard too, intellectually spendthrift men, who squandered what was offered them in preparation for their futures. But was it an accident that the film I saw with Mrs. Bunting—it was a documentary of Harvard-Radcliffe life—just before I terminated my visit, had been made at Harvard, not Radcliffe, by two male, not female, students in Alice's department and that, whatever its shortcomings, it was sufficiently accomplished to be under consideration for use by the Harvard Alumni Office? There was money to be earned from a training in visual studies: this the young men in the department had been quick to see. Even in a period of extraordinary narcissism—which is how I judged it—among college students, the students at Harvard apparently recognized the extent to which the search for personal identity depends on the way in which we earn our livings and they refused the existential imperative, which has so often rationalized the cessation of function among dropouts from our society, that we not be defined by our function. It is the fierce imperative of money, the need to earn a living not for one year or five but always, that gives men their immeasurable advantage over women in the quest for identity. And in this far at least, that a man's most unimpressive excursion into education improves his capacity to earn the money by virtue of which he holds his place as the family head, it must be said, however wryly, that he needs his degree more than most women need theirs. I am told that at the Harvard Commencement exercises in 1971—I was not present, having already left Cambridge—many members of the Radcliffe graduating class signalized their ever-growing assimilation into the male institution by demanding yet another evidence of sexual justice: equal admissions with men. The demand was peaceably made: they indicated their wish not by shouting or stampeding the ceremonies nor yet by taking off their clothes but by wearing conspicuous equal-signs on their academic gowns. It is doubtful that this particular demand will be as quickly met as, in their current enthusiasm for their rights, some of these girls expect: the liberated students of Radcliffe may not be familiar with the sexual character of money but I suspect that the Harvard Corporation understands that the farther Harvard moves from being a bachelor's club, the less money it can count on from its alumni. How interesting it would be, though, if—oh, most crass and pernicious fantasy!—Harvard decided to distribute its places in the college wholly on the strength of a student's certified need and wish to be a wage earner, with sex no factor. So far as male enrollment is concerned it would at once eliminate the millionaire minority, which is sufficient disaster to guarantee that such an experiment will never be tried, but in the case of women what a powerful change in the direction of seriousness and intellectual self-respect it would bring about in women's view of themselves and of their educational purpose! What would have begun as an act of sexual invidiousness, because it would dramatically reduce the number of women admitted to the university, would conclude as the most substantial advance in the emancipation of women since university degrees were first put in their reach.

At any rate, these were the irresponsible thoughts which chased through my mind as I studied a little newspaper called *Radcliffe News from the College* which followed me to the country a month or two after the 1971 graduation exercises. The paper, full of happy pictures, was a report of Commencement activities; the self-approval it managed to communicate without the vulgarity of outright boastfulness was not unfamiliar to me from other promotional material I had received from my own and other colleges over the years, and not for the first time it occurred to me to wonder if all educational institutions had to admire themselves this inordinately: was it a hazard of the trade? One story particularly held my attention, suggesting as it did that there was far more reason for collegiate self-doubt than complacency. Captioned "Three Seniors," it carried the subhead "Three Radcliffe seniors are photographed as they pursue activities typical of Commencement Week." One of these seniors was half-American, half-Asian, and one could guess that she had been focused upon for this ethnic interest. This graduating student had been among the group wearing an equal-sign in advertisement of its desire for equal admissions with men; her confidence in her protest had been qualified, however, by her sense of a world not yet ready for so much enlightenment: " 'The chance of the University accepting an equal number of men and women is nil,' " she told the reporter, " 'partly because of Harvard's inertia, but largely because of very little societal pressure for equality for women.' " After this quotation, the report continues: "She hopes to travel around Europe with friends next year, then to Africa and India. 'I feel restless right now,' she admits. 'It sounds corny, but ultimately I do want to use my life to affect others in a positive way, although right now I'm not really sure exactly how.' "

"To affect others in a positive way." Clearly, the vocabulary of self-hallucination has changed since I was in college. I and my Radcliffe contemporaries wanted to "do" something, or at most we wanted to "be" something. What we meant by this was that we wanted to have some form of activity which would justify the confidence that we were set apart from the general run of women who lacked our gifts and educations and were thus retrograde to ourselves. That most of us failed to achieve this distinction didn't eliminate our wish for it but only made it more acute. Now a Radcliffe graduate is apparently satisfied that she *is* something. Her aim, therefore, is to share her advantages; sure of herself or, at any rate, sustained by the illusion of her superiority to much of the world, she wishes to change the lives of others. The difference isn't a negligible one. It perhaps suggests an arrogance which isn't especially attractive if we separate it from other aspects of the female undergraduate personality. But seen in conjunction with the confusion which it partners, it is at last only saddening.

Confusion, however, is the element which has persisted through the years since I was a student, up until today, and it proposes at least one reason why the cause of female equality, which we suppose has made such notable advances, is still a very fragile venture. For if the purportedly outstanding women's college of America can do no better for its students than to encourage and advertise such flaccid sentimental idealism as was voiced by its recent graduate, what chance, I must wonder, have we for a female social force equal to the task of claiming full citizenship for the second sex?

[1971–72]

Lawrence
and the
Movements of
Modern Culture

as our modes of feeling and perception alter, and while Lawrence has continued to be received equivocally, the ground for acceptance or rejection of his books, even the order in which we rank them, has regularly shifted. Indeed it is possible to trace certain of the major developments in culture over the last forty years by examining how people have read him and what they chose to take from his work.

Thus, remarkable as it seems today, in the thirties what was thought to be at the center of Lawrence's doctrine was an appeal—as simple as that—for the release of sexuality, and the book of his which was most fully responded to was one which, if it is now discussed at all, is assigned a relatively minor place in the canon, *Lady Chatterley's Lover*. It was *Lady Chatterley*, not *Women in Love* or *The Rainbow* or even *Sons and Lovers*, which was regarded as his most significant achievement, also as his chief doctrinal pronouncement, and it was read as a rousing call to sexual freedom from a writer who had perhaps too often wandered in the dark bypaths of myth and metaphor but who had at last, near the close of his career, emerged into the brighter air of human actuality. It was of great point that the book had been suppressed: the public charge of indecency underwrote its worth as a document of the serious life; just as a few years earlier it had been one's high literary duty to bootleg a copy of Joyce's *Ulysses* and struggle with its innovative techniques, now it became one's high moral duty to acquire a copy of *Lady Chatterley* and put oneself to its sexual schooling. This was a period in which sexologies were coming to be widely read: mistakenly, Lawrence's novel was taken to offer a similar if more elevated instruction although, in fact, far from providing a manual of eroticism, Lawrence drew a curtain on his single scene of sexual excursion or improvisation, leaving the reader to guess what had gone on, and dealt with the detailed physiology of intercourse only insofar as he wished to describe the possibility of failure, which he then went on to blame on the female partner. But women in the thirties and forties, virtually in the degree that they thought of themselves as culturally advanced, and certainly in the degree that they were available to the teachings of psychoanalysis, were not unfamiliar with the accusation that they were lacking in proper submissiveness to men and therefore at fault in most situations of unhappiness. Lawrence's harshness to women, instead of alienating his female readers, seems to have stimulated their unhealthy appetite for self-criticism.

Outspoken as he was about sex, Lawrence was solemnity itself; he never intended Lady Chatterley—or sex—to be fun nor was either of them taken by his readers as anything except a thoroughly no-nonsense business. Despite his insistence on a language of lovemaking which would rid sex of its shames and shams and present it in its naked purity, the sexuality of Lady Chatterley could not have been more cloaked in portentous emotion. Lawrence's erotic manifesto had little or nothing to do with the investigation of pleasure, everything to do with the deep connections of body and spirit and the subtle resonances of love. But the thirties were of course the years of economic depression and of the rising tide of totalitarianism, and in a world of deprivation and fear the abrogation of the pleasure principle in favor of a new emotional economics, a new dialectic of male-female relations, was not particularly noteworthy—whatever proposed a personal transcendence of material circumstance was a gift of the imagination. In Lady Chatterley Lawrence offered his readers a world which, actual as it was with the actuality of explicit sex, led one beyond the banal universe of economic and political necessity. Under circumstances in which politics, or at least the politics of intellectuals, had become an egregiously moral enterprise, Lawrence's sexual novel was licensed by the fact that it similarly charged the erotic life with morality, to the point indeed—as was eventually said—of puritanism.

When his critics of the fifties accused Lawrence of puritanism they meant something other than this would mean today. The word is now seldom used but when it is it refers to any view of sexuality which proposes a hindrance to the pursuit of gratification. In the fifties it meant a view of sexuality in which freedom was circumscribed, perhaps even defined, by those values of love and responsibility which had been traditionally supposed to curb our sexual instincts. Especially in response to the atomic bomb, a mood of profound if unchanneled despair had seized the advanced sections of culture; the young in particular were borne down with the sense of having destinies already arranged for them, of being controlled by governments in which they were unable to make themselves heard and of being implicated in decisions in which they had no voice. It was this sense of fatedness, of having lost all freedom of social will, of social choice, which was now to be corrected, or at any rate countered, by a new and unlimited freedom of sexual will; in the advanced fiction of the period as almost ever since, only a single expression of self–directedness is permitted the characters who speak for the authors, that of their sexual desire.

But if an unconditioned sexuality, which is to say a sexuality with no goal except its own fulfillment, was the reply of the fifties to a society which had created conditions so coercive that nothing was left to the individual save the existential self, so long as even that was permitted, then clearly Lawrence provided small comfort. It required no exigent reading to understand that the sexuality for which Lawrence spoke was nothing if not conditioned, and not merely by the full-scale emotions which he insisted upon both as its source and justification but also by the larger social purpose to which he thought sexuality must minister. No more than Lady Chatterley's affair with her gamekeeper was to be read as an essay in pleasure was her escape from her crippled and impotent husband, who represents our modern civilization, to be read as the negation of society as such; it is only the society which produces a Clifford Chatterley which Lawrence rejected. Because, as his work progresses, there is less and less of the furniture of society in Lawrence's novels and because the social ideal becomes increasingly abstract, the thirties and forties commonly read an antisocial intention into his books. Indeed, in the thirties, this helped account for the emphasis that was put upon the sexual doctrine—if one thought of Lawrence as only an advocate for sexual freedom one could the more readily forgive his neglect of its social context. The fifties were more accurate in their comprehension: they recognized that behind Lawrence's demand that we surrender to the dark imperative of the blood and return to a more primitive consciousness than that of the contemporary world there lay not a wish for the annihilation of society but a vision of social regeneration. A renovated state of personal being would issue in a renovated state of social being.

For the fifties, however, the fact that Lawrence looked to sex as an instrument of social revision wasn't the sole evidence of a retrograde stance. For readers who came to his books from, say, Henry Miller, or even from Colette, the ultimate proof of Lawrence's puritanism and of his willingness to accept a regressive social authority was the stress he put upon marriage. "Your most vital necessity in this life," Lawrence had written in 1914 to Thomas Dunlop, British consul at Spezia, "is that you shall love your wife completely and implicitly and in entire nakedness of body and spirit. . . . You asked me once what my message was. . . . This that I tell you is my message as far as I've got any." Obviously at another moment Lawrence might have put the matter less simplistically or made more of the connection between personal and social modes of feeling but this doesn't alter the truth of his brief prescriptive summary. In the first instance Lawrence was always in search of a transcendent meeting of man and woman: *a* man, *a* woman. Except as seen in its metaphoric meaning which is also its largest social dimension, the whole of his doctrine, whatever its transmutation into religion or politics or anthropology, boils down to Lawrence's imagination of the perfect embodiment of woman in wife.

Two short decades after Lawrence's death in 1930, the Wagnerian heroism with which he had invested this quest had lost its splendid overtones of moral grandeur and become only embarrassing. As I have said, the importance which Lawrence gave to the relation of man-woman or husband-wife, the generation which had come of age in the war years gave to a quite other sort of relation, that of self and society. In the face of society's manifest ascendancy over the self, withdrawal and passivity became the order of the day in politics—witness the fact that McCarthyism, instead of being at once resisted and destroyed, as surely it might have been, was allowed to run its unrestricted course for several disastrous years—while in the more personal sphere the call went out, fundamentally different in kind from Lawrence's, for attainment to a new consciousness through drugs, on the one hand, and, on the other hand, through a reversion to the polymorphous perversity of infant life, before civilization makes its claim on the body and its instincts. Throughout his writing Lawrence frequently uses the phrase "lapsing back" to describe the process by which mankind must regenerate itself. The concept was always and only a figurative one, however fiercely he might insist upon its actuality. How to define the precise intention of such writers as Norman Mailer or Norman O. Brown, whether their work, too, was to be read as metaphor or whether a new cultural generation was issuing a literal command that we rid ourselves of the restraints of civilization as we are familiar with it, might be open to disagreement. But one thing was certain: the resounding entrance upon the literary scene of writers such as these announced a new social era and yet another assessment of Lawrence.

At no time in Lawrence's life or since his death had there been so sharp a swing away from the established culture and from the priorities of modern competitive society as developed in the late fifties and sixties. Although this movement, especially as we have known it in America, shows signs of abatement as we advance into the seventies, many of the changes it brought about, particularly in the sphere of sexual conduct, are probably irreversible. Casual or merely companionable sex, sexual experience as an end in itself, indulgence of the desire for sensation: all of these had been deeply distasteful to Lawrence and we can suppose that he would have loathed a culture which encouraged them in the name of radical progress. But the rejection by the young of the values and ambitions and rewards of modern industrial society should, in logic, have been sympathetic to him.

Yet even the logical connection between Lawrence's views and those of a present generation of readers is perhaps not as firm as at first appears. To be sure, the part played by Lawrence's hatred of the First World War in his rejection of modern life is paralleled by the part played by the Vietnam War in the rejection of the power structure of the nation by many young people today. Indeed, in the force with which it states the difference between that which increases and that which diminishes life, the slogan of the sixties, "Make love, not war," is close to the heart of Lawrence's doctrine. But Lawrence never made slogans nor, had he been offered one, would he have been willing to rest in it, which is an oblique way of saying that he had no impulse to the facile. More directly to the point, the lovemaking to which one was being encouraged in the use of this slogan, though presumably dedicated to the same social goals as Lawrence's, was of a very different order of personal experience and thus proposed a different social outcome. The sexuality which Lawrence celebrated was mating, but, by and large, what a present generation means by love-making is coupling. Coupling, as distinct from the unique sexual-affectional connection of a particular man and woman in mating, is to be understood in various ways; it can mean anything from the unimpeded satisfaction of the sexual appetites to an attempt to escape from singleness, from isolation. But one thing it doesn't mean is ultimate or transcendent emotion such as Lawrence was proposing when he spoke of loving your wife "completely and implicitly and in entire nakedness of body and spirit." Therefore, while it can put itself in opposition to the established society, it cannot regenerate it in any way that would accord with Lawrence's moral vision.

Aware of Lawrence's antagonism to Freud one is reluctant to adduce a Freudian concept, that of the superego, to explain what is surely the chief difference between Lawrence's view of sex and the view which now becomes increasingly salient in our culture, connected though the two may seem to be by their common aversion from the kind of eroticism which, to borrow Auden's famous line, has built our cities. If we accept Freud's definition of the superego as the sum and source of our ideals, our conscience, our guilts, the repository of the parental teachings in obedience to or defiance of which we shape the character of our mature lives, then Lawrence must be recognized as one of the most superego-ridden people who yet managed to be a literary genius. The sexuality preached by Lawrence, attached as it was to idealism and to high social purpose, was but minimally a function of the Freudian id and even less a reversion to the polymorphous perversity of infancy. It was a clear product of the superego, which in fact is why it was so perfectly tailored to the thirties when diminution of confidence in the existent social organization was so well compensated for by faith in the ability of man to solve his social problems through selfless social action. The revolutionary ardor of the Marxist thirties, optimistic, orderly, submissive to idea and discipline, readily found its corollary in the disciplined and ideology-bound sexual ardor of Lawrence. In fact, as was demonstrated by the changes in sexual dictate in the Soviet Union in the course of the thirties, the responsible mating for which Lawrence was a spokesman was far more appropriate to the continuing Communist effort than the earlier promises of free love, free abortion, free divorce had been. It represented a reassertion in the personal life of the rigors which are always involved in political as distinct from cultural revolution.

For much the same reason that in the Western world ours is a time of revolutions in and through culture rather than of revolution along strict ideological lines, it is a time when there is

also likely to be a considerable resistance to any view of the
world which, like Lawrence's, is heavily charged with superego; that is to say, with stern demands for discipline. While
there was often a kind of grandiosity in Lawrence's projection
of the social scene which consorted with his vision of a super-
nal personal quest and which probably underlay his fascina-
tion with protofascist posturings, actually one is misled in supposing that his image of the hero was itself larger than life. He
was a slight man, much given to domestic occupations, and he
always entrusts his doctrine to men of similar body and inclina-
tion, also to men of more or less the same class as his: his
leading male characters are regularly thin, wiry, fierce, home-
centered men of the working class. These protagonists stand,
however, full in the heroic tradition: they think of life as a test
or challenge to be faced up to and overcome. Even the clothes
in which Lawrence dresses them or in which he would ideally
wish them to be dressed make *figures* of them, molding their
bodies, encouraging the swagger of masculinity. Young men
today are much concerned with dress, but they have scorn for
the defined maleness which led Lawrence to his interest in
outward appearance and which made for him a first condition
of the heroic. There is a way to put the difference, finally,
which while it may seem unflattering to those who are shaping
our advanced contemporary culture, is surely not an unqualified judgment on Lawrence: whereas the representatives of
the advanced culture of the present decade find it difficult to
bring sex into happy conjunction with character, for Lawrence
it was rather dismally impossible to separate the two.

[1973]

Portrait of
a Marriage

NOW that I know everything, I love her the more, as my father did, *because* she was tempted, *because* she was weak. She was a rebel. . . ." Nigel Nicolson is summing up his response to the sexual vagaries of his mother, the writer Vita Sackville-West, but his statement, which expectably enough is quoted on the dust jacket of the latest of our best-selling English literary biographies, is no less misleading than it is high-minded: as Mr. Nicolson himself makes plain in *Portrait of a Marriage*, Vita Sackville-West was not "tempted" by homosexuality, she gave herself to it throughout her life, with zest, and was often—very much so in the notable instance of Virginia Woolf—far more the seducer than the seduced. As to being "weak" and a "rebel," how is anyone either weak or a rebel who, child of Knole, one of the greatest of English houses, has both within and in back of her the fullest power and license of her class? The hallmark of Vita's world, not alone the aristocratic world of her birth but the Bloomsbury society in which she elected to live, was indulgence of the personal will, particularly of the sexual will—we remember from a recent biography of the Bloomsbury painter Carrington that when Carrington and the homosexual Lytton Strachey, with whom she was passionately in love and with whom she shared a house in the country, had weekend visitors, she would watch at bedtime from the garden until all the upstairs lights had gone off and on again and then off again so that she could have a rough floor-plan of who was sleeping with whom of whichever sex. Lady Sackville, Vita's mother, had suffered no loss of station because she was the illegitimate child of an earlier Lord Sackville or through the protracted residence at Knole of a wealthy admirer whose happy participation in the life of the Sackvilles did a great deal to ease the financial strains of the costly household. She was not only informed but also busily kept others informed of her daughter's exotic elopement with Violet Keppel, daughter of Edward VII's favorite mistress, and she was scarcely ignorant of Vita's transvestite excursions in London and on the Continent in the role of "Julian," a young wounded war veteran. When Lady Sackville attempted, as she unsuccessfully did, to persuade Vita to give up Violet and return to her husband, Harold Nicolson, and to their two small sons, it was not because she was shocked by Vita's desertion of her family or by her liaison within her own sex—the lesbian preference was only curious—or because she thought that a husband, even a husband who, like Harold Nicolson, was himself homosexual, had a claim on his wife or that children had need of their mothers. Simply, she was worried that the newspapers might get the story and make Vita's escapade a matter of public discussion rather than what it miraculously remained, a subject of private titillation within her own class. Apparently the worst, the one really bad thing that could happen to a Sackville, as to Virginia Woolf, was exposure to the judgment of ordinary persons.

Portrait of a Marriage turns out to be a fascinating extended footnote to British upper-class habits and advantages. But this is inadvertent. Mr. Nicolson gives no sign of having any greater awareness of the uncommon social authority his mother could bring to her sexual desires than of the complex emotional requirements which were served in Vita and Harold's marital arrangements or those of Violet and the man she eventually married, Denys Trefusis. Surely had he been conscious of how different the situation would have been if

Vita, with her homosexual urgency, had been trapped in the conventions of middle-class marriage, he could not have made his pious appeal to our (presumed) present-day tolerance, portraying his mother as a pioneer of the freedom which is now supposedly available to all of us and implying that it asked merely the passage of time for her conduct to be countenanced more readily than it was in her lifetime. Vita's sexual behavior was thoroughly countenanced in her lifetime. It could not have been more so, short of holding parades in her honor. She suffered no iota of social or economic pain because of it. True, it is now permissible as it would not have been in the England of earlier years of this century to publish a book about one's parents' sexual deviations. Yet it is in our own enlightened day that an English sexual scandal, the Profumo case, cost Profumo his career and Stephen Ward his life. One's English friends protest that Profumo was discredited and disgraced not by his sexual behavior but solely by his lie in the House. But Ward was a chiropractor, he had no public office in which to be truthful or untruthful, and yet the censure directed to him was so harsh that he was unable to sustain existence. Objectively measured, there may of course have been insufficient ground for the ultimate fear or shame which drove Ward to suicide; but according to the morality engendered in his own class origins there was obviously ground enough.

In Mr. Nicolson's re-creation of his parents' marriage the middle class with its cruel moral judgments, its duties, its demands and exigencies, its cautions and its limitations on freedom is only an offstage rumble. Harold and Vita Nicolson had a family word for the way life is lived on a level lower than their own: they called it "bedint"—the very sound is ugly—and their joint eschewal of everything which smacked of the bedint undoubtedly helped cement their remarkable alliance. Knole with its 365 rooms was manifestly not bedint. Their own more modest establishment, Long Barn, in which they could manage with the help of only three indoor and two outdoor servants, was not bedint. Sissinghurst Castle, a later residence—it was here, in Vita's tower retreat, that after her death Nigel Nicolson found his mother's Byronic record of the affair with Violet which, together with family letters and diaries, makes the basis of his narrative—was not bedint. The famous Sissinghurst gardens which Vita and Harold designed together and which Vita planted with no small skill and effort were anything but bedint. Least of all were the Nicolsons' marital contrivances bedint, or the rearing of their sons. It may have been impossible for Vita to mask her restiveness when the children were brought to her for their daily audience but she had the substantial virtue of never being worn and irascible like a bedint mother with the wash still to do and supper to get, and—so Nigel tells us—there was always Harold to be genuinely interested in the boys when, having exchanged diplomacy for a literary career in London, he was able to come home with fair regularity for weekends; for the rest, the children had their nannies, their games, their Eton, and they even had their Granny. It was Granny Sackville, indeed, who told Ben, older of the two boys, about his mother's affair with Violet Trefusis—this was when Ben was sixteen. From Nigel Nicolson's description of the episode it is hard to say whether Lady Sackville was being vicious, senile, or just making the small talk of her set.

With *Portrait of a Marriage* pursuing its conspicuous way in America one hears the relation of Vita and Harold Nicolson celebrated as a triumph of bisexuality. Actually, it was bisexual only in its short first years when the children were being produced; once the family was established, Vita and Harold made no pretense of sexual interest in each other. Their nonsexual devotion nevertheless steadily grew, increasing in intensity virtually in proportion to their sexual distance from each other and to their conscientious disregard of each other's extramarital activity—and we gather from Nigel Nicolson's account that their extramarital ventures, with the single exception of Vita's passing involvement with Geoffrey Scott, author of the widely

praised *Architecture of Humanism,* were always, for each of
them, homosexual. Far more than the marriage was an instance
of how bisexuality can be made to work, the marriage was an
example of the supremacy of friendship between the sexes
over sex between the sexes—and this, I suspect, is why Mr.
Nicolson's book is so attractive to the present-day public, especially an American public. From Freud, that most bedint of
psychologists bred in middle-class Vienna, Americans have
now for some years learned that a properly ongoing marriage
is built upon the kind of love which is nurtured in, also expressed in, sexuality, "mature" (i.e., reciprocally genital) sexuality. Fundamental to marriage, in the Freudian view, is sexual fidelity; where fidelity breaks down, neurosis is believed to
have taken over. More recently, however, this imperative of an
invigorating monogamy has lost much of its force as a troubling ideal of marital health. In fact, our American post-
Freudian culture is in many ways coming to resemble the still-
ruling pre-Freudian culture of England, a country whose personal choices continue to be largely determined by a class in
which the arrangement of family life meets few of the conditions which the middle-class Freud took for granted. Not only
for the American young or for the consciously "free" but for
many classes of Americans, even, one is told, in solid suburbia,
the assumption that love is exclusive, like the idea that it is
limited to persons of opposite gender and is properly rooted
in "normal" appetites, loses the reassuring grip it was once
thought to have on the imagination. It constitutes no new or
radical insight to recognize that if sex makes the foundation of
a marriage and something goes wrong sexually between a husband and wife, perhaps only that they no longer have mystery
for one another, inevitably the whole of the relation is dam-
aged; what Mr. Nicolson's book provides is welcome evidence
that sex and love do not necessarily even have to combine, let
alone bolster each other. In any culture at any time a relation
such as existed between Mr. Nicolson's parents, the enduring
affection and respect and sympathy they had for each other,

would represent a rare attainment; and it is understandable that at the present time, when we try to persuade ourselves that there are fresh and lasting solutions for old woes in all departments of life, we like to think that the success they made of their marriage contains a generally applicable lesson. Certainly in Vita and Harold's situation, in which both the husband and the wife were predominantly homosexual, the elimination of sex from the relation provided not just a first but an absolute condition of their enduring peace and happiness with each other. But the sexlessness of the marriage was also what it seldom, if ever, could be in the unalleviated marriage of two heterosexuals or even of one heterosexual and one homosexual: it was a *possible* condition of enduring peace and pleasure.

It is a shortcoming of *Portrait of a Marriage* that Mr. Nicolson makes it almost wholly Vita's story and that he glides too smoothly over his father's sexual history both before and during the marriage. This leaves many questions unanswered, among them the interesting one of why Harold was impelled to marriage in the first place, and committed to it, once Vita had become his wife, to the extent of wanting to win her back from Violet. Harold and Vita were married and parents when Vita eloped with the woman to whom she had already been attached in girlhood. If Harold had married only in order to perpetuate the line, this had now been accomplished; he no longer had need of a wife for purposes of procreation. But so simplistic a view of what moved him, while it offers the quickest explanation of why an active homosexual would wish to marry, conforms not at all to Mr. Nicolson's account of Harold's need to keep the marriage from breaking up. Mr. Nicolson quotes extensively from his father's correspondence with Vita during the period of greatest threat to the marriage: although Harold's pleas to Vita to come back to him are rather more literary (even in their self-pity) than impassioned, they at least arrived in a steady stream and they are bafflingly uncynical; they sound no slightest note of sexual slyness or collusion such as one might expect in a communication from one admitted homosexual to another. They are the letters of a person who, although uncertain of his right to his marriage, unmistakably wants it, and on unchanged terms.

Then there is Violet to be explained, and her relationship with Denys Trefusis or, rather, his to her, and Vita's response to *their* marriage. Violet had no impulse to be wed but both she and Vita, in the fashion of well-placed young heroines of nineteenth-century fiction, recognized that, as Vita put it, "she would gain more liberty by marrying." (Though how she could use more liberty than she already had, it is hard to say.) Denys's motive in wanting to marry Violet, on the other hand, had no such time-honored social-economic source. For reasons which Mr. Nicolson doesn't undertake to explore, Denys was a self-entrapped prisoner of the perverse circumstance: the more Violet was given to Vita, the more he was determined to capture her: he went so far, in fact, as to vow never to claim his conjugal rights. Once Violet actually became his wife, Denys broke this promise or very likely only attempted to, probably only once and with Violet's encouragement. At any rate, the gross imposition was reported to Vita by Harold; it was his master stroke in getting back his wife: Vita, who had never been touched with sexual jealousy in her relation with Harold, was seized with a jealousy so acute as to amount to revulsion—the news put an effective end to her attraction to Violet. As for the erring husband, Denys apparently didn't persist in his marital transgression; we are not told what substitutes he had recourse to although we are told that the Trefusis's marriage, despite the strength of feeling which had made it so compulsory for Denys, Violet's hesitations driving him near to madness, turned out to be not at all of the same affectional order as that of the Nicolsons. And thereby hangs, of course, a strange text for these times of our confusion: while it may indeed be that sex is a primary cause of marital incompatibility, it takes more than the abandonment of sex—need it be said?—to ensure love between a man and woman.

The story of an aristocratic bohemia which seems no longer to exist, or not with anything of its old arrogance and flourish, *Portrait of a Marriage* is also a useful if unintended guide to English habits of feeling which have managed to survive extreme shifts in the political climate of the nation and which in fact cut across class lines although proclaiming themselves most clearly where class privilege is most marked. In America, for instance, it would be difficult even today to imagine a writer, even an "advanced" writer, being as forthright and unashamed about his own father's homosexuality as Mr. Nicolson is about the homosexuality of Harold Nicolson—we have no books in this country like J. R. Ackerley's fascinating *My Father and Myself*. This is because Americans, unlike the British, have until now always regarded homosexuality as a monolithic pathology, a bourn from which no man returns to woman. Were the British to share this view, what with the traditional early and long separation of the sexes in school and the consequent restriction of early sexual activity to members of one's own sex, there would surely be no England. It would also push our famous American permissiveness farther than it is yet prepared to go for a respectable middle-class publisher-author to delve as publicly as Mr. Nicolson does into the sexual deviations of his own parents. In England, too, Mr. Nicolson's revelations about his parents have not been entirely immune to disapproval. But, in general, criticism of the author of *Portrait of a Marriage* has been addressed not so much to Mr. Nicolson's divulgence of his parents' sexual digressions as to his intrusion into their privacy: what would not be the case here, it is regarded in England as almost as unmannerly to speak so openly about normal as about abnormal intimacies, whether it is the case of a school fellow or of one's own mother or father. This is a quintessential difference in national character: for the English still, as for Lady Sackville, it is not what one does that matters; what matters is to keep what one does to oneself or to one's own kind. A corollary—or perhaps even a cause—of the English emphasis on privacy is the extraordinary inwardness of the English people, what David Riesman might have called their inner-directedness were its origin not so clearly "other," arising from the old well-defined class structure of English society and perhaps primarily from an imperialism which demanded that one have the inner strength, principle, conviction, resource to maintain power among strangers. No American reader can fail to remark in *Portrait of a Marriage* what to the English reader is probably as unnoteworthy as Mr. Nicolson's comfortable use of his own language: his cool detachment from these parents whom he professes to have loved very much and whom he no doubt did truly love. In America, at any rate until recently, love as detached, as seemingly impersonal and remote as this would at once be spotted for an emotional insufficiency; it would be isolated as a "symptom," blamed on Mr. Nicolson's upbringing, on the distance at which he had been kept from his parents, his reliance upon nannies for his early education in responsiveness, even upon his traumatic discovery of his parents' unsanctified sexual tastes. The English have no such diagnostic fervor nor do they prize, as Americans do, a life of expressed feeling, of emotion always on the boil. But they have a not negligible alternative for easily accessible personal emotion: a sense of self, a definition of self, which Americans do not readily come by.

[1974]